Pollock Memories: A Collection Of Chess Games, Problems, &c., &c., Including His Matches With Eugene Delmar, Jackson Showalter, And G. H. D. Gossip...

William Henry Krause Pollock

Nabu Public Domain Reprints:

You are holding a reproduction of an original work published before 1923 that is in the public domain in the United States of America, and possibly other countries. You may freely copy and distribute this work as no entity (individual or corporate) has a copyright on the body of the work. This book may contain prior copyright references, and library stamps (as most of these works were scanned from library copies). These have been scanned and retained as part of the historical artifact.

This book may have occasional imperfections such as missing or blurred pages, poor pictures, errant marks, etc. that were either part of the original artifact, or were introduced by the scanning process. We believe this work is culturally important, and despite the imperfections, have elected to bring it back into print as part of our continuing commitment to the preservation of printed works worldwide. We appreciate your understanding of the imperfections in the preservation process, and hope you enjoy this valuable book.

In Memoriam.

W. H. K. Pollock.

Born, 21st February 1859.
Died, 5th October 1896.

Frederick W. Klamp

Pollock Memories:

A collection of

CHESS GAMES, PROBLEMS,

&c., &c.

Part I—Portrait, Biography, and 70 Games, played in England, Ireland, and Holland, selected, annotated, and illustrated by the late W. H. K. POLLOCK.

Part II—A selection of Games played in the United States, and Canada, including his matches with EUGENE DELMAR, JACKSON SHOWALTER, and G. H. D. GOSSIP; End Games, Problems, and items of interest connected with the Chess career of the late Master.

EDITED BY MRS. F. F. ROWLAND.

DUBLIN:
Mrs. F. F. Rowland, 6 Rus-in-Urbe, Kingstown.
1899.

HARVARD COLLEGE LIBRARY
BEQUEST OF
SILAS W. HOWLAND
NOVEMBER 8, 1938

Printed by W. W. Morgan,
Chess Player's Chronicle Office,
New Barnet, London.

PREFACE.

THE following biography of the late W. H. K. Pollock is compiled from personal recollections, and from the *British Chess Magazine* and the Dublin *Evening Mail*. The English games were selected, annotated, and diagrammed by Mr. Pollock, in 1895-6, possibly with a view of publication, but there is no record of any expressed wish on his part concerning them. Of the games played in America and Canada, the majority have not been hitherto published in this country. Many were kindly contributed by Mr. Miron Hazeltine, Chess Editor *New York Clipper*, and Professor Howard J. Rogers, Albany, New York. Others were selected from interesting MSS. books, belonging to Mr. Pollock, which contained about 3,000 games entered by himself, and played by Masters and distinguished amateurs, with critical remarks by Mr. Pollock.

This work is issued as a small tribute to the memory of a dear friend, who was one of the brightest ornaments in Caissa's diadem.

Here I thank those who have so kindly aided me in its publication.

FRIDESWIDE F. ROWLAND.

KINGSTOWN, IRELAND,
    November 1899.

W. H. K. POLLOCK.

W hen round Caissa's board we meet,
I n pensive evening's hour,
L oved friends and hands to warmly greet
L inked by her magic power.
I n vain we seek amidst the scene
A genius rare as thine hast been,
M arvels to weave with insight keen.

H allowed by fire divine thou wert,
E 'er bright thy smile—thy heart
N e'er changed, through all the waste of years
R emembered still thou art,
Y et is that memory fraught with tears.

K een critic; oft thy sparkling wit
R egilt the classic page,
A nd in Chess lore thy games are writ
U ndimned by change or age.
S o brief thy life—an April day,
E arly its sunshine passed away.

P erchance death's shadow oft was strewn
O 'er youthful sunny days,
L ike clouds that flit across the moon
L oom darkly near her rays.
O h, still to thee, and scenes of yore,
C ling hearts and friends on distant shore,
K ing in our game till time be o'er.

A

BIOGRAPHICAL NOTES.

WILLIAM HENRY KRAUSE POLLOCK was a son of the Rev. William J. Pollock, M.A., formerly Rector of St. Saviour's, Bath, but now Chaplain of the Blind Asylum, Bristol. He was born at Cheltenham, on 21st February 1859, and was educated at Clifton College and Somersetshire College, Bath. He was intended for the medical profession, and made considerable progress with his studies from 1880-2, during which period he was a resident pupil at Dr. Steeven's Hospital, Dublin. He qualified in 1882 as a licentiate of the Royal College of Surgeons, Dublin.

Pollock learnt to play Chess early in life; in 1878 he had a reputation as a good player in the local Chess circles of Bristol and Dublin. His first published game and problem appeared during 1882, in "The Practical Farmer," the only newspaper in Dublin which then contained Chess news.

The year 1885 found him competing in the Master Tournament of the British Chess Association's first Congress, and this Tournament was the first really important public contest in which he took part. Being somewhat nervous, he made a bad start, and lost successively to Messrs. Bird, Gunsberg, Donisthorpe, and the late Rev. G. A. MacDonnell. After these reverses his play improved, and he defeated Messrs. Rumboll, Mackeson, Mills, and Mortimer, closing his first week's engagements with 4 wins and 4 losses. The next week he showed to better advantage, and scored 6 out of the 7 games played—the seventh, with Mr. Guest, being drawn. In the final score he was fourth, with 10½ out of a possible 15; after Messrs. I. Gunsberg, 14½; H. E. Bird and A. Guest, 12; but above Messrs. MacDonnell and Loman, 10 each. Mr. Pollock also competed in the "Tennyson" competition, in the same Congress, and won the first prize (a copy of the Poet Laureate's works, with his autograph), with the fine score of 6½ out of a possible 7. In the same year (1885) he played in the Master Tournament at the Hereford Congress of the Counties Association, but fared badly. In 1885 he also played in the Master Tournament of the Irish Chess Association, coming out first, with 9 points, thereby winning the Irish championship. Mr. Porterfield Rynd (of Dublin) was second, with 8½. In the Handicap, however, Mr. Pollock only tied for second and third places, Mr. Rynd being first.

In 1886 Mr. Pollock played in the Master Tournament of the British Chess Club, but did not secure a prize, Messrs. Blackburne, Bird, Gunsberg, and Mason being the prize-winners, in the order named. He also took part in the International Master Tournament of the

British Chess Association, and opened his score well, defeating Blackburne in the first round, drawing with Gunsberg in the second, and defeating Herr Lipschutz in the fourth; but he lost to the late Herr Zukertort in the third round. In the subsequent play he did badly, and finally only scored 4½ out of a possible 12, and was not placed. During 1886 he played for Ireland in a correspondence match against Sussex, his opponent being Mr. L. Leuliette. In 1886 he took part in the Nottingham Congress of the now defunct Counties' Chess Association, but was unplaced in the prize list. He also played in the 1886 Master Tournament of the Irish Chess Association, and secured the first prize, with the exceptionally brilliant score of 8 points out of a possible 8. Mr. J. H. Blackburne was second with 7, and Mr. Amos Burn third with 6. In the Handicap, Mr. Pollock came out second, with a score of 11½, Mr. Burn being first, with 13.

In 1886 Mr. Pollock joined the City of London Chess Club, and played in the Winter Handicap, yielding odds to all the players of his section. He made a good score, but did not secure any material prize. He also gave a very fine exhibition of simultaneous play. In the match City v. St. George's, May 1887, he played at the first board, drawing his game with the late Rev. W. Wayte, the captain of St. George's.

In the Master Tournament of the British Chess Association, in 1887, he finished fifth, after Messrs. Burn, Gunsberg, Blackburne, and Zukertort, but with a higher score than Messrs. Bird, Lee, and Mason.

In 1888 Mr. Pollock played in the Handicap at Simpson's, tieing with Mr. Sellon for fifth place—score, 11 each—after Messrs. Gunsberg, 16½; Mason, 15½; Bird, 13; and Gibbons, 11½; but before Messrs. Zukertort and Mortimer, 10½ each; and Muller, 8½. He took part in the International Master Tournament of the Bradford Congress, 1888, but did badly, only scoring 7 out of 16.

Early in 1889 he visited various Chess centres in Ireland, giving exhibitions of simultaneous play with marked success. He took part in the Dublin Chess Congress, 1889, and in the Major Tournament came out second, with 6½ out of 8; Mr. Amos Burn being first, with 7½; and Mr. J. Mason third, with 5½. In the year 1889 Mr. Pollock left England for America, and since then his record is mainly identified with American and Canadian Chess. He received a very handsome testimonial from the members of the Belfast Chess Club, just previous to his departure. This mark of appreciation, together with the fact of having won the Irish Championship, induced him to represent Ireland in the American Congress of 1889. He therefore took part in this International contest at New York—a two-round Tournament—finishing eleventh with 17½, after Messrs. Tchigorin (29), Weiss (29), Gunsberg (28½), Blackburne (27), Burn (26), Lipschutz (22), Mason (22), Judd (20), Delmar (18), and Showalter (18). Below him in the score sheet were Messrs. Taubenhaus, Lee, Baird, Gossip and Burille. He divided with Mr. Max Judd a special prize offered for the best score in the second round against the prize-winners; and for his game against Herr Max Weiss, of Vienna, he was awarded the special prize of 50 dollars, offered for the most brilliant game played in the Tournament. The game, given later on, was a masterpiece in every respect, and ranks high amongst those which are regarded as classic.

Mr. Hoffer, in the "Chess Monthly" says: "The latter part is worthy to rank amongst the few immortal games we possess. It is a perfect gem."

Soon after the conclusion of the New York Tournament, Mr. Pollock went to Baltimore, Maryland, U.S.A., and here for some time he made his home, and conducted the Chess column in the "Baltimore Sunday News." In 1890 he played at the St. Louis meeting of the United States Chess Association, coming in second to Showalter (first), but above Lipschutz (third).

Mr. Pollock played for Maryland at the Lexington meeting of the United States Chess Association, in 1891, and tied with Showalter for the championship of the United States—score, 5 each—but on the play off Mr. Showalter won. Mr. Pollock next played a match with Mr. Delmar, of New York, the final score being Delmar 5, Pollock 3. In 1891 Mr. Pollock played for the championship of the Brooklyn Club, defeating all the best New York players of that day, except Lipschutz and Steinitz.

In 1892 Mr. Pollock played in the Lexington meeting of the United States Chess Association, coming in second, after Showalter (first), but above Hanham (third); shortly after this contest he made an extended professional tour through parts of the States and Canada, giving most successful exhibitions of simultaneous and blindfold play, and he was received everywhere with great cordiality, especially in Montreal, in which city he took up his abode. He played in the New York Tournament of 1893, but did not do himself full justice, and was not placed. He only scored 5 out of a possible 13; Herr Lasker being first with an absolutely unbroken score of 13 won games. In the early part of 1895 Mr. Pollock played a match with Mr. Gossip, which ended in a draw, each side scoring 6 wins, with 5 draws and 1 cancelled game.

In 1895 Mr. Pollock returned to England, to compete in the International Master Tournament, held in August 1895, at Hastings, as the accredited representative of Canada. His health even then was far from being good, and his play was irregular and fitful, though there were occasional glimpses of the old fire. His aggregate score was only 8—a moderate total—but he defeated such opponents as Albin, Bird, Gunsberg, Steinitz, and Tarrasch. The games against the two last-named players are fine specimens of Mr. Pollock's skill, and will be found in another part of this volume.

AT HASTINGS.

"Punctually at seven o'clock the director's bell rings, the forces are placed in correct position, the move recorded on suspending play is made, the clocks set in motion, and the games are in progress. During the interval I have heard reports of several critical positions, and visit first board 2, where W. H. K. Pollock, a tallish good looking fellow, courteous and pleasant, with poetic fancies both in Chess and words, and who sits far back with arms resting on his knees and face almost touching the board, so that it seems hardly possible for him to view the whole, is faced by M. Tchigorin, the Russian master, of moderate height, well-knit frame, dark olive complexion, high round forehead, jet black hair, and most penetrating eyes, very quiet and affable in manner, with hands clasped and the fore part of the arms resting on the table, and whose slight trembling of the right leg resting on the toes indicates the excitement of mind. Just before the adjournment, Pollock's attack seemed exhausted, and in the following position Tchigorin played 27 Kt-B5, to which 28 R(B7)-QB7 seems most satisfactory, but the game proceeded 27 . . . Kt-B5, 28 B-B5 R-Q4, 29 B-B8 Kt-Q7, 30 B-R3 R-KB4, in which position the game was adjourned; continued by 31 KR-B7 R-Kt4ch, 32 K-R3 B-B3, and White shortly resigned. By the winning of this game M. Tchigorin secured the "Evans" special prize, a handsome emerald ring, set in diamonds." (B.C.M., Oct. 1895).

BLACK (Tchigorin).

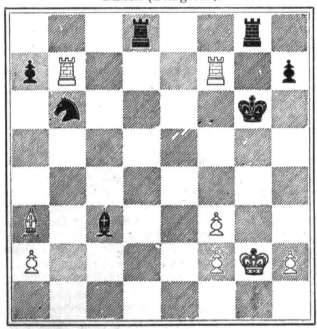

WHITE (Pollock).
Black to play his 27th move.

After the tournament, Mr. Pollock made a professional tour through the Midlands, the North of England and Dublin, giving several exhibitions of simultaneous play. His friends were, however, much pained with his altered appearance, for signs were evident that the fell disease, consumption, was sapping his constitution. Despite the appeals of his relatives and many friends, Mr. Pollock returned to Canada in

February 1896, and resumed his Chess work, again taking up his abode in Montreal. Not for long, however, was he destined to remain abroad. His physical weakness growing apace, he decided to return home. Prior to his departure for England he visited the different Chess Clubs in Montreal, and universal regret was expressed at his being obliged to leave owing to the severe breakdown of his health. On the 8th August 1896, he started for Old England, on board the "Vancouver." What appears to have hastened the course of his disease was the shock caused by the collision of the "Vancouver" and another vessel in the St. Lawrence. So serious was the injury done to the vessel he was on board of that she was obliged to at once return to Quebec for repairs. Some idea of the great peril the passengers were in may be formed by the picture of the "Vancouver" on her arrival at Quebec, which was published in the "Strand Magazine." So great was the damage that when Capt. Jarman was consulted about it, that great expert took time to consider whether he was looking at the bow or the stern! It is the bow of the "Vancouver" that is shown, however, or rather where the bow had been. The bow of the vessel had literally been carried clean away, but was recovered. Part of it, quite detached, is seen on the left, below the anchor. Observe how the timbers are shattered and cut, and the plating cracked and twisted.

THE "VANCOUVER" ON ARRIVAL AT QUEBEC.
From a photograph, from the "Strand Magazine" (by permission).

Taking passage in another vessel he reached England in due course, but reached it only to die. He was taken straight to his father's house at Clifton, and tended with all care that love could bring to his aid. But it was too late, for he sank slowly but surely, until death released him on the 5th of October, in the 38th year of his age. To the last he himself was hopeful of partial recovery. His mortal remains were interred at Arno's Vale Cemetery, Clifton, on Friday, 9th October 1896.

A friend in Montreal wrote: "As to the commencement of the trouble, I am inclined to date it further back than others. Sometime in the late winter—I have not the exact date—in February or March 1895, on returning from a long drive out to a Scotch entertainment in the suburbs, when the thermometer was down to 20 below zero, he found a fire in progress near his lodgings. A poor woman was being burnt out of house and home, and his quick sympathies being excited, he did much to help in saving both her, and her little sticks of furniture. He got home sodden with water, which was hanging icicles from his hair, hat, and coat. No wonder he caught a severe cold, which laid him up for some time, and from which I do not believe he ever really recovered. For he suffered all that summer, from what he euphemistically called "Hay fever." Anyway, I firmly believe that he came by his death in the service of others."

In a letter received from Mr. F. J. Lee he says: "A very interesting fact concerning the young days of W.H.K.P. was his undoubted ability as a 'Cricketer.' Long before he went to America, and at the time of his first appearance in London, Pollock often went with me to witness great cricket matches at Lord's ground in London.

On one notable occasion, previous to the commencement of a match—'M.C.C. and ground v Australians,' Mr. A. G. Steel (at that time about amateur champion bat of England) was practising at the nets. Mr. Steel made a gigantic lofty drive, and Pollock caught the ball, to the astonishment and applause of a large assembly."

Mr. Pollock distinguished himself in several matches in which he took part in Baltimore, Washington, &c., and interesting accounts of the play are in his MSS. books.

Mr. I. M. Brown, in his obituary notice in the B.C.M. for November 1896, wrote: "A scholar and a gentleman, Mr. Pollock was an excellent writer on all subjects connected with Chess. He had a 'sweet turn' for literary effect, and a happy wit that made his writings enjoyable. As a Chess expert he was brilliant rather than profound. He was a fanciful player, delighting in prettiness, and therefore apt to lose games to the dull players of the exact school. He had a habit of over-refining his play, which not unfrequently resulted in defeat. In a word he was an artist rather than a scientist, and the poetry of Chess was more to him than its prose. In tournaments he was always "a dreaded antagonist," even for the strongest Masters to meet, yet he threw away games to weaker players; but with all these faults of his environments, his best efforts reached the high water mark of genius. He won good games in many important tournaments from most of the Masters he met, notable exceptions being Messrs. Lasker and Zukertort. He constructed a few problems, but they were only vagaries, at least he so termed them. During his Chess editorship in the States he won two of Loyd's prizes in New York, against the best solvers.

In the early days of Mr. Pollock's Chess career, many people thought that in him a future English champion would be forthcoming, and the glories of Staunton and Blackburne be revived if not eclipsed. But this expectation was not fulfilled, and Pollock's Chess career must be regarded as a fragment rather than a whole. Yet it is a fragment no British lover of Chess would willingly part with, for it is full of beautiful promise and adorned with many Chess gems of rare brilliancy. With great gifts for the game he never attained the highest rank among the Masters, though it may be doubted whether any one of them excelled him in actual and potential genius for the game. In Chess, however, as in life, he was an idealist. He worshipped at the shrine of the beautiful. He was not content to do what he could do easily and well, but strove after the absolute—his own perception of the perfect. He was above all an artist at the Chess-board. It was not merely "the mate" that he pursued, but the beauty of the mate; he did not merely want to win, he always wanted to win in the most artistic manner. And in this pursuit of the ideal, the practical often suffered. Had he been more self-seeking, the Chess world would have heard more of him personally. Neither nature nor art had fitted him to be his own trumpeter; he loved Chess for its own sake, and not for the gain it might bring him, or the reputation he might attain by its means.

We have spoken of the Chess player, we must now speak of the man, and at the grave of all that is mortal of our lamented co-worker, we desire to pay the last tribute of affection and esteem to the memory of one whom we ever found upright, true, and gentle; generous, high-spirited, and unselfish. Not without faults—who is?—yet with and above all faults, an Englishman of a noble type."

Few have been dowered with a tenderer, warmer disposition. The genuineness and tenacity of his friendship and affection is proved by many. He had the power of attracting strangers to himself by a magnetic influence. In a strange land he could win a group of friends who would never cease to love him whilst life lasted.

One of his confrères wrote—" Any fault he possessed was completely overshadowed by his many good qualities. He was always ready and willing to help a brother professional."

What one would most admire in his character was his self-abnegation, and self-surrender to the cause of Chess. He sacrificed a high position, and all that would make life most attractive to another man, to pursue professionally a Chess career. His genius, and the fascination he felt for the game, seemed to impel him on to his fate. A man who sacrifices his life in any cause will always attract and excite admiration. In his own Chess column his personal achievements were never set forth, but the advancement of the game he loved. He saw in Chess a charm—a variety and depth of beauty quite unthought of, and unnoticed by the average player. Had he remained at home to plod on in a conventional path he might be still amongst us.

If the world think it a pity such genius and talent as he undoubtedly possessed were thrown away on Chess, we can only answer that Chess was his chosen profession, and as such he gave to it all his best art. The originality and depth and yet brilliance of his play was but the outcome of a mind singularly susceptible to beauty, and of an ideality and intellectuality as far above the "common herd" as his Chess genius.

The following is from the "Illustrated London News" Chess column of 17th October 1896:—"The news of the death of Mr. W. H. K. Pollock will be received with sincere regret by everyone who knows what a peculiar place he filled in the Chess world. While not a successful player as counting by results, he was one of the finest the game has yet known, and some of his performances will not readily be forgotten. His classic contest with Weiss in the New York Congress is familiar to everybody, and raised him to the fellowship of the 'Immortals,' while even as recently as the Hastings Tournament last year he scored off both Steinitz and Tarrasch in a scarcely less striking fashion."

One of the most interesting and lengthy notices appeared in "The Witness," Montreal, of 17th October. "The news of his death, though more sudden than was expected, will hardly be unexpected; though it will bring grief to the heart of many a friend in and out of Montreal Chess circles, not to mention that far wider circle whom his genial and kindly ways drew around him at every point in his Bohemian wanderings." After a brief summary of Mr. Pollock's career and fatal illness, it concludes with the following:—

As a Chess editor and analyst Pollock was also in the front rank, and his columns in the "Baltimore News" and "Albany Journal" were eagerly sought after by Chess editors the world over, and his opinions were quoted and referred to with a deference most flattering. For some time in the early nineties he was intimately associated with Steinitz in the preparation of his "Modern Chess Instructor," which owes much both in analysis and literary polish to Pollock's indefatigable enthusiasm wherever Chess was concerned.

Here is a fairly complete list of his achievements over the board, without counting blindfold and simultaneous exhibitions.

1883.—First prize, second class, Counties Chess Association, at Birmingham; C. D. Locock, 2nd.

1884.—First prize, first class, B Division, C.C.A. meeting, Bath; defeating Fedden, Loman, Blake, Locock, and others.

1885.—Fourth prize, B.C.A. National Tourney, London; Gunsberg 1st; Bird and Guest, 2nd; and also won Tennyson prize.

1885.—First prize, Irish C.A. meeting, at Dublin.

1886.—First prize, International Tournament of Irish C.A., at Belfast; Blackburne, 2nd; Burn, 3rd.

1887.—Tied with Bird in Bradford International Tournament.

1888.—Tied with Thorold for third prize in C.C.A. meeting, at Stamford; Blake, 1st.

1889.—Second prize, International Tourney of Irish C.A., at Dublin; Burn, 1st; Mason, 3rd.

1889.—Brilliancy prize for game Pollock vs. Max Weiss, in sixth American Chess Congress in New York, and tied with Max Judd for highest score against prize winners in second round.

1890.—Second prize in United States Championship Tourney at St. Louis; Showalter, 1st; Lipschutz, 3rd.

1891.—Third prize, Open Tourney at Chicago; Showalter, 1st; Wedemann, 2nd.

1891.—Won match against Charles Moehle by 7 games to 6.

1892.—Won championship of Brooklyn, in two-round Tourney in Brooklyn Chess Club.

1892.—Second prize in United States Championship Tournament at Lexington, Ky.; Showalter, 1st; Hanborn, 3rd.

1893.—Second prize, New York State Association Tourney at Staten Island.

1895.—Draw match with Gossip at Montreal Chess Club.

1895.—Played in Hastings Tournament, winning his games against Steinitz, Bird, Tarrasch, and others.

A LETTER FROM PROFESSOR HOWARD J. ROGERS.

State of New York Department of Public Instruction,
Superintendent's Office, Albany,
17th January 1898.

Mrs. Frideswide F. Rowland,
6 Rus-in-Urbe, Kingstown, Ireland.

Dear Madam: I am in receipt of your letter asking me to send you some "reminiscences" of our old friend Pollock while he was in America. I will, with pleasure, send you a letter containing a few random recollections, but have not the time to prepare anything so elaborate as to be entitled "Reminiscences."

I think the American people had a particularly friendly feeling towards Mr. Pollock when he appeared at the 6th American Chess Congress in 1889 as the Irish Champion. This feeling was heightened by the manly, vigorous style of Chess which he played, and by his splendid victory over Weiss which won the brilliancy prize. We considered that American Chess had made an enviable acquisition when Mr. Pollock, in the summer of 1889, decided to remain in this country and began the editing of a Chess column in the Baltimore "News."

Personally, I did not meet him till 1891. I was at that time Secretary of the New York State Chess Association, of which organisation Mr. Charles A. Gilberg, of New York, was the President. As an added attraction to the midsummer meeting of the Association at Skaneateles, N.Y., we hit upon a match between the New York State Champion,

Eugene Delmar, and Mr. Pollock, the Champion of the South. I conducted the correspondence, which was very pleasant, and awaited with much interest my first meeting with Mr. Pollock. The match was to begin on Monday, and up to Sunday noon we were uncertain of the whereabouts of the Southern Champion. About five o'clock a few of us were sitting on the broad piazza overlooking the beautiful waters of Skaneateles lake, when a dusty figure in a brown suit, freckled face and wealth of reddish chestnut hair, approached the hotel. "Pollock," we shouted in a breath, "where on earth did you come from?" "Well, you see," said he, shaking hands all round with beaming cordiality, "I brought up in Syracuse early in the morning; I really couldn't spend the day loafing around there, so I thought I would take a bit of a tramp across the hills and tone myself up a little for the match." His "bit of a tramp" was a hard walk of over 20 miles in a hot August day. Pollock lost that match, by the way, but took his defeat with the utmost good humour. "It isn't to be wondered at," said he, "I am entirely out of the way of good Chess in Baltimore; and the games that I won in this match are worse Chess than those I lost in the 6th American Congress."

In the early spring of 1893, my duties as Superintendent of New York's Educational Exhibit at the Chicago Exposition took me to that city for eight months. I proposed to Pollock that he come to Albany, take charge of my Chess column in the "Albany Evening Journal," and try life in the North for a time. His letters to me had shown a desire to leave Baltimore, and during a professional tour the winter previous he had made Albany a visit, liked the city, and made a great hit with our Chess players. The year '93 I think was Pollock's most prosperous year in America. He edited both the "Baltimore News" and "Albany Journal" Chess columns, and was also given a half-time assignment as reporter on the "Journal" staff. This combined, gave him a weekly income of about sixteen dollars. His life in Albany seemed very pleasant, and on my return from Chicago in November of that year, I found him established quite like an old resident.

Of his life in Albany, I must touch lightly, or I shall become prolix. He was a steady attendant at the Chess Club, and many were the struggles we had over the board. He was of a nervous temperament, easily impressed, and would often dwell strangely on one idea. He often called me a mind-reader, because I seemed to anticipate his line of play in Chess, and block it. Curiously enough, although he was easily my superior at the game, it was with difficulty that he made even games in our personal tilts. His erratic and Bohemian ways were the delight of his brethren on the reporting staff of the "Express," the morning edition of the "Journal." Pollock would usually appear at the reporting rooms about 10 or 11 p.m., and calmly settle himself for a deep Chess analysis or other work. He was ready to chat with anybody, from managing editor to galley-boy, at any time, and finally when the morning editions were going to press in the small hours of the night, he would betake himself to his rooms and go to bed. He never arose till about 10 a.m. When assigned to report a particular occurrence, he was as likely to report another totally different, which happened to take his fancy, or perhaps forget about it entirely. As might be imagined, this resulted in the end in his discharge from the reporting staff. As an instance of his delight in pursuing investigations of a scientific nature may be mentioned his interest in meteorology and in the practical working of the Weather Bureau. He struck up a warm acquaintance with Mr. Sims, Chief of the Department at Albany, and himself a Chess player, and might be found many a night occupying the signal tower in the government building with his friend. About this time also, I believe in January '94, he had the misfortune to slip on an icy pavement, and break the small bone of his leg just above the ankle. This laid him up in the city hospital for nearly five weeks, where his chief amusement was annotating Chess games and chatting with his daily callers, of whom he had many. Pollock roomed in the house of Dr. Southworth, who took a most kindly interest in him, on Eagle Street, and after he left the hospital spent most of his time in his room for a number of weeks. I had many long visits with him at that time, and he told me in confidence much of his past history. It was during this spring that his throat seemed to trouble him, but with the coming of warm weather it seemed to disappear.

In May 1894 Mr. Pollock went to Montreal to report the Lasker-Steinitz match. He dined with me on the evening of his departure for Montreal, and I accompanied him to the train. At that time he expected to return to Albany, but he never did, and I never saw him again.

His letters to me from Montreal were frequent, and I edited the local news for his Chess column. The tone of his letters, however, indicated discouragement, and I could see that he was not getting on well in Canada. He seemed to dislike the idea of returning to the States, though he undoubtedly would have done so had a good opportunity presented itself. Of his life in Montreal, I know little, as his letters said scarcely anything concerning his personal affairs. With his visit to England in the fall of 1895, and his return to Canada in the early part of 1896, you are conversant. I tried hard, not knowing the extremity of his health, to induce him to come to the midsummer tournament of the New York State Association, held at Ontario Beach, on Lake Ontario, in July 1896. His last letter to me, from which I quote, was written July 24th, and throws much light on his physical condition and upon his unsatisfactory life in Montreal. "To me nothing would be more delightful than a trip to Rochester for the Ontario Beach meeting, though it would be questionable if I could play decently. But it is impossible; I cannot seem to get the better of my trouble. Barring accidents, I must sail on August 1st. Three or four days in the land of Cousin Jonathan, who, for the most part treated me exceedingly well, would indeed have been a pleasure to take the taste of these half-breeds out of my mouth before sailing. Please convey to the committee my extreme regret at being prevented from coming, through illness."

The next news we had of him was the tidings of his death, in October, at the home of his parents.

Mr. Pollock will be chiefly remembered in America for his genial, unaffected manner, his devotion to the royal game, and as a Chess writer of remarkably pure and vigorous English. His style of play was of the old school, and he lacked the impassiveness necessary to conduct the "drawing matches," so prevalent at the present time. His analytical powers were conceded to be of the highest order, and had his health permitted he would undoubtedly have contributed much of worth to the literature of the game of Chess. We have the kindest memories of his stay amongst us.

Trusting that these few rambling thoughts may be something of the nature you desire, I beg to remain,

Very sincerely yours,

HOWARD J. ROGERS.

A copy of the last Chess column compiled by W. H. K. Pollock.

NEWS CHESS COLUMN.

Baltimore, August 8, 1896.

TO ALL READERS.

IMPORTANT NOTICE.

With very great regret, I have to announce that I am obliged to abdicate the chair of Chess editor of this column. Serious and prolonged trouble of (at least) a bronchial nature has compelled my severance from my many delightful Chess associations in this country, and I am due to sail for my paternal home in Bristol on this day, if perchance complete rest and home treatment may effect a restoration. Any personal communication must be addressed to me at 5 Berkeley Square, Bristol, Eng., only,

"Farewell!"

Problem No. 1553.

Black—Three Pieces.

White—Six Pieces.

White to play and mate in three moves.

(White K-Qsq, R-QB4 and K4, B-QB8, P-K3 and KKt4. Black K-Q6, P-Q7 and K3.)

This problem is calculated to torment anyone moving the pieces before "catching the idea." It was "said" to have been declared unsolvable by Pillsbury and is a noted puzzler. We do not know its further history.

Problem No. 1554.

By P. F. Blake, Manchester, England.
First prize in Liverpool Weekly Mercury.

Black—Six Pieces.

White—Ten Pieces.

White to play and mate in two moves.
(White K-QKt5, Q-QRsq, R-Q2 and K8, B-QKt4 and QB4, Kt-Q6, P-QKt3, KKt2 and 3. Black K-K6, R-K3, B-QKt3, Kt-Q8 and KKt8, P-K2.)

Solutions.

Problem 1550. By Lissner.

1. Q-QKt7.

The Nuremberg Congress.

The following was the first game finished in the great tournament at Nuremberg. Although it proceeds on book lines for some 15 moves, it is extremely interesting, the problem-like draw forced by Blackburne being worthy of that master, and not the least pretty part of the game.

Game No. 1435—Two Knights Defence.

White, Blackburne.	Black, Teichmann.
1 P to K4	1 P to K4
2 Kt to KB3	2 Kt to QB3
3 B to B4	3 Kt to B3
4 P to Q4	4 PxP
5 Castles	5 B to B4 (a)
6 P to K5	6 P to Q4
7 PxKt	7 PxB
8 R to K sq ch	8 B to K3
9 Kt to Kt5	9 Q to Q4
10 Kt to QB3	10 Q to B4
11 P to KKt4 (b)	11 Q to Kt3 (c)
12 QKt to K4	12 B to Kt3
13 P to B4	13 Castles QR
14 P to B5	14 BxP
15 PxB	15 QxP (B4) (d)
16 K to R sq (e)	16 PxP
17 Q to B3 (f)	17 QxQ ch
18 KtxQ	18 Kt to Kt5
19 KtxBP (g)	19 KtxBP
20 B to B4	20 KtxQR
21 RxKt	21 P to B6 (h)
22 PxP	22 PxP
23 R to QB sq	23 R to Q6
24 Kt to K sq	24 R to Q7
25 Kt to B2	25 R to K7
26 Kt to Q5	26 B to R4
27 Kt to Q4	27 RxP
28 KtxP(B3)	28 BxKt
29 RxB	29 P to QB3
30 Kt to B5	

Black—Teichmann.

White—Blackburne.

	30 K to Q2
31 R to Q3 ch	31 K to K3
32 Kt to Kt7 ch !	32 K to K2 (k)
33 R to K3 ch	33 K to Q sq
34 R to Q3 ch	34 K to K2
35 R to K3 ch	35 K to Q sq
36 R to Q3 ch	36 K to K2

Drawn game.

Notes.

(a) This is the original "Max Lange" position. Black could avoid it by 5...KtxP.

(b) Nothing better, we believe, has been discovered. The move leads to the gain of a piece, against which Black has a great superiority in pawns and position.

(c) If QxP at B3 White can obtain a smart attack either by Kt-Q5 or Kt-K4.

(d) The "Handbuch" here dismisses the variation as in Black's favor.
(e) White plays a purely defensive game. We prefer 16 R-B sq and if P-Q6 ch. 17 K-Kt2, PxP. 18 QxP; or Q-Q4. 17 Q-Kt4 ch, followed by R-B5.
(f) If 17 KtxBP, QR-Ksq, etc.
(g) A masterly move, hampering the adverse Rooks.

(h) The real object of this is to bring the Rooks into play down the Q file.
(i) Now the plot unfolds itself, and Black can scarcely win but by surrendering one of his Rs for a minor piece.
(k) If K-B3. 33 R-Q6 ch and the K must return to K2 or be mated.

An engrossed copy of the following was sent to the Rev. W. J. Pollock, Clifton, Bristol (the father of Mr. Pollock):

BALTIMORE CHESS ASSOCIATION.

At a meeting of the Baltimore Chess Association, held October 21st, 1896, the following resolutions were unanimously adopted:—

"Whereas this Association has learned of its loss through death of an esteemed and highly gifted member, Dr. William H. K. Pollock, which occurred in Bristol, England, October 5th, 1896, and, whereas we deem it proper to place upon record this expression of our sorrow, therefore be it resolved—That we have lost in him a true friend, endowed with the deepest sense of honour, a generous nature, and a modest and unassuming disposition; resolved, that as an organisation devoted to the ennobling game of Chess, we record our indebtedness, as well as that of the whole Chess playing world, to him as one of the most brilliant and original Chess Masters of his time, whose labours as Chess editor of the "Baltimore News," and as Chess instructor, have done much to elevate the standing of the Association, and improve the play of the members. Resolved, furthermore, that a page of our minutes be set apart for recording these resolutions, and that a copy be sent to his bereaved family."

E. L. TORSCH, President.
JOHN HEINRICHS, Vice-President.
HARRY E. GARNER, Secretary.

DUBLIN CHESS CLUB.

The following vote was passed by the Managing Committee (Dublin Chess Club) on behalf of the Club, Jan. 27, 1897:—Proposed—"That this club do place on record its deep sense of the loss the cause of Chess has recently sustained by the death of our brilliant young Master, Mr. W. H. K. Pollock, who represented Ireland in the game, and who, for several years, while studying medicine in Dublin, was a member of this Club, and even then showed great originality and grasp of the game, and by his genial and warm-hearted nature had won for himself the esteem of his fellow-members, to all of whom his after—though too short career—was a matter of lively interest." A copy of above was forwarded to Rev. W. J. Pollock, Bristol.

In Memoriam.

W. H. K. POLLOCK, Died October 5, 1896.

"Only the hours serene are numbered."—Virgil.

The various memories that crowd
  The mind when retrospective,
The thoughts of other days allowed
  To throng me when reflective,
Continue still a friendship rare
  Though death has come between;
And in that mood no thought I spare
  But for the hours serene.

No space for bickering was there,
  Where hearts were close entwined:
And naught but harmony could dare
  Prevade the one in mind;
So much alike in good or ill,
  In character and mien,
'Twere strange if aught but passing chill
  Came over hours serene.

Each guessed at what the other thought,
  And knew the thought his own;
Each laboured that the talk be fraught
  With kind, congenial tone;
And if a word too swiftly flew,
  (The fault must mine have been,)
No answering anger either knew
  In those sweet hours serene.

So in these hours serene I think
  Of those—not passed away,
But chained to these by link on link
  Of memories that stay;
And pleasures oft I gather yet,
  From pleasures that have been,
More sweet by far that I forget
  All but the hours serene.

        GABRIEL BREEZE, Montreal.

GAME 1.—Played at Bristol, May 1883. White, Mr. Pollock; Black, Mr. J. Burt.

Evans Gambit Declined.

WHITE.	BLACK.	WHITE.	BLACK.
1 P-K4	1 P-K4	29 K-Kt4	29 Kt-B4
2 Kt-KB3	2 Kt-QB3	30 B-B5	30 BxB
3 B-B4	3 B-B4	31 KtxB	31 Kt-K6ch
4 P-QKt4	4 B-Kt3	32 K-Kt3	32 KR-B7
5 P-Kt5	5 Kt-R4	33 Q-K5	33 RxPch
6 BxPch(A)	6 KxB	34 K-R4	34 P-Kt4ch
7 KtxPch	7 K-Bsq	35 QxPch	35 RxQ
8 B-R3ch	8 P-Q3		
9 P-Q4	9 B-K3		
10 Castles	10 Kt-K2		
11 Q-B3ch	11 K-Ksq		
12 Q-R5ch	12 P-Kt3		
13 Q-Kt5	13 PxKt		
14 QxKP	14 BxQP		
15 QxQB	15 BxR		
16 Kt-Q2	16 B-B6		
17 R-Qsq	17 R-KBsq		
18 Kt-Bsq(B)	18 R-B2		
19 RxQch	19 RxR		
20 Kt-K3	20 R-Q7		
21 P-R3	21 QRxKBP		
22 Kt-Q5	22 B-Q5		
23 KtxPch	23 K-Bsq		
24 Q-B8ch	24 K-Kt2		
25 Kt-K6ch	25 K-R3		

and as Black threatens mate on the move in four different ways White resigns.

Position after Black's 25th move.

(See Diagram below.)

26 Q-QKt8(c)	26 R-B8ch
27 K-R2	27 B-Kt8ch
28 K-Kt3	28 B-B7ch

NOTES.

(A) This is altogether unsound, not so much on account of the sacrifice of material as in that the attack is premature and short lived.

(B) White has contrived, deftly enough, to win the Queen, but of course at an exorbitant price.

(c) Truly a strange plight! This is the only move to prevent the immediate loss of the game. Compare diagram.

GAME 2.—Played at Purssell's, 18th October 1883. White, Mr. S. Tinsley; Black, Mr. Pollock.

Queen's Fianchetto.

WHITE.	BLACK.	WHITE.	BLACK.
1 P-QKt3	1 P-K4	2 B-Kt2	2 Kt-QB3

WHITE.	BLACK.	WHITE.	BLACK.
3 P-K3	3 P-Q4	27 Kt-K2	27 Q-B7
4 B-Kt5?	4 B-Q3	28 Kt-Q4	28 Q-B4ch
5 P-KB4	5 P-B3	29 K-R2	29 R-Ktsq
6 BxKtch(A)	6 PxB	30 Q-Ktsq	30 Q-Kt5
7 P-Kt3(B)	7 Kt-K2(C)	31 Q-QBsq	31 B-B5(K)
8 Q-K2	8 Kt-Kt3	32 Q-B2	32 QxRPch
9 Kt-QB3	9 Castles		
10 Castles	10 P-QR4		
11 P-QR4	11 B-R3		
12 Q-B3	12 Q-K2		
13 K-Ktsq	13 QR-Ktsq		
14 P-B5(D)	14 P-K5		
15 Q-B2	15 Kt-K4		
16 K-R2	16 RxP(E)		

and wins.

Position after Black's 16th move.

(See Diagram below.)

17 PxR(F)	17 Kt-Q6
18 Q-Kt2(G)	18 Kt-Kt5ch
19 K-Rsq(H)	19 Kt-B7ch
20 K-Ktsq	20 B-Q6
21 K-Bsq	21 B-R6
22 Kt-Ktsq(I)	22 Q-B4(J)
23 BxB	23 KtxBch
24 K-Kt2	24 KtxKt
25 RxKt	25 Q-B7ch
26 K-R3	26 QxR

NOTES.

(A) White may have purposed subsequently sacrificing his B for KP, but found it would not work.

(B) This move makes it the more likely, as its only possible object could be to prevent Q-B5ch. It is of course very bad Chess.

(C) Kt-R3 would answer present purposes equally well, and is very probably a better move.

(D) Mr. Tinsley does not often play in this manner. The game is only given on account of the very interesting play arising from White's 16th move.

(E) Sound or unsound, this sacrifice of a Rook is particularly startling, as there appears to be nothing whatever in it, viewing the game at this stage.

(F) If 17 KxR B-B5 mate.

(G) The only move to save the Queen.

(H) K-R3 would of course mean submitting to Black the choice of a draw. Or he might proceed as follows: 19 K-R3 B-Q6, 20 KKt-K2 R-Ktsq, 21 Kt-Q4 B-K4, 22 Kt-Ktsq Kt-B7ch, 23 K-R2 BxKt, 24 BxB Q-Kt5, and wins. If 19 K-Ktsq B-Q6ch, and the result is practically the same as in the actual game.

(I) The only available move.

(J) He could also win by BxBch followed by R-Ktsq.

(K) This apparently was a slip, for White could take off the Bishop and victory would again hang in the balance.

GAME 3.—Played at the Counties' Chess Association, Birmingham, 1883. White, Mr. Pollock; Black, Mr. C. D. Locock.

Vienna Opening.

	WHITE.		BLACK.		WHITE.		BLACK.
1	P-K4	1	P-K4	11	K-Qsq	11	QxQ
2	Kt-QB3	2	Kt-KB3	12	PxQ	12	Kt-B6
3	P-B4	3	P-Q4	13	P-K6(e)	13	P-KB3?
4	BPxP	4	KtxP	14	P-Q3!	14	Castles
5	Kt-B3	5	B-KKt5(A)	15	B-R3	15	K-Ktsq(F)
6	Q-K2(B)	6	Kt-QB3(C)	16	R-Bsq	16	Kt-K4(G)
7	KtxKt	7	Kt-Q5?	17	B-K3(H)	17	Kt-B5
8	Q-Q3	8	BxKt	18	B-Bsq	18	B-B4
9	PxB(D)	9	PxKt	19	K-K2	19	Kt-K4
10	QxP	10	Q-R5ch!	20	B-K3	20	BxB
				21	KxB(I)	21	R-Q3
				22	R-KKtsq	22	R-B3
				23	RxP	23	RxBP
				24	QR-KKtsq	24	Kt-Kt3
				25	P-K7	25	RxRP
				26	B-Q7	26	KtxP
				27	RxKt	27	RxP
				28	RxP	28	R-KBsq
				29	R-B7	29	R-Qsq
				30	RxP	30	RxP
				31	P-K5	31	P-B4
				32	P-K6	32	K-B2
				33	R-Kt7	33	R-R6
				34	B-R4ch	34	K-Ktsq
				35	B-Kt5	35	P-B5
				36	BxP		Resigns.

Position after Black's 10th move.

BLACK.

WHITE.

NOTES.

(A) B-K2 is perhaps the safest move here.

(B) In order to dislodge the Knight from K5.

(C) If KtxKt, 7 KtPxKt, greatly strengthening White's centre. Another move is 6 Kt-Kt4. The text move is erroneous.

(D) Immediately after the game Mr. Locock pointed out that retreating the Kt to B2 (or Kt3) wins a clear piece. The position is very peculiar, and well illustrates Steinitz's rule, "When you have found a very good move, don't make it, but look for a better one." Not only did I make the very same oversight in an offhand game in London a year or two later, but the identical position occurred between Blackburne and Paulsen in the Breslau tournament seven years later, the self-same mistake being again perpetrated by Black and overlooked by White. Mr. Hoffer on that occasion pointed out White's proper reply, 9 Kt-B2. It is easy to discern the process of thought which led to the "let-off." White, whether failing to reckon on the opponent's extremely ingenious 10th move, or not, sees that the plan of his game is a good one, and that he will remain with a strong Pawn centre and both Bishops on the board.

(E) In order to isolate a Pawn. Black ought of course to have taken it.

(F) B-K2 looks somewhat stronger.

(G) If KtxP, 17 R-B2 B-Q3, 18 B-B4 BxB, 19 RxB P-KKt4, 20 RxP P-Kt5, 21 B-Kt2, or White might play 20 R-B2.

(H) White ought to play K-K2 at once.

(I) The King is now well posted and victory merely a matter of time.

GAME 4.—Played at the Counties Chess Association, Birmingham, 1883. White, Mr. Pollock; Black, Mr. F. P. Wildman.

Four Knights' Game.

WHITE.	BLACK.	WHITE.	BLACK.
1 P-K4	1 P-K4	20 RxQ	20 PxR
2 Kt-QB3	2 Kt-QB3	21 BxB	21 RxB
3 Kt-B3	3 Kt-B3	22 R-Ksq	Resigns.
4 B-Kt5	4 B-Kt5		
5 Castles	5 Castles		
6 Kt-Q5	6 B-B4		
7 P-Q4(A)	7 KtxQP(B)		
8 KtxQKt	8 PxKt		
9 B-Kt5	9 B-K2		
10 KtxBch	10 QxKt		
11 QxP	11 P-Q3		
12 P-KB4	12 P-B4(c)		
13 Q-B3	13 QxP		
14 BxKt	14 PxB		
15 QxKBP	15 Q-Kt3(D)		
16 Q-R4	16 B-B4(E)		
17 R-B3	17 K-Rsq		
18 R-KKt3	18 Q-K3		
19 B-Q7(F)			

(See Diagram below.)

19 Q-Kt3

Position after White's 19th move.

NOTES.

(A) A powerful attack, invented by Blackburne.

(B) KtxKt might perhaps be played here. PxP is also better than the text move.

(C) Black's game is badly constrained, nor does this help matters. If R-Qsq, 13 P-K5 PxP, 14 QxKP Q-Q3, 15 QR-Qsq Q-Kt3ch (QxR, 16 BxKt), 16 K-Rsq B-Kt5, with a much better prospect.

(D) White threatened both R-B3 and B-Q3.

(E) If QxBP, 17 R-B3 QxKtP, 18 QR-Qsq with a crushing attack. Q-Kt5, however, held out some slight chances.

(F) Neat and conclusive. B-B4, on the other hand, would have enabled Black to prolong the game by P-Q4.

GAME 5.—Played at the Bath Chess Club, January 1884. White, Mr. J. Burt; Black, Mr. Pollock.

Four Knights' Opening.

WHITE.	BLACK.	WHITE.	BLACK.
1 P-K4	1 P-K4	\multicolumn{2}{l}{Position after Black's 21st move.}	
2 Kt-KB3	2 Kt-QB3		
3 Kt-B3	3 Kt-B3		
4 B-Kt5	4 P-QR3		
5 B-R4(A)	5 B-Kt5		
6 Castles	6 Castles		
7 P-Q3	7 P-Q3		
8 P-KR3(B)	8 Kt-K2(C)		
9 Kt-K2	9 Kt-Kt3		
10 Kt-Kt3	10 P-Q4		
11 Q-K2	11 B-Q3		
12 B-KKt5	12 P-R3		
13 BxKt(D)	13 QxB		
14 PxP	14 Kt-B5		
15 Q-K4	15 P-KKt4		
16 Kt-R2	16 P-KR4		
17 Q-B3	17 P-Kt5		
18 PxP	18 PxP		
19 KtxP	19 Q-R5		
20 Kt-K3	20 P-KB4	22 Q-Kt3ch	22 K-B2
21 Kt-Rsq	21 P-K5(E)	23 QxQ	23 Kt-K7 mate.

NOTES.

(A) 5 BxKt QPxB, 6 KtxP affords a stronger attack.

(B) A weak move.

(C) Black should have taken the Kt off first, although he makes a pretty good case of it as it is.

(D) The attack to which he is subjected shows the gain of the Pawn to be a loss.

(E) Leading to a comical and evidently unexpected crisis.

GAME 6.—Played at the Counties Chess Association, Bath, 1884, in playing off the tie. White, Mr. Pollock; Black, Mr. R. J. Loman.

Sicilian Defence.

WHITE.	BLACK.	WHITE.	BLACK.
1 P-K4	1 P-QB4	9 B-Bsq	9 P-B4(D)
2 Kt-QB3	2 Kt-QB3	10 PxP	10 QBxP
3 Kt-B3	3 P-KKt3	11 Castles	11 Q-B2
4 B-Kt5(A)	4 B-Kt2(B)	12 Kt-Kt3	12 Kt-K4
5 BxKt	5 QPxB(C)	13 KtxKt(E)	13 BxKt
6 Kt-K2	6 Kt-B3	14 P-KB4	14 B-Kt2
7 P-Q3	7 Castles	15 Q-K2	15 QR-Ksq
8 B-K3	8 Kt-Kt5	16 KtxB	16 RxKt

WHITE.	BLACK.	WHITE.	BLACK.
17 Q-K6ch	17 K-Rsq	39 R-K8	39 QxR
18 P-KKt4	18 R-Q4	40 QxQch	40 R-Ktsq
19 R-Ktsq	19 R-Q3(f)	41 Q-K5ch	41 R-Kt2
20 Q-Ksq	20 Q-Q2	42 QxP	42 R-QB2
21 Q-Kt3	21 P-K4	43 Q-B8 mate. (o)	
22 P-B5(g)	22 PxP		
23 RxP	23 R-Kt3(h)		
24 B-K3	24 P-K5		
25 B-Q2(i)	25 PxP		
26 PxP	26 Q-Q5ch		
27 K-Rsq	27 RxP		
28 Q-KB3(j)	28 R-KKtsq		
29 B-B3	29 Q-R5		
30 R-B8(k)			

(See Diagram below.)

	30 BxB		
31 PxB	31 QxP		
32 RxRch	32 QxR		
33 P-B4(l)	33 R-Kt3		
34 Q-B4(m)	34 P-Kt4		
35 Q-K5ch	35 R-Kt2		
36 R-KBsq	36 Q-Qsq(n)		
37 R-B7	37 Q-KKtsq		
38 R-K7	38 P-Kt5		

Position after White's 30th move.

BLACK.

[Chess diagram]

WHITE.

NOTES.

(A) Strangely enough this excellent move seems to have passed out of memory, and does not seem to have been had recourse to at all in the days of the revival of the Sicilian Defence by Messrs. Bird, Lasker, and others, in the form of the King Fianchetto, in conjunction with P-Q3.

(B) Kt-Q5 is preferred by some, but the move at least gives White considerable latitude.

(C) The capture with KtP would leave the doubled Pawns more awkwardly fixed, unless the QBP could be advanced to B5 and supported with the QP. In the Ruy Lopez the doubled QBP is considered no disadvantage to Black. But in the present case both Pawns are advanced a square, and therefore the two front Pawns of the phalanx of three cannot both be defended by Pawns, unless the foremost is advanced to B5. It is on the forced position of these adverse Pawns that White gives up his Bishop, and we shall see how far he was justified in trying so fine a plan.

(D) This gives Black considerable freedom for his pieces, but does not improve his Pawn position.

(E) There was also Kt-Kt5 to be considered, but White is determined upon following the plan indicated, remote as it seems.

(F) Black makes great efforts to advance his KP. Could it have been played to K4 on the 15th move?

(G) This will leave White two Pawns to one on the King's side for the ending.

(H) This move and the next (especially) is very well managed by Black, and the position of the first player becomes exceedingly precarious.

(I) It is remarkable that White should succeed in repairing a mistake of such magnitude as that of his 24th move. If 25 BxP B-Q5ch, 26 BxB QxBch, 27 K-Rsq PxP, and should win.

(J) Threatening to win a piece by B-B3.

(K) Both sides play most ingeniously, and the attack changes like a kaledioscope. See diagram.

(L) To prevent the exchange of Queens.

(M) Threatening to win the QBP safely.

(N) This loses the game forthwith. P-KR3!

(O) A very curious and interesting game, of its kind.

GAME 7.—Played at the Counties Chess Association, Bath, 1884. White, Mr. C. D. Locock; Black, Mr. Pollock.

Ruy Lopez.

WHITE.	BLACK.	WHITE.	BLACK.
1 P-K4	1 P-K4	26 Q-Q4	
2 Kt-KB3	2 Kt-QB3		
3 B-Kt5	3 P-QR3		
4 B-R4	4 Kt-B3		
5 P-Q4	5 PxP		
6 Castles	6 B-K2		
7 P-K5	7 Kt-K5		
8 KtxP	8 Castles		
9 Kt-B5	9 P-Q4(A)		
10 PxP en pass	10 BxKt		
11 BxKt	11 BxP		
12 BxP	12 Q-R5(B)		
13 P-KKt3!	13 Q-R6		
14 Q-B3(C)	14 QR-Ksq		
15 B-K3	15 R-K3		
16 Kt-Q2	16 Kt-B3!		
17 P-B4	17 P-B3		
18 BxP	18 B-QKt5		
19 B-Q5(D)	19 BxKt		
20 BxR	20 PxB		
21 Q-Kt2	21 BxB		
22 PxB	22 Q-R3		
23 KR-Ksq	23 B-K5		26 KtxP(E)
24 Q-Q2	24 B-B6	27 Q-K5	27 Kt-K7ch
25 R-KBsq	25 Kt-K5	28 K-B2	28 Q-R5ch
		29 Q-Kt3	29 KtxQ

Position after White's 26th move.

and mates directly.

NOTES.

(A) This game was played in Section 1B. It was of considerable importance, and the last game of the tournament. By winning it Mr. Pollock tied for first place with Messrs. Fedden and Loman. Had he lost it he would have tied for fourth place with Mr. Burt, half-a-point below Mr. Blake. Hence the "heroic treatment" of the defence. Black deliberated 20 minutes over this move, the time limit being one hour for 20 moves.

(B) The plan, of course, seems a bold one, if not at first blush a desperate one.

But Black was in no humour to reck of a sacrifice of the exchange. It may just be noticed that KtxKBP would be foiled by Q-B3.

(c) It must be confessed that here reality coincides with appearances. White seems to gain nothing by disdaining to take the Rook. It is, of course, "another thing" in actual play, with the clocks ticking their warning of the approach of the hour's expiration, when many things that are not are seen. After 14 BxR RxB, 15 Q-B3 R-Ksq, 16 Q-Kt2 Q-R4, 17 R-Ksq! Black has no better move than R-K3. A comparison then of this position with that after Black's 17th move in the actual game will show at once which of the two is the more manageable game to play.

(D) Black here gains a piece prettily, while the opponent is striving to prevent B-K5. If 19 Q-Kt2 RxB.

(E) This either wins the Queen or mates. See diagram.

GAME 8.—Played at the Counties Chess Association, Bath, 1884. White, Mr. Pollock; Black, Mr. R. J. Loman.

Four Knights' Opening.

WHITE.	BLACK.	WHITE.	BLACK.
1 P-K4	1 P-K4	14 KxKt	14 P-KKt3
2 Kt-QB3	2 Kt-QB3	15 Q-R6	15 PxPch
3 Kt-B3	3 Kt-B3	16 K-Ktsq	16 P-Q3
4 B-Kt5	4 B-B4	17 B-B4ch	17 B-K3
5 KtxP	5 KtxKt	18 B-KKt5	18 Q-Q2
6 P-Q4	6 B-Q3	19 BxBch	19 QxB
7 PxKt	7 BxP	20 R-KBsq	20 P-Q4
8 Castles	8 BxKt	21 QR-Ksq	21 P-K5
9 PxB	9 Castles	22 B-K3	22 P-Kt3(E)
10 P-K5	10 Kt-K5(A)	23 B-Q4	23 Q-K2
11 Q-R5	11 Q-K2(B)	24 RxRch	24 RxR
12 R-Ksq	12 KtxKBP(c)	25 R-KBsq	25 RxRch
		26 KxR	26 Q-Bsqch(F)
		27 QxQch	27 KxQ
		28 B-K5	28 P-B3
		29 K-K2	29 K-K2
		30 K-K3	30 K-K3
		31 B-Kt8	31 P-QR3
		32 P-Kt4	32 P-KKt4
		33 P-B4	33 K-Q2
		34 PxP	34 PxP
		35 K-Q4	35 K-K3
		36 P-QR4	36 P-Kt4
		37 P-R5	

and wins.

Position after Black's 12th move.

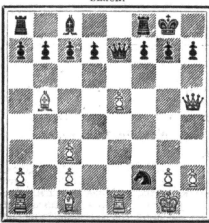

| 13 B-Bsq! | 13 P-KB3(D) |

NOTES.

(A) Black has played the opening indifferently. His 4th, 6th and 8th moves are open to question, and here Kt-Ksq is safer.

(B) If KtxQBP, 12 B-Q3 P-KKt3, 13 Q-R6, followed by B-KKt5, and wins.

(c) The loss of the piece can hardly be prevented: thus, if Q-B4, 13 RxKt QxB, 14 R-KB4 P-KR3, 15 BxRP, and wins. Or KtxQBP, 13 B-Q3. Or Kt-B4, 13 B-Kt5 Q-K3, 14 R-K3 P-QB3, 15 B-B6, and wins. It will be noticed that White made the only move, if 13 B-R4 Q-B4, 14 B-K3 Q-B5, 15 B-Kt3 Q-KKt5!

(D) Black now makes desperate efforts to retrieve matters, and the greatest care becomes necessary to prevent it, for he obtains a third Pawn for the piece minus.

(E) In order to drive away the B when it reaches Q4. But it does not improve his Pawn position.

(F) Labouring under the impression that he could draw the game.

GAME 9.—CURIOSITIES OF CHESS. "It is curious to note, how a little novelty in a well worn opening often succeeds in completely leading the opponent astray. The following game was played at Simpson's Divan, London, in 1884, and is worth a perusal." White, Mr. Pollock; Black, Mr. W.

Muzio Gambit.

WHITE.	BLACK.	WHITE.	BLACK.
1 P-KB4	1 P-K4(A)	12 RxKt(D)	12 Q-B4ch
2 P-K4	2 PxP	13 K-Rsq	13 QxR
3 Kt-KB3	3 P-KKt4	14 Kt-Q5	14 Q-Qsq(E)
4 B-B4	4 P-Kt5	15 B-B3	15 P-Q3
5 Castles	5 PxKt	16 B-B6	16 Kt-B3
6 QxP	6 Q-B3	17 BxQ	17 KtxB
7 P-K5	7 QxP	18 Kt-K7ch	18 K-Rsq
8 P-Q3	8 B-R3	19 KtxB	
9 B-Q2	9 Kt-K2(B)	and wins, for if RxKt, 20 Q-KR3.	
10 R-Ksq	10 Q-KB4(C)	Or if B-Kt4, 20 Q-Kt4, followed by	
11 Kt-B3	11 Castles	Q-Q7.	

NOTES.

(A) Starting for From's Gambit, which White, by refusing, converts into a King's Gambit; and presently the regular Muzio appears.

(B) If 9 QxP, 10 Q-K4ch any, 11 B-B3 Q-Kt3ch, 12 B-Q4 and wins a piece.

(C) This seems unsuitable in the present instance. The idea of White's novelty, 10 R-Ksq, is to abandon the assault up the blocked KB file, and to seize instead a file which is more open and valuable.

(D) Probably quite unexpected.

(E) If 14 Q-R5, 15 B-B3, threatening B-B6.

GAME 10.—Played in a match between Bath and Bristol, February 1885. White, Mr. Pollock; Black, Mr. W. H. Harsant.

Four Knights' Opening.

WHITE.	BLACK.	WHITE.	BLACK.
1 P-K4	1 P-K4	6 B-KKt5	6 P-Q3
2 Kt-QB3	2 Kt-QB3	7 B-Kt5	7 B-Q2
3 Kt-B3	3 Kt-B3	8 Castles	8 BxKt
4 P-Q4	4 PxP	9 PxB	9 Castles
5 KtxP	5 B-Kt5	10 P-KB4	10 KtxKt

D

WHITE.	BLACK.	WHITE.	BLACK.
11 BxB	11 QxB	15 Q-Kt5ch	15 K-Rsq
12 BxKt	12 Kt-B3	16 Q-B6ch	16 K-Ktsq
13 Q-R5	13 PxB	17 R mates. (A)	
14 R-B3	14 P-B4		

NOTES.

(A) A strange little story enough!

GAME 11.—Played at Bristol, April 1885. White, Mr. Pollock; Black, Mr. J. Burt.

Two Knights' Defence.

WHITE.	BLACK.	WHITE.	BLACK.
1 P-K4	1 P-K4		
2 B-B4	2 Kt-KB3		
3 Kt-KB3	3 Kt-B3		
4 Kt-Kt5	4 P-Q4		
5 PxP	5 KtxP		
6 KtxBP	6 KxKt		
7 Q-B3ch	7 K-K3		
8 Kt-B3	8 Kt-K2		
9 P-Q4	9 P-B3		
10 B-KKt5	10 Q-R4(A)		
11 PxP	11 Kt-Kt3		
12 CastlesKR	12 B-Kt5		
13 KR-Ksq(B)	13 BxKt		
14 Q-Kt4ch	14 K-B2		
15 P-K6ch	15 K-Ksq		
16 PxB	16 QxBP		
17 QR-Qsq	17 R-Bsq		
18 BxKt	18 PxB		
19 Q-R4ch	19 Q-B3		22 PxB(D)
20 RxP	20 Kt-K2	23 Q-KKt4	23 BxR
21 R-Q7(C)	21 R-B3	24 PxBch	24 QxP(E)
22 BxR		25 Q-Kt8 mate.	

Position after White's 22nd move.

NOTES.

(A) A somewhat unusual move.

(B) White preserves his KP for the persecution of the adverse K as soon as it is set free.

(C) The game is not without its pretty points. White again threatens mate, in three moves.

(D) If QxQ, 23 RxKtch K-Bsq, 24 R-B7ch K-Ksq, 25 RxKKtP BxP, 26 RxBch K-Bsq, 27 R(K6)-K7; White cannot lose, and ought to win.

(E) An oversight. K-Qsq best, when after 25 Q-Kt7 QxQP, 26 QxBP he would not find it easy to win.

GAME 12.—Played at the British Chess Association, London, 1885. White, Mr. Pollock; Black, Mr. H. E. Bird.

Sicilian Defence.

WHITE.	BLACK.	WHITE.	BLACK.
1 P-K4	1 P-QB4	37 Q-R6(H)	37 Kt-Kt4
2 Kt-QB3	2 Kt-QB3	38 QxRP	38 P-Q5
3 Kt-B3	3 P-KKt3	39 Q-B7	39 K-Kt2
4 P-Q4(A)	4 PxP	40 R-Rsq	40 P-K3
5 KtxP	5 B-Kt2	41 Q-Kt8	41 Kt-K5
6 B-K3	6 P-Q3	42 B-R5	42 P-K4
7 B-QB4	7 Kt-B3	43 B-B7	43 Kt-B7ch
8 Castles	8 Castles	44 K-Ktsq	44 P-K5
9 Q-Q2	9 Kt-KKt5	45 B-K5ch	45 K-R3
10 KtxKt	10 PxKt	46 K-R2	46 P-K6
11 QR-Qsq	11 B-K3	47 P-QKt4	47 KtxP
12 BxB	12 PxB(B)	48 PxKt	48 QxBPch
13 B-Kt5	13 R-B2	49 K-Rsq	49 Q-K5ch
14 P-KR3	14 Kt-B3	50 K-Ktsq	50 R-B7
15 Q-K2(c)	15 Q-R4	51 B-Kt7ch	51 KxB
16 B-Q2	16 Q-Kt5	52 R-R7ch	52 K-R3
17 R-Ktsq(D)	17 QR-KBsq(E)	53 RxPch	53 KxR
18 Kt-Qsq	18 Q-R5		
19 P-QKt3	19 QxRP	and wins.	
20 R-Bsq(F)	20 Q-R6		
21 P-KB4	21 Kt-Q2	Position after Black's 30th move.	
22 Q-Kt4	22 Kt-B4		
23 Kt-B2	23 B-Q5		
24 P-B5	24 KPxP		
25 PxP	25 BxKtch		
26 RxB	26 RxP		
27 RxR	27 RxR		
28 Q-Q4	28 Kt-K3		
29 Q-KR4	29 Q-B4ch		
30 K-Rsq	30 R-B3(G)		
(See Diagram below.)			
31 Q-K4	31 P-Q4		
32 Q-QR4	32 Q-B7		
33 Q-QKt4	33 P-B4		
34 Q-Kt8ch	34 R-Bsq		
35 Q-K5	35 Q-B4		
36 Q-K2	36 R-B2		

NOTES.

(A) An excellent move here is B-Kt5. See game 8, Pollock v. Loman, p. 24.

(B) The opening appears to result a little in Black's favour.

(c) Intending to proceed with P-K5 or Q-B4.

(D) It does not appear that White missed anything here, sc., by Kt-Q5. The text move is therefore a good one, and the least disturbing to his Pawn position.

(E) This prevents Kt-Q5, Kt-B7, &c.

(F) White seems to have fallen into the temptation of playing for a trap hoping to have time to play B-QB3 and win the Q by R-Rsq. He also perhaps preferred to sacrifice the Pawn for a K side attack, for he could probably have recovered it by 20 Kt-B3 Q-R4, 21 R-Rsq Q-B2, 22 Q-B4 Q-Q2, 23 R-R6, bringing the pressure from the Queen's side. The play now becomes animated enough.

(G) Black holds his Pawns together very skilfully.

(H) White gives a great deal of trouble, but the end of it is fairly visible.

GAME 13.—Played at the British Chess Association, London, 1885. White, Mr. Pollock; Black, Mr. J. Mortimer.

Three Knights' Opening.

WHITE.	BLACK.	WHITE.	BLACK.
1 P-K4	1 P-K4	27 R-K2(E)	27 Q-R5
2 Kt-QB3	2 Kt-QB3	28 RxKtch	28 K-Qsq
3 Kt-B3	3 B-B4?	29 Q-K2	29 Q-Kt4ch
4 KtxP(A)	4 KtxKt	30 B-Kt2	30 QxP
5 P-Q4	5 B-Q3	31 B-Q6	31 Q-Kt3
6 PxKt	6 BxP		
7 B-Q3(B)	7 BxKtch?		
8 PxB	8 P-Q3		
9 Castles	9 P-KR3		
10 P-K5 !	10 P-Q4(C)		
11 B-R3	11 Kt-K2		
12 P-KB4	12 P-KKt3		
13 Q-B3	13 P-QB3		
14 QR-Ksq	14 B-K3		
15 P-Kt4(D)	15 P-KR4		
16 P-R3	16 PxP		
17 PxP	17 Kt-Ktsq		
18 P-B5	18 PxP		
19 PxP	19 Q-R5		
20 R-B2	20 B-Bsq		
21 P-K6	21 P-B3		
22 QR-K2	22 Kt-K2		
23 R-R2	23 R-Ktsqch		
24 QR-Kt2	24 Q-K8ch		
25 B-Bsq	25 BxP		
26 RxRch	26 BxR		

and White mates in four moves.

Position after Black's 31st move.

NOTES.

(A) Nearly always the "coup juste" in kindred positions, as leading to rapid development, of the Pawn centre especially. Black should have played the other Knight. This game is a good example of the rule: Black's KB quickly becomes embarrassed and presently he is fain to exchange it off for an inferior piece.

(B) The Bishop is snugly placed here should Black, as in the present case, take off the QKt, which, however, is by no means commendable.

(C) PxP is perhaps as good. The Pawn, however, could in no way be held.

(D) White's opening is perfectly played, and the attack which he pursues, without respite from this to the mate, is absolutely sound.

(E) The moves all explain themselves. The late Herr B. Horwitz expressed himself several times as greatly pleased with White's management of this game.

GAME 14.—Played in the Tennyson Prize Tournament, London, 1885. White, Rev. G. A. MacDonnell; Black, Mr. Pollock.

Irregular Opening.

WHITE.	BLACK.	WHITE.	BLACK.
1 P-KB4	1 P-KB4	31 RxR	31 RxR
2 P-QKt3	2 P-K3	32 KtxP!	32 Q-Ksq
3 B-Kt2	3 Kt-KB3	33 KtxB	33 PxKt
4 P-K3	4 B-K2	34 K-B2	34 Q-K8
5 Kt-KB3	5 Castles	35 K-B3	35 R-R5(H)
6 P-B4	6 Kt-K5		
7 Q-B2	7 B-R5ch(A)		
8 P-Kt3!	8 B-B3		
9 P-Q4(B)	9 P-QKt3		
10 B-Kt2	10 B-Kt2		
11 Kt-B3	11 P-B4		
12 CastlesQR	12 Q-K2		
13 KR-Ktsq	13 P-QR3(C)		
14 Q-K2	14 KtxKt		
15 BxKt	15 P-QKt4		
16 Kt-Q2	16 Kt-B3		
17 Kt-Ktsq	17 BPxP		
18 KPxP	18 PxP		
19 P-Q5	19 Kt-Qsq(D)		
20 P-Q6	20 Q-B2		
21 PxP	21 QBxB		
22 RxB	22 Kt-B3		
23 Q-Q3	23 KR-Ktsq		
24 QR-Q2	24 Kt-Kt5		
25 BxKt	25 RxB		
26 R-QB2	26 QR-Ktsq		
27 Kt-B3	27 Q-R4(E)	36 Q-Kt2(H)	36 Q-K6ch.
28 KR-Q2	28 P-K4(F)	37 K-B2	37 RxRPch
29 R-QKt2(G)	29 P-K5	38 K-Qsq	38 Q-Kt6ch
30 Q-Q5ch	30 K-Bsq	Resigns. (I)	

Position after Black's 35th move.

R-R5—The blunder that decided the coveted Tennyson Prize.

NOTES.

(A) The object of this is to open the entire diagonal for the action of the QB.

(B) In this class of opening it is essential to remember that the Pawns constitute the framework of the game, and should be self-supporting. White has therefore already a slight disadvantage in position.

(C) It is true that Black is violating the rule just laid down. But the rule naturally applies to fixed Pawns, and Black is here advancing with a view to exchanging Pawns for attack against the castled King.

(D) Any other move with the Knight loses a piece.

(E) Threatening BxKt R-Kt8ch, &c.

(F) Here is a gross violation of the principle! The proper method of pursuing the attack is Q-R6, followed by the advance of the KRP. The text move was made without due preparation and should have cost the game.

(G) Well devised (29 PxP B-Kt4, winning the exchange).

(H) This extraordinary double blunder is accountable to both parties being much pressed by the time limit. Black's move is a blunder, and White could have won the Rook by simply attacking it with his King.

(I) If K-Bsq R mates. If K-K2 RxRch, &c. If K-Ksq Q-Kt8ch, &c. If R-B2 R-R8ch, followed by QxRch, &c.

GAME 15.—Played in the Tennyson Prize Tournament, London, 1885. White, Mr. W. Donisthorpe; Black, Mr. Pollock.

Irregular Opening.

WHITE.	BLACK.	WHITE.	BLACK.
1 P-QKt3	1 P-K4	26 Kt-B7ch	26 K-Ktsq
2 P-K4	2 Kt-KB3	27 Kt-Q6	27 B-B2
3 Kt-QB3	3 B-Kt5(A)		
4 B-Q3	4 Castles		
5 KKt-K2	5 P-Q4		
6 B-Kt2	6 PxP		
7 BxP	7 KtxB		
8 KtxKt	8 P-KB4		
9 QKt-Kt3	9 Kt-B3(B)		
10 P-QB3	10 B-R4(c)		
11 Q-B2	11 P-K5		
12 CastlesQR(D)	12 Kt-K4		
13 Kt-B4	13 Kt-Q6ch		
14 KtxKt	14 PxKt		
15 Q-Ktsq	15 P-B5		
16 Kt-K4	16 B-B4		
17 P-B3	17 P-QKt4!		
18 P-QKt4(E)	18 B-QKt3		
19 P-QR4	19 P-QR4(F)		
20 Q-R2ch	20 K-Rsq		
21 PxRP	21 RxP		
22 P-R4	22 RxP		
23 Q-Kt3	23 Q-Rsq	28 B-R3(G)	28 RxQ
24 Kt-Kt5	24 P-B4	Resigns.	
25 QxP	25 R-QKtsq		

Position after Black's 27th move.

"Will he make any terms?"

NOTES.

(A) A Ruy Lopez "au second." P-QKt3 has, by the way, been suggested as a defence to the Ruy Lopez. So that White is "second player with a move ahead." I doubt if it is a move of much use to him.

(B) Besides having both Bishops, Black has the freer game by far.

(C) Preventing P-Q4.

(D) There seems no available means of preventing the damaging entry of the Knight at Q6.

(E) Rather desperate, as it obviously plays Black's game.

(F) This practically settles matters, as White's stronghold on the Q side is destroyed, and he can never escape across the invested centre of the board.

(G) A dying thrust! If Black took the Bishop instead of the Queen White would deliver mate in seven moves—the well-known smothered mate.

GAME 16.—Played at Simpson's Divan, October 1885. White, Mr. Kvistendahl; Black, Mr. Pollock.

Evans Gambit.

WHITE.	BLACK.
1 P-K4	1 P-K4
2 Kt-KB3	2 Kt-QB3
3 B-B4	3 B-B4
4 P-QKt4	4 KtxP
5 P-B3	5 Kt-QB3
6 P-Q4	6 PxP
7 Castles	7 P-Q3
8 PxP	8 B-Kt3
9 P-Q5(A)	9 Kt-R4
10 B-Kt2	10 KtxB(B)
11 Q-R4ch	11 B-Q2
12 QxKt	12 P-KB3
13 P-QR4(C)	13 Kt-K2
14 P-R5	14 B-QB4
15 P-K5	15 BPxP
16 KtxP	16 Castles
17 Kt-Q3	17 P-QKt3
18 KtxB	18 KtPxKt
19 Kt-B3	19 R-Ktsq
20 R-Ktsq(D)	20 R-Kt5
21 Q-K2	21 Kt-Kt3!
22 B-Rsq(E)	22 R-Kt5
23 P-Kt3	23 Kt-B5
24 Q-Q2	24 Q-R5
25 Kt-K2(F)	25 Kt-R6ch
26 K-Rsq(G)	26 B-B4!
27 P-B3(H)	27 BxR(I)

(See Diagram below.)

28 PxQ(K)	28 RxBP!
29 RxR(L)	29 Kt-B7ch!
30 RxKt	30 B-K5ch
31 R-Kt2	31 RxR

(See Diagram below.)

32 Kt-B3(M)	32 RxQch
Resigns.	

Position after Black's 27th move.

Position after Black's 31st move.

NOTES.

(A) The QP should never be advanced beyond the 4th square without great caution, especially early in the game. This is all but a case in point, and the text move has for many years been discarded in favour of Morphy's attack, 9 Kt-B3.

(B) This looks almost like a blunder, but it is not. The usual move is Kt-K2. The idea of the text move is shown in the following variation: (10 KtxB), 11 BxP P-KB3, 12 Q-R4ch? Q-Q2, 13 QxQch BxQ, 14 BxR K-B2. I have adopted it several times with success.

(c) An ingenious but harmless continuation.

(D) Hardly a good move, as Black could also gain an advantage by B-B4.

(E) It is curious to note that 22 B-Bsq instead, with a view of preventing Kt-B5, would have given Black another opportunity of winning the exchange by B-QKt4.

(F) Another defence lay in playing the King, but Black's attack would remain very strong.

(G) If 26 K-Kt2, Black may continue Kt-Kt4, threatening QxRPch.

(H) If 27 PxQ B-K5ch, 28 P-B3 RxBP, and mates directly.

(I) It is rare indeed that we meet with a case where one party, in a winning combination, sacrifices Queen, Rook, and Knight in three successive moves.

(K) White will otherwise lose the game, more prosaically, through loss of material.

(L) 29 Kt-Kt3 would not redeem the game.

(M) 32 Q-B4 prolongs but does not save. Thus, 32 Q-B4 R-Kt5ch, 33 QxB RxQ, 34 Kt-Ktsq R-R5, 35 B-B3 R-R6, 36 B-Ksq R-Q6, 37 K-Kt2 RxP, 38 Kt-K2 K-B2, 39 K-B3 R-Q8 would probably be the "modus op."

GAME 17.—Played in the International Tournament, Hereford, 1885. White, Mr. Pollock; Black, Mr. J. Mason.

Irregular Opening.

WHITE.	BLACK.	WHITE.	BLACK.
1 P-KB4	1 P-Q4	24 P-Q4	24 Q-B5
2 P-K3	2 P-K3	25 P-Q5	25 Q-QB8ch
3 Kt-KB3	3 P-QR3(A)	26 B-Bsq	26 P-K4
4 P-QKt3	4 P-QB4	27 Q-Kt6	27 K-Ksq
5 B-Kt2	5 Kt-KB3	28 Q-K6ch	28 K-Bsq
6 Kt-B3	6 Kt-B3	29 P-Q6	29 Q-K6ch
7 B-Q3(B)	7 B-K2	30 K-Rsq	30 Q-B7
8 Castles	8 P-QKt4(c)	31 Q-K7ch	Resigns.
9 Kt-K5	9 B-Kt2		
10 P-QR4	10 P-B5		
11 PxKtP	11 RPxP		
12 B-K2	12 RxR(D)		
13 QxR	13 Q-Kt3		
14 PxP	14 QPxP		
15 R-Ktsq			

(See Diagram below.)

	15 KtxKt(E)		
16 PxKt	16 Kt-Q2		
17 B-R3	17 KtxP		
18 RxP	18 Q-B3		
19 P-K4	19 P-B3		
20 BxB	20 KxB		
21 Q-R7!	21 Kt-Q2		
22 RxB	22 Q-Q3		
23 BxP	23 R-Qsq(F)		

Position after White's 15th move.

NOTES.

(A) This precaution is hardly necessary.

(B) A move sometimes adopted by Tschigorin and others, with the object of bringing the QKt round by K2. If Black reply Kt-QKt5 White allows the B to be captured, retaking with the Pawn, which then keeps the other Kt from entering at K5.

(C) In order to prevent Kt-K2, which would cost the Bishop, through P-QB5.

(D) Black ought not to have neglected to Castle; he is now subjected to a very harrassing and enduring fire.

(E) The QKtP is in danger, and a little examination will show that Black could not now Castle.

(F) If QxQP, 24 Kt-Q5ch K-Bsq, 25 R-Kt8ch, &c.

GAME 18.—Played at Simpson's Divan, London. White, Mr. Pollock; Black, Mr. A. Burn.

Four Knights' Game.

WHITE.	BLACK.	WHITE.	BLACK.
1 P-K4	1 P-K4	12 B-Q3	12 PxP
2 Kt-QB3	2 Kt-KB3	13 KtxP	13 R-Ksq
3 Kt-B3	3 Kt-B3	14 Q-K2	14 QKt-K4
4 P-Q4	4 PxP(A)	15 CastlesQR	15 KtxBch
5 KtxP	5 B-Kt5(B)	16 RxKt	16 Q-K2
6 Kt-B5(C)	6 Castles	17 QR-R3	17 Kt-R3
7 B-KKt5	7 BxKtch	18 R-K3(E)	18 Q-R6ch
8 PxB	8 P-KR3	19 K-Ktsq	19 B-Kt5(F)
9 P-KR4(D)	9 P-Q4	20 Kt-B6ch	20 PxKt
10 Kt-Kt3	10 PxB	21 RxRch	21 K-R2
11 RPxP	11 Kt-KKt5	White mates in four moves.	

NOTES.

(A) This capture turns the Opening into a complicated branch of the Scotch Gambit, but it is nevertheless good play.

(B) The pinning of the Queen's Knight is quite as sound here as on the previous move.

(C) White cannot reap any advantage from the changed order of moves, either by this enterprise or by the following steadier line of play: 6 KtxKt KtPxKt, 7 Q-Q4 Q-K2, 8 B-Q3 P-Q4, 9 Castles P-QB4 (not BxKt, 10 PxB PxP, on account of 11 R-Ksq), 10 B-Kt5ch K-Bsq, 11 Q-Q3 BxKt, 12 PxB PxP, 13 Q-Kt3 B-K3 all in Black's favour, and the branch referred to in note (A), viz., 6 B-KKt5 Q-K2, 7 P-B3 P-Q4, 8 KtxKt PxKt, 9 Q-Q4 P-B4, 10 B-Kt5ch K-Bsq, 11 Q-Q2 (the student ought also to examine 11 Q-B2) P-Q5, 12 CastlesQR B-Kt2, in spite of its mazes, is to be thwarted by a careful resistance.

(D) The attack must be kept up at any cost. The game now becomes extremely animated.

(E) The skilful combination of White's 17th and 18th moves wins back the Knight, but against the best play it ought not to do more.

(F) Mr. Burn, whose parrying strokes have so far been full of force and meaning, here makes a fatal slip. The best defence appears to be 19 B-K3, 20 P-QB4 Q-Kt5ch, 21 K-Rsq QxP (if BxP, 22 Kt-B6ch, &c.), 22 QxQ BxQ, 23 PxKt P-KB4, 24 Kt-Kt3 RxR, 25 PxR P-KKt3, &c.

GAME 19.—Played in the International Tournament, British Chess Association, London, 1886. White, Mr. J. H. Zukertort; Black, Mr. Pollock.

Ruy Lopez.

WHITE.	BLACK.	WHITE.	BLACK.
1 P-K4	1 P-K4	32 R-Q3	32 B-Kt4
2 Kt-KB3	2 Kt-QB3	33 K-Rsq	33 B-B5
3 B-Kt5	3 P-Q3	34 PxP	34 QxKKtP
4 P-Q4	4 B-Q2	35 Kt-B5	35 R-KKtsq
5 PxP	5 PxP	36 Q-B2	36 Q-QB3
6 Castles	6 B-Q3	37 Q-Ksq	37 Q-KKt3
7 Kt-B3	7 KKt-K2	38 Q-KBsq	38 Q-QB3
8 B-QB4	8 Castles	39 Q-K2	39 Q-KKt3
9 B-K3	9 B-KKt5	40 R-Qsq	40 Q-KB3
10 P-KR3	10 B-R4	41 R-Q7	41 Q-KKt3
11 P-KKt4	11 B-Kt3	42 Q-Kt4	42 Q-Kt3
12 Kt-KR4	12 Kt-R4	43 R-Kt7	43 Q-K3
13 B-Q3	13 Kt-Q4	44 P-Kt3	44 P-QR4
14 Kt-B5	14 KtxB	45 P-B4	45 B-B8
15 KtxKt	15 Q-R5	46 P-R3	46 P-B3
16 K-Kt2	16 Kt-B3	47 P-B5	47 B-B5
17 Kt-K2	17 QR-Ksq	48 P-Kt4	48 P-R5
18 Kt-Kt3	18 Kt-Q5	49 RxRch	49 QxR
19 Kt-B5	19 BxKt	50 Q-Qsq	50 B-Kt4
20 KtPxB	20 K-Rsq	51 Q-Q7	51 B-B3
21 P-QB3	21 Kt-B3	52 QxKtP	52 B-Qsq
22 B-Kt5	22 P-KKt3	53 QxP	53 Q-B2
23 Q-Kt4	23 Q-B3	54 Q-Q5	54 Q-B3
24 K-R2	24 B-B4	55 Q-Q7	55 P-R3
25 QR-Qsq	25 R-Qsq	56 Q-Q6	56 Q-Kt4
26 BxKt	26 QxB	57 QxRPch	57 QxQ
27 P-KB4	27 RxR	58 KtxQ	58 K-Kt2
28 RxR	28 B-Q3	59 Kt-Kt4	59 B-B2
29 PxKtP	29 BPxP	60 P-B6	
30 P-B5	30 Q-Kt3	and wins.	
31 Q-K2	31 B-K2		

GAME 20.—Played in the International Tournament, London, 1886. White, Mr. H. E. Bird; Black, Mr. Pollock.

Scotch Gambit.

WHITE.	BLACK.	WHITE.	BLACK.
1 P-K4	1 P-K4	6 P-QB3	6 KKt-K2
2 Kt-KB3	2 Kt-QB3	7 B-K2	7 BxKt
3 P-Q4	3 PxP	8 PxB	8 P-Q4
4 KtxP	4 B-B4	9 Kt-B3	9 B-K3
5 B-K3	5 Q-B3	10 P-K5	10 Q-Kt3

WHITE.	BLACK.	WHITE.	BLACK.
11 Castles	11 P-KR4(A)	37 PxR	37 P-Q5
12 K-Rsq	12 R-Qsq(B)	38 R-KKtsq	38 P-B4
13 Kt-R4	13 Kt-B4	39 P-B5	39 P-B5
14 Kt-B5	14 B-Bsq	40 R-Kt4	40 K-R3
15 R-Bsq	15 P-R5	41 RxP	41 R-B2
16 B-Q3	16 P-R6(C)	42 R-Q7	42 R-B4
17 P-KKt3	17 P-Kt3	43 P-K7	43 RxP
18 Kt-Kt3	18 Kt-Kt5(D)	44 R-Qsq	Resigns.
19 B-Ktsq	19 B-R3		
20 Q-B3(E)	20 Kt-Q6		
21 KR-Qsq	21 KtxB		
22 PxKt	22 R-Q2		
23 Kt-Q2(F)	23 P-KB4		
24 R-B3	24 KtxKtP		
25 BxP	25 Castles(G)		
(See Diagram below.)			
26 BxQ	26 RxQ		
27 R-QKtsq(H)	27 R-B7		
28 RxKt	28 B-K7		
29 P-K6	29 R-K2		
30 B-B7ch	30 K-R2		
31 R-Bsq	31 B-Q6		
32 Kt-B4(I)	32 R-B6		
33 Kt-K5	33 RxP(K6)		
34 KtxB	34 RxKt		
35 R-KB2	35 RxQP		
36 R-KB4	36 RxR		

Position after Black's 25th move.

NOTES.

(A) This seems compulsory, as White threatened to win the Queen for a minor piece by 12 B-R5 Q-B4, 13 P-KKt4.

(B) A well opened game on both sides, considering its nature.

(C) An advance of this kind ought to be made only with great caution. In the first place the Pawn as it stood exercised considerable restraint on White's game, which would be enhanced by the advance of either of the three White Pawns. In the second place, the advanced Pawn at R6 can now never be exchanged, and the K side becomes partly blocked in favour of White. P-KR6 was not good.

(D) Initiating a long combination of moves that results only in the loss of a piece to Black.

(E) White plays very steadily and forcibly: if 20 R-Ksq B-Q6, 21 BxB? KtxB, 22 QxKt? KtxPch, winning the Q.

(F) Preventing Q-K5.

(G) A very curious and interesting position.

(H) Quiet, but masterly.

(I) Again very ably played.

GAME 21.—Played at the British Chess Association, London, 1886. White, Mr. Pollock; Black, Mr. J. H. Blackburne.

French Defence.

WHITE.	BLACK.	WHITE.	BLACK.
1 P-K4	1 P-K3	36 Q-B2	36 Q-Q4
2 P-K5(A)	2 P-KB3(B)	37 RxRP	37 Kt-Kt3
3 P-Q4	3 P-QB4(B)	38 R-B6	38 Kt-B5
4 B-Q3	4 P-KKt3	39 RxKBP	39 QxP
5 P-KR4	5 P-B4(C)	40 R-R5	40 Q-Kt2(I)
6 B-KKt5(D)	6 B-K2	41 R-Kt5	41 Q-Rsq
7 BxB	7 QxB	42 P-R5	42 R-Q2
8 Kt-QR3	8 PxP	43 Q-B3	43 Q-R3
9 Kt-Kt5	9 K-Qsq	44 P-B4	44 Kt-Q7ch
10 Q-Q2	10 Kt-QB3	45 K-Rsq	45 Kt-K5
11 Kt-Q6	11 P-Kt3(E)	46 R-Kt6	46 QxR
12 Kt-B3	12 P-KR3(F)	47 PxQ	47 KtxQ
13 P-B3	13 Q-Kt2	48 PxKt	48 K-B2
14 PxP	14 KKt-K2(G)	49 P-B5	49 K-Qsq
15 CastlesQR	15 K-B2	50 P-B6	50 K-Ksq
16 Kt-Kt5ch	16 K-Ktsq	51 R-Rsq	51 R-Q7
17 K-Ktsq	17 B-Kt2	52 P-B7ch	52 K-K2
18 B-B4	18 P-R3	53 R-Ksqch	Resigns.
19 Kt-Q6	19 Kt-Bsq		
20 KtxB	20 KxKt		
21 P-Q5	21 PxP		
22 BxP	22 KKt-R2		
23 BxKt	23 PxB		
24 P-K6	24 QR-Ksq		
25 KR-Ksq	25 R-R2		
26 Q-B4	26 Q-QB2		
27 Q-Q4	27 Q-Kt2		
28 Q-QB4	28 Q-B3		
29 R-Q6	29 R-QB2		
30 Kt-K5	30 P-QKt4		
31 Kt-Q7(H)			
(See Diagram below.)			
	31 Q-Kt2		
32 Q-B5	32 Kt-Bsq		
33 R-QBsq	33 RxP		
34 RxR	34 QxKt		
35 RxKtP	35 Q-Q6ch		

Position after White's 31st move.

BLACK.

WHITE.

NOTES.

(A) This was adopted several times by Steinitz in the London Tournament of 1883. The idea is to exchange off KP for QP, and by P-Q4 and P-KB4 to keep Black's KP " depressed " at K3, and his game thereby cramped.

(B) Compare notes to Game 61, Pollock v Tarrasch.

(C) If QBPxP, 6 P-R5 Q-R4ch, 7 K-Bsq QxKP, 8 PxP P-KR3, 9 Kt-KB3 Q-Q4, 10 KtxP QxKt?, 11 P-Kt7 BxP, 12 B-Kt6ch, and wins.

(D) As will be seen it is excellent play to get rid of the adverse KB.

(E) Of course KtxP would cost the Knight.

(F) Again, KtxP, 13 KtxKt QxKt, 14 Kt-B7ch, winning the Q for two Knights.

(G) If KtxQP, 15 KtxKt QxPch, 16 B-K4, and wins.

(H) It is remarkable how persistently White maintains his attack throughout this game. A good move seems to be always forthcoming.

(I) Black certainly makes a heroic resistance.

GAME 22.—Played in the British Chess Association, London, 1886. White, Mr. Pollock; Black, Mr. J. Mason.

French Defence.

WHITE.	BLACK.	WHITE.	BLACK.
1 P-K4	1 P-K3	31 B-Q3	31 R-Kt2
2 Kt-KB3	2 P-QB4(A)	32 RxRch	32 KtxR
3 P-Q4	3 PxP	33 Q-R6	33 Q-Kt4
4 KtxP	4 Kt-KB3	34 QxQ	34 KtxQ
5 Kt-QB3	5 B-Kt5	35 P-B4	35 Kt-B2
6 P-K5	6 Kt-Q4	36 P-Kt3	36 Kt-Q3
7 KKt-Kt5	7 P-QR3	37 K-B2	37 K-Ktsq
8 Kt-Q6ch	8 BxKt	38 R-Ksq	38 B-B3
9 PxB	9 KtxKt	39 P-QB5	39 PxP
10 PxKt	10 Kt-B3	40 BxP	40 Kt-K5ch
11 B-Q3(B)	11 Q-R4	41 K-K2	41 RxP
12 Castles	12 Castles(C)	Resigns.	
13 R-Ksq(D)	13 P-B4		
14 Q-R5	14 P-QKt3		
15 R-K3(E)	15 P-Kt3		
16 R-Kt3	16 Kt-K4		
17 B-Q2	17 B-Kt2		
18 R-Ksq	18 R-B2		
19 Q-Kt5(F)	19 QR-KBsq		
20 P-QB4!	20 Q-B4		
21 B-B3	21 Kt-Kt5(G)		
22 R-K2	22 Kt-B3		
23 P-KR4	23 QxQP		
24 P-R5	24 Q-K2(H)		
25 PxP	25 PxP		
(See Diagram below).			
26 B-Kt4(I)	26 QxB		
27 QxPch	27 K-Rsq		
28 R-R3ch	28 R-R2		
29 QR-K3	29 Q-K2		
30 BxP	30 R-B2		

Position after Black's 25th move.

NOTES.

(A) P-Q4 is a better reply; with the text move Black drifts into an unfavourable form of the Sicilian Defence.

(B) White has already a splendid game, with two Bishops and plenty open spaces for the play of his Rooks presently.

(c) If QxP White would probably continue with R-Ktsq, threatening B-Kt2, and Black would have no peace.

(D) Rather an attacking than a developing move; it also keeps the Kt at B3, for if Kt-K4 White might continue 14 BxPch.

(E) Which looks like carrying the position by storm.

(F) In order to introduce a new factor, the KRP, into the attack.

(G) Mr. Mason defends with great patience and dexterity.

(H) If KtxP, 25 B-K5 Q-B3, 26 QxKt, &c.

(I) An altogether unaccountable and crazy blunder. He had only to play BxP and the day was won.

GAME 23.—Played in the Master Tournament of the British Chess Club, Spring, 1886. White, Mr. Pollock; Black, Mr. H. E. Bird.

Sicilian Defence.

WHITE.	BLACK.	WHITE.	BLACK.
1 P-K4	1 P-QB4	33 Kt-Q5	33 BxKt
2 P-Q4	2 PxP	34 PxB	34 QxP
3 Kt-KB3	3 P-KKt3(A)	35 R-R3	35 P-K6ch
4 QxP	4 Kt-KB3	36 P-B3	36 Q-Q7(H)
5 P-K5	5 Kt-B3		
6 Q-KB4	6 Kt-Q4	37 R-Qsq	37 QxRch
7 Q-K4	7 P-K3(B)	38 BxQ	38 RxBch
8 Kt-B3(c)	8 KtxKt	39 K-Kt2	39 Kt-Kt3
9 PxKt	9 P-Q4	40 R-R4	40 P-K7
10 PxP en pass	10 B-Kt2	41 R-K4	41 Kt-B5ch
11 Q-Q3	11 Castles	42 RxKt	42 P-K8(Q)
12 B-K2	12 P-K4	43 R-K4	43 R-Q7ch
13 Castles	13 B-B4	44 K-R6	44 Q-B8ch
14 Q-Qsq	14 P-K5	45 K-Kt3	45 Q mates.
15 Kt-Ksq	15 BxP		
16 R-Ktsq	16 B-K4		
17 RxP	17 BxQP		
18 K-Rsq(D)	18 R-Ktsq		
19 R-Kt3(E)	19 Q-K2		
20 Q-Q2	20 QR-Qsq		
21 Q-R6	21 B-K4		
22 B-R3	22 B-Q3		
23 P-Kt4(F)	23 B-K3		
24 R-R3	24 P-B3		
25 B-Kt2	25 R-B2		
26 Kt-Kt2	26 Kt-K4(G)		
27 Kt-K3	27 Q-Kt2		
28 B-Rsq	28 R-Kt2		
29 P-QB4	29 Kt-B2		
30 Q-R4	30 P-Kt4		
31 Q-R5	31 B-K4		
32 BxB	32 KtxB		

Position after Black's 36th move.

NOTES.

(A) Kt-QB3 is usually played here and is probably advisable.

(B) Black has not a good opening. As is well known, P-Q3 and not P-K3 is the proper accompaniment to P-KKt3.

(C) Here 8 B-QB4 is indicated, preserving the QKt for subsequent attack. Another line of play was 8 P-QR3 B-Kt2, 9 P-B4 KKt-K2, 10 Kt-B3 P-QR3, 11 B-B4, with a very fine game. The course adopted may be compared with that in a game Pollock v Mortimer, the disadvantage of the doubled BP being fully counterbalanced, especially in gain of time in development.

(D) This or P-Kt3 is necessary here.

(E) A good position for the Rook, which would not suffer by being exchanged.

(F) Although this gives some attack it was probably a case of miscalculation, White imagining it to be unanswerable.

(G) From this point Mr. Bird plays to the end with consummate skill.

(H) A really pretty situation; "one of the olden time."

GAME 24.—Played in the International Tournament, Nottingham, 1886. White, Mr. J. Taubenhaus; Black, Mr. Pollock.

Thorold-Allgaier Gambit.

WHITE.	BLACK.	WHITE.	BLACK.
1 P-K4	1 P-K4	18 K-B3	18 QxR
2 P-KB4	2 PxP	19 B-K3	19 Q-K8ch
3 Kt-KB3	3 P-KKt4	20 Kt-Q2	20 P-Kt8(Q)
4 P-KR4	4 P-Kt5	21 BxQ	21 QxR
5 Kt-Kt5	5 P-KR3	22 Q-Kt6ch	22 K-Qsq
6 KtxP	6 KxKt	23 Q-B6ch	23 K-Bsq
7 P-Q4	7 P-B6	24 QxR	24 K-Q2
8 B-B4ch	8 P-Q4	25 Q-R7ch	25 B-K2
9 BxPch	9 K-Ksq	26 P-K6ch	26 BxP
10 PxP	10 P-Kt6	27 BxBch	27 KxB
11 P-KB4	11 Kt-KB3	28 P-Q5ch	28 KxP
12 B-B4	12 P-Kt7	29 Q-B5ch	29 Kt-K4
13 R-Ktsq	13 B-KKt5	30 QxKtch	30 K-B3
14 Q-Q3	14 Kt-B3	31 QxB	31 QxB
15 P-K5	15 Kt-K5	32 Q-K6ch	32 K-Kt4
16 QxKt	16 QxPch	33 P-R4ch	33 K-R4
17 K-Q2	17 Q-B7ch	and White mates in two moves.	

GAME 25.—Played in the International Tournament, Nottingham, 1886. White, Mr. P. Rynd; Black, Mr. Pollock.

Scotch Gambit.

WHITE.	BLACK.	WHITE.	BLACK.
1 P-K4	1 P-K4	6 B-K2(A)	6 P-Q3
2 Kt-KB3	2 Kt-QB3	7 Castles	7 KKt-K2(B)
3 P-Q4	3 PxP	8 Kt-B3	8 Castles
4 KtxP	4 B-B4	9 Kt-R4(c)	9 P-B4
5 Kt-Kt3	5 B-Kt3	10 KtxB	10 RPxKt(D)

WHITE.	BLACK.	WHITE.	BLACK.
11 PxP	11 BxP	29 BxQch	29 RxB mate.
12 P-QB3	12 B-K3		
13 P-KB4	13 K-Rsq		
14 P-QR3	14 Q-Ksq		
15 Kt-Q2(E)	15 Kt-Q4		
16 Kt-K4	16 B-B4		
17 KtxP(F)	17 PxKt		
18 B-R5	18 P-Kt3		
19 QxKt	19 PxB		
20 B-Q2	20 Q-Kt3		
21 QR-Ksq	21 QR-Ksq		
22 P-B4	22 K-Kt2		
23 B-B3ch	23 K-R3		
24 R-Qsq	24 R-K7		
25 QxP	25 RxPch		
26 K-Rsq	26 B-K5		
27 QxRch			
(See Diagram below.)			
	27 Q-Kt2(G)		
28 R-B3	28 BxR		

Position after White's 27th move.

NOTES.

(A) Necessary, unless the risky advance of P-QB4 be selected. For if 6 Kt-B3 Black may answer with Q-B3.

(B) An exception to the rule against playing out the Knights to self-protecting squares. Here it would not do to allow the Kt to be pinned on KB3, as Black has no very good means of keeping the Kt from Q5. Again, it is important, as will be seen, to be able to throw forward the KBP at an early stage.

(C) The Bishop, indeed, is strong, but the exchange weakens White's QRP, which causes loss of time on his 14th move.

(D) Both Black's Rooks are now brought passively into action.

(E) A slip apparently.

(F) This part of the game is incomprehensible.

(G) See diagram of this extraordinary position:

GAME 26.—Played at Simpson's Divan, November 1887. White, Mr. Pollock; Black, Mr. F. J. Lee.

French Defence.

WHITE.	BLACK.	WHITE.	BLACK.
1 P-K4	1 P-K3	7 Kt-B3	7 P-R3
2 P-QB4(A)	2 P-Q4	8 Castles	8 B-K2
3 BPxP	3 PxP	9 P-Q4	9 Kt-KB3
4 PxP	4 QxP	10 B-KB4	10 P-B3
5 Kt-QB3	5 Q-K3ch	11 R-Ksq	11 Q-Kt5
6 B-K2	6 P-QR3	12 Q-Q2	12 B-K3

WHITE.	BLACK.	WHITE.	BLACK.
13 Kt-KKt5	13 Q-B4	19 BxPch	19 K-B2
14 B-Q3	14 Q-R4	20 Kt-K4	20 Kt-Q2
15 KtxB	15 PxKt	21 Kt-Q6ch(B)	21 K-Ktsq
16 RxP	16 K-Bsq	22 B-B4ch	22 K-R2
17 QR-Ksq	17 B-Kt5	and White mates in four moves.	
18 RxKtch	18 PxR		

NOTES.

(A) Good diversion.

(B) Beautiful end.

GAME 27.—An off-hand game, played at London, April 1887. White, Mr. A. Burn; Black, Mr. Pollock.

Ruy Lopez.

WHITE.	BLACK.	WHITE.	BLACK.
1 P-K4	1 P-K4	26 B-K3	26 P-K5
2 Kt-KB3	2 Kt-QB3	27 B-Q4	27 KtxB
3 B-Kt5	3 P-Q3	28 KtxKt	28 Q-Kt5ch
4 Castles	4 B-Q2	29 K-Ksq	29 PxP
5 P-B3	5 KKt-K2	30 QxBP	30 R-K7ch
6 Kt-R3	6 Kt-Kt3	31 K-Qsq	31 R-QB7ch
7 P-Q3	7 B-K2	Resigns. (C)	
8 Kt-B4	8 Castles		
9 Kt-K3	9 P-B4(A)		
10 B-B4ch	10 K-Rsq		
11 PxP	11 BxP		
12 KtxB	12 RxKt		
13 B-K6	13 R-Bsq		
14 P-KKt3	14 P-Q4		
15 Kt-Ksq	15 B-B4		
16 Q-Kt3	16 RxP(B)		
(See Diagram below.)			
17 RxR	17 BxRch		
18 KxB	18 Q-B3ch		
19 K-K2	19 QxB		
20 QxKtP	20 R-KBsq		
21 B-K3	21 R-QKtsq		
22 QxBP	22 RxPch		
23 K-Qsq	23 P-Q5		
24 B-Ktsq	24 PxP		
25 Kt-B3	25 P-KR3		

Position after Black's 16th move.

BLACK.

[chess diagram]

WHITE.

NOTES.

(A) The opening has not proceeded on usual lines, White omitting to attack in the centre. Black has now a very good position.

(B) Diagram of this unexpected coup.

(C) An entertaining little game.

GAME 28.—Played at Simpson's Divan, June 1887. White, Mr. R. J. Loman; Black, Mr. Pollock.

Scotch Gambit.

WHITE.	BLACK.	WHITE.	BLACK.
1 P-K4	1 P-K4	31 P-B4	31 P-Kt4
2 Kt-KB3	2 Kt-QB3	32 B-K5	32 P-B4
3 P-Q4	3 PxP	33 P-B5ch	33 BxP(F)
4 KtxP	4 Q-R5		
5 Kt-Kt5	5 B-B4		
6 Q-B3	6 Kt-Q5		
7 KtxKt(A)	7 BxKt		
8 B-QB4	8 Kt-B3		
9 Castles	9 B-K4!		
10 P-KKt3	10 Q-R6		
11 B-KKt5(B)	11 BxQKtP		
12 P-K5	12 Q-Kt5		
13 BxPch	13 KxB		
14 Q-Kt3ch	14 Kt-Q4(C)		
15 QxKtch	15 Q-K3		
16 QxQch	16 KxQ		
17 Kt-Q2	17 BxR		
18 RxB	18 P-KR3		
19 B-K3	19 KxP		
20 R-Ksq	20 K-Q4		
21 P-B4ch	21 K-B3		
22 B-Q4	22 R-KKtsq		
23 R-K7	23 K-Q3(D)	34 Kt-B4ch	34 K-Kt4
24 RxKtP	24 RxR	35 PxB	35 KxP
25 BxR	25 P-KR4	36 B-B7	36 P-Kt5
26 Kt-K4ch	26 K-K3	37 K-B2	37 R-QBsq
27 Kt-B6	27 K-B2	38 B-Q6	38 R-B3
28 KtxP	28 K-Kt3	39 B-Kt8	39 R-QR3
29 P-Kt4	29 P-Q4(E)	40 Kt-K2	40 RxP
30 P-KR3	30 PxP	Resigns.	

Position after Black's 33rd move.

NOTES.

(A) Or the following: 7 KtxPch K-Qsq, 8 Q-B4 QxQ, 9 BxQ KtxPch, 10 K-Qsq KtxR, 11 KtxR, and in all probability "Jack is as good as his master."

(B) An enterprising move which gives a lively character to the game. On the 12th move it is noteworthy that no fewer than four of White's pieces are "en prise."

(C) This curious looking move ensures at least the gain of the exchange; the calculation is of course quite simple.

(D) It certainly seems as though Black would live to rue his venturesome play.

(E) White ought to have included this move in his forecast. It decides the game.

(F) Black is quite justified in the sacrifice, although it can hardly be called a sacrifice. The Rook comes in at the death very neatly.

GAME 29.—Played at Simpson's Divan, July 1887. White, Rev. G. A. MacDonnell; Black, Mr. Pollock.

Muzio Gambit.

WHITE.	BLACK.	WHITE.	BLACK.
1 P-K4	1 P-K4	27 QxKRP	27 R-B3
2 P-KB4	2 PxP	28 P-R4	28 K-K6
3 Kt-KB3	3 P-KKt4	29 P-R5	29 Kt-K4
4 B-B4	4 P-Q4(A)	30 P-K7	30 R-B8ch
5 BxP	5 P-Kt5	31 K-Kt2	31 R-B7ch
6 Castles	6 PxKt	32 K-R3	32 R-B8
7 QxP	7 Q-K2	33 Q-Q3ch	
8 Kt-B3	8 P-QB3		
9 B-Kt3	9 B-K3	and wins.	
10 P-Q4	10 BxB		
11 RPxB	11 Kt-QR3	Position after Black's 16th move.
12 P-K5	12 Castles		
13 BxP	13 RxP		
14 RxKt(B)	14 RxB		
15 RxPch	15 K-Ktsq !		
16 QxR	16 PxR		
(See Diagram below.)			
17 P-K6ch	17 Q-Q3		
18 QxP	18 Kt-K2		
19 K-Rsq	19 Kt-Kt3		
20 Q-K8ch	20 K-B2		
21 R-Qsq	21 B-K2		
22 Q-B7	22 R-KBsq		
23 RxQ	23 KxR(C)		
24 Kt-K4ch	24 K-K4		
25 Q-Kt7ch	25 KxKt		
26 P-Kt3	26 B-B4		

NOTES.

(A) This, in conjunction with the seventh move and sequel, forms something of a novelty in the defence to the Muzio Gambit.

(B) Perhaps a little rash, but he must make some show of attack.

(C) Probably done for a jest.

GAME 30.—Played in the National Tournament, British Chess Association, London, 1887. White, Mr. Pollock; Black, Mr. J. Mortimer.

Three Knights' Game.

WHITE.	BLACK.	WHITE.	BLACK.
1 P-K4	1 P-K4	5 P-Q4	5 B-Q3
2 Kt-QB3	2 Kt-QB3	6 PxKt	6 BxP
3 Kt-B3	3 B-B4(A)	7 B-QB4	7 BxKtch
4 KtxP	4 KtxKt	8 PxB	8 P-Q3

WHITE.	BLACK.
9 Castles	9 Kt-K2
10 Q-R5	10 Kt-Kt3
11 B-KKt5	11 Q-Q2(B)
12 P-KR3	12 Castles
13 P-B4	13 K-Rsq
14 P-B5	14 Kt-K4
15 P-B6	15 P-KKt3
16 Q-R6	16 R-KKtsq
17 R-B4	17 Kt-B6ch
18 RxKt	18 Q-Ksq
19 R-B4	19 Q-Bsq

(See Diagram below.)

20 QxPch

and wins. (C)

Position after Black's 19th move.

NOTES.

(A) See notes to Game 13.

(B) Black has at least a very awkward game. If P-KB3, 12 P-B4, with a strong attack.

(C) Always a pleasing finish to the eye.

GAME 31.—Played in the National Tournament, British Chess Association, London, 1887. White, Mr. J. Mason; Black, Mr. Pollock.

Greco Counter Gambit.

WHITE.	BLACK.	WHITE.	BLACK.
1 P-K4	1 P-K4	22 Q-K3	22 R-Bsq(D)
2 Kt-KB3	2 P-KB4	23 P-KKt4	23 PxP
3 P-Q4	3 PxKP	24 PxP	24 KtxP(E)
4 KtxP	4 Kt-KB3		
5 B-QB4(A)	5 P-Q4		
6 B-Kt3	6 B-Q3		
7 B-Kt5?	7 P-B3		
8 Castles	8 Castles		
9 Kt-QB3	9 Q-B2(B)		
10 B-KB4	10 K-Rsq		
11 B-Kt3	11 P-QKt3(C)		
12 Q-Q2	12 P-QR4		
13 P-QR3	13 B-R3		
14 Kt-K2	14 P-B4		
15 P-QB3	15 P-R5		
16 B-R2	16 QKt-Q2		
17 KtxKt	17 QxKt		
18 QR-Ksq	18 BxB		
19 BPxB	19 BxKt		
20 RxB	20 QR-Ksq		
21 R-B4	21 Q-Kt4		

Position after Black's 24th move.

WHITE.	BLACK.	WHITE.	BLACK.
25 RxRch(F)	25 RxR	29 B-Ktsq	29 P-Kt3
26 Q-Q2	26 P-K6	30 Q-Q3	30 Q-B5
27 Q-B2	27 Q-R3	31 PxKt	31 RxR
28 P-R3	28 R-B7	Resigns.	

NOTES.

(A) Loss of valuable time; B-K2, followed by Castling, is the natural course.

(B) Q-Ksq appears to be stronger. The reply 10 P-B4 would be compelled, as if 10 B-B4 Kt-R4.

(C) A less complicated plan was to dislodge the Kt by QKt-Q2.

(D) All this play on Black's part is directed towards working his Pawn majority.

(E) Springing a surprise!

(F) If 25 RxKt QxR, and wins.

GAME 32.—Played in the National Tournament, British Chess Association, London, 1887. White, Mr. H. E. Bird; Black, Mr. Pollock.

Giuoco Piano.

WHITE.	BLACK.	WHITE.	BLACK.
1 P-K4	1 P-K4	27 Q-K2	27 Kt-Kt3
2 Kt-KB3	2 Kt-QB3	28 KR-Qsq(E)	28 Q-Kt2
3 B-B4	3 B-B4	29 KtxB	29 QxKt
4 P-B3	4 Q-K2	30 B-Bsq	30 Kt-B5
5 P-QKt4	5 B-Kt3	31 BxKt	31 KtPxB
6 P-QR4	6 P-QR4(A)	32 R-Q5(F)	32 Castles
7 P-Kt5	7 Kt-Qsq	33 QR-Qsq(G)	33 R-Kt2
8 Castles	8 P-Q3	34 Q-B3(H)	34 Q-Ktsq(I)
9 P-Q4	9 P-KB3(B)	35 K-Rsq	35 Q-Ksq
10 B-R3	10 B-Kt5	36 Q-K4	36 Q-R4
11 B-K2	11 Kt-K3	37 P-B3	37 R-B3
12 Kt-R4	12 BxB	38 Q-Ksq	38 R-R3
13 QxB	13 PxP(C)	39 Q-Ktsq	39 Q-R5(K)
14 Kt-B5	14 Q-Q2	40 P-Kt6(L)	40 PxP
15 R-Qsq!	15 P-Kt3	41 RxP	41 RxR
16 KtxP(Q4)	16 Kt-B5?	42 RxR	42 R-Kt3
17 Q-B3	17 Kt-K3	43 RxRch	43 PxR
18 P-K5	18 BPxP	44 Q-Qsq	44 Q-B7
19 KtxKt	19 QxKt	45 P-R3	45 K-R2
20 QxP	20 R-Qsq	46 Q-QKtsq	46 K-R3
21 Q-B6ch	21 R-Q2	47 Q-K4	47 Q-B4
22 Kt-Q2	22 Kt-K2	48 Q-Ksq	48 K-Kt4
23 Q-B4	23 Q-Q4	49 P-R4ch	49 K-B3
24 Q-K4	24 Q-B2(D)	50 Q-Q2	50 K-K2
25 R-KBsq	25 P-Kt4	51 Q-Q3	51 K-B3
26 Kt-B4	26 Q-Q4	52 K-R2	52 Q-B3

WHITE.	BLACK.	WHITE.	BLACK.
53 Q-K4	53 Q-B4(M)	54 Q-Q3	54 Q-B3
		55 Q-B2	55 K-K2
		56 K-R3	56 Q-K3ch
		57 P-Kt4	57 Q-B5
		58 K-Kt2	58 P-QKt4
		59 PxP	59 QxKtP
		60 P-B4	60 Q-B4
		61 P-Kt5	61 Q-K6
		62 Q-Kt2	62 P-R5
		63 Q-Kt7ch	63 K-Qsq
		64 Q-Kt8ch	64 K-Q2
		65 Q-Kt5ch	65 K-Q3

Position after Black's 53rd move.

Drawn game.

NOTES.

(A) In the customary form of the Evans Gambit Declined (where the fourth moves of the present game are not made) this is not so good as P-QR3, although adopted by some masters. For after P-Kt5 the Kt must go to Q5, whereupon White exchanges, with gain of time to form a strong centre.

(B) The position is in favour of Black, who here plays correctly.

(C) Rather shortsighted and losing his advantage. Kt-KR3 or P-Kt3 are better moves.

(D) The play on both sides is rather pretty. White's object is to play Kt-B4 and take the Bishop, so long as he can oblige Black to recapture with P, leaving the QP assailable.

(E) Now KtxB would give Black a rather threatening attack on the K side.

(F) Threatening RxPch.

(G) Again menacing the Pawn.

(H) Necessary, to prevent P-B6.

(I) Black is aware that his Queen is getting shut out from the fun.

(K) Apparently intending to push P to K5.

(L) Very well played, although truly he has little else to do.

(M) QxQ, followed by P-QKt4, wins at once.

GAME 33.—Played at the British Chess Association, London, 1887. White, Mr. Pollock; Black, Mr. J. H. Zukertort.

Staunton's Opening.

WHITE.	BLACK.	WHITE.	BLACK.
1 P-K4	1 P-K4	6 Castles	6 B-Q2(A)
2 Kt-KB3	2 Kt-QB3	7 PxP	7 KtxP
3 P-B3	3 P-Q4	8 P-Q4	8 P-QR3
4 Q-R4	4 P-B3	9 Q-Kt3	9 PxB
5 B-Kt5	5 Kt-K2	10 QxKt	10 PxP

WHITE.	BLACK.	WHITE.	BLACK.
11 R-Ksqch	11 B-K2	31 Kt-Q4ch	31 K-B4
12 Q-R5ch(B)	12 P-Kt3	32 Kt-Kt3ch	32 K-B5
13 Q-R6	13 K-B2	33 Kt-Q2ch	
14 Q-R4	14 Kt-K4	Drawn game. (F)	
15 RxKt(c)	15 PxR		
16 KtxPch	16 K-Ksq		
17 QxP	17 B-KB3		
18 B-Kt5	18 R-KBsq(D)		
19 B-R6	19 R-Rsq		
20 Kt-Q2	20 B-B4		
21 Q-K3	21 Q-K2		
22 R-Ksq	22 QxKt		
23 QxQ	23 BxQ		
24 RxBch	24 K-Q2		
25 P-KKt4	25 B-K3		
26 Kt-K4	26 RxP		
27 Kt-B5ch	27 K-Q3		
28 B-B4	28 B-Q4		
(See Diagram below.)			
29 Kt-Kt3(E)	29 KR-Rsq		
30 R-R5ch	30 K-B3		

Position after Black's 28th move.

NOTES.

(A) Steinitz advocates playing the B to K3 where possible in this and similar positions.

(B) 12 PxP simply, followed, unless P-Kt5, by Kt-B3, would have given White an excellent game.

(C) A very energetic stroke, but unsound.

(D) He could have won here by BxB, if 19 KtxB KR-Ktsq.

(E) The draw is extremely neatly brought about.

(F) Black can only escape the perpetual check by moving away from the protection of his Bishop.

GAME 34.—Played at Simpson's Divan, 1887. White, Mr. Pollock; Black, Mr. J. Hirschfeld.

Three Knights' Opening.

WHITE.	BLACK.	WHITE.	BLACK.
1 P-K4	1 P-K4	10 B-K3	10 B-Q2(c)
2 Kt-QB3	2 Kt-QB3	11 R-Ktsq	11 B-B3
3 Kt-B3	3 B-B4(A)	12 B-Q4	12 Q-R3
4 KtxP	4 KtxKt	13 P-KB4	13 Kt-K2
5 P-Q4	5 B-Q3	14 P-B5(D)	14 P-B3
6 PxKt	6 BxP	15 Q-B3	15 P-KKt4
7 B-Q3	7 BxKtch	16 PxP en pass	16 PxP
8 PxB	8 P-Q3	17 P-KR3	17 R-KBsq
9 Castles(B)	9 Q-B3	18 Q-Kt4	18 P-B4

WHITE.	BLACK.
19 PxP	19 PxP
20 B-Kt7	20 Q-K6ch
21 K-R2	21 PxQ
22 RxRch	22 K-Q2
23 RxR(E)	

(See Diagram below).

Black mates in four moves.

NOTES.

(A) Not a good move.

(B) See Game 30, Pollock v Mortimer.

(C) If QxP, 11 B-Q4, winning the Rook.

(D) Here Q-Kt4 is the "coup juste."

(E) A rather ludicrous termination. There is, however, little to be done. If 23 KR-Bsq P-Kt6ch, 24 K-Rsq Q-Q7, 25 R-KKtsq R-KKtsq, and if 26 B-Q4 Q-R3, or 26 QR-Qsq BxPch, and wins.

Position after White's 23rd move.

GAME 35.—Played at the Counties Chess Association, Stamford, 1887. White, Rev. G. A. MacDonnell; Black, Mr. Pollock.

Ruy Lopez.

WHITE.	BLACK.	WHITE.	BLACK.
1 P-K4	1 P-K4	24 Q-Q3	24 P-KB4
2 Kt-KB3	2 Kt-QB3	25 B-Q2	25 Q-R4
3 B-Kt5	3 P-Q3	26 Q-K2	26 B-B3
4 P-Q4	4 B-Q2	27 Q-K6ch	27 K-Rsq
5 BxKt	5 BxB		
6 Kt-B3	6 P-B3(A)		
7 Castles	7 Q-K2		
8 P-QKt4(B)	8 P-QR3(C)		
9 B-K3	9 Q-B2(D)		
10 P-QR4	10 P-KKt4		
11 Q-K2	11 Kt-K2		
12 KR-Qsq	12 Kt-Kt3		
13 P-Kt5	13 B-Q2		
14 KtPxP(E)	14 KtPxP		
15 Kt-Q5	15 B-K3		
16 Q-B4	16 BxKt		
17 PxB	17 Q-Q2		
18 QR-Ktsq(F)	18 B-K2		
19 R-Kt7	19 P-K5		
20 Kt-Ksq(G)	20 B-Qsq		
21 P-KB3(H)	21 PxP		
22 KtxP	22 Castles		
23 R-KBsq	23 Q-Kt5(I)		

Position after Black's 27th move.

WHITE.	BLACK.	WHITE.	BLACK.
28 QxBP(K)	28 BxPch	36 Kt-K4(M)	36 R-B6(N)
29 KtxB	29 RxQ	37 R-Ktsq	37 QxKt
30 KtxR	30 R-QBsq(L)	38 R-B8ch	38 R-Bsq
31 B-B3ch	31 K-Ktsq	39 RxRch	39 KxR
32 P-R3	32 P-R3	40 R-Ksq	40 Kt-B6ch
33 R-Ksq	33 R-Bsq	41 PxKt	41 QxQP
34 RxP	34 Kt-K4	42 B-Kt4ch	42 K-B2
35 KtxQP	35 Q-R5	and wins.	

NOTES.

(A) The maintenance of the centre in this way has always been allowed by experts to be in harmony with the spirit of this form of defence to the Ruy Lopez. At the same time they have generally fought shy of adopting it in serious Chess. Steinitz has always laid it down as a principle that the support of the KP by P-KB3 is advisable where there is no danger from the adverse KB. And at all events Black's game is not more cramped than by PxQP, B-K2, &c.

(B) A much better preparation to meet Black's intention of Castling on the Q side would be 8 B-K3.

(C) P-Kt5, followed by Kt-Q5, was threatened.

(D) Naturally, a very good place for the Queen.

(E) It would be more advantageous to let Black capture first, and here Kt-Q5, supported by P-B4, looks more consistent with the advance of the Pawns.

(F) A pretty sharp attack is now looming up.

(G) It is not quite certain that White cannot play as follows : 20 RxP Q-Kt5, 21 P-R3 Q-R4, 22 Q-B6ch K-B2, 23 QxQP PxKt, 24 Q-K6ch K-Kt2, 25 RxBch KtxR, 26 QxKtch Q-B2, 27 QxQch KxQ, 28 P-B4, and should win. Yet it was necessary for Black to advance the KP, for if B-Qsq, 20 PxP QPxP, 21 P-Q6. We shall therefore have to confess that Black's game is too backward and that his judgment was at fault on the 10th move, the time for which he could not afford.

(H) This helps Black, but it was not otherwise easy to get the Knight again into play.

(I) Releasing the Q from the masked battery, and presumably intending an attack by Q-K5 and Kt-Q2, if allowed.

(K) Splendidly conceived and well meriting success. See the illustration.

(L) An abject looking defence !

(M) If RxKt Black could draw by perpetual check.

(N) A happy resource indeed !

GAME 36.—Played in the Handicap Tournament, Counties Chess Association, Stamford, 1887. White, Mr. Pollock; Black, Mr. J. H. Blake.

Four Knights' Opening.

WHITE.	BLACK.	WHITE.	BLACK.
1 P-K4	1 P-K4	6 B-KKt5	6 BxKtch(A)
2 Kt-QB3	2 Kt-QB3	7 PxB	7 Q-K2
3 Kt-B3	3 Kt-B3	8 B-Q3	8 Q-B4
4 P-Q4	4 PxP	9 Kt-B5(B)	9 QxQBPch
5 KtxP	5 B-Kt5	10 B-Q2	10 Q-K4

WHITE.	BLACK.	WHITE.	BLACK.
11 KtxPch	11 K-Bsq	32 Kt-B5ch	32 PxKt
12 Kt-B5	12 KtxP	33 Q-K6ch	33 K-B2
13 B-R6ch	13 K-Ksq	34 B-B4ch	34 K-Kt3
14 Kt-Kt7ch	14 K-Qsq	35 Q-Kt3ch	
15 Castles	15 Kt-B6(c)		
16 Q-Q2	16 P-Q3		
17 QR-Ksq	17 Q-Q5		
18 Q-Kt5ch	18 P-B3		
19 Q-KR5	19 Kt-K4		
20 P-KR3	20 P-B3		
21 B-B5(d)	21 Q-Q4		
22 P-B4	22 Kt-B2		
23 Q-R4	23 BxB		
24 QxPch	24 K-B2		
25 R-K7ch	25 K-Kt3		
26 RxKt	26 B-K5(e)		
27 QxKt	27 QxR		
28 Q-Kt4ch	28 K-B2		
29 QxB	29 KR-KKtsq		
30 Kt-K6ch	30 K-Q2		
31 P-B5(f)			

and wins.

Position after White's 31st move.

(See Diagram below.)

31 Q-R4

NOTES.

(A) There is no necessity for this capture. Black should Castle or play P-KR3.

(B) Black must have overlooked this. It precludes Castling, on account of the fatal reply BxKt.

(c) There was hardly another move in face of BxKt or R-Ksq.

(D) Keeping up the attack actively. If BxB, 22 QxB, threatening a fatal check with Kt at K6.

(E) The defence is valiant but clearly ineffectual.

(F) A subtle move. See Diagram.

GAME 37.—Played in the Handicap Tournament, Counties Chess Association, Stamford, 1887. White, Mr. Herbert Jacobs; Black, Mr. Pollock.

Vienna Opening.

WHITE.	BLACK.	WHITE.	BLACK.
1 P-K4	1 P-K4	7 PxP	7 KtxP
2 Kt-QB3	2 Kt-KB3	8 Kt-B3	8 B-QKt5
3 P-B4	3 P-Q4	9 B-Q2	9 Castles
4 P-Q3	4 Kt-B3	10 B-K2	10 Kt(Q4)-B5
5 BPxP	5 QKtxP	11 Castles	11 B-Kt5
6 P-Q4	6 Kt-Kt3	12 B-B4	12 KtxP

WHITE.	BLACK.	WHITE.	BLACK.
13 K×Kt	13 Kt-R5ch	18 Kt-Kt5	18 Q-B3
14 K-Kt3	14 QB×Kt	19 R-KBsq	19 Q-Kt4ch
15 R×B	15 Q×P	20 K-R3	
16 B-Q3	16 B-Q3ch	White mates in four moves.	
17 B-KB4	17 P-KB4		

GAME 38.—Played at the Counties Chess Association, Stamford, 1887. White, Mr. Pollock; Black, Mr. J. H. Blake.

Two Knights' Defence.

WHITE.	BLACK.	WHITE.	BLACK.
1 P-K4	1 P-K4	37 Q×R	37 R-Ksq
2 Kt-KB3	2 Kt-QB3	38 K-Q2	38 Q×RP
3 B-B4	3 Kt-B3	39 Q-QKt5	39 Q-K3
4 Kt-Kt5	4 P-Q4	40 R-K3	40 R-Qsqch
5 P×P	5 Kt-QR4	41 K-B2	41 Q-Kt3ch
6 P-Q3	6 P-KR3	42 K-Kt3	42 K-Bsq
7 Kt-KB3	7 P-K5	43 Q-B5ch	43 K-Ktsq
8 Q-K2	8 Kt×B	44 Q-B7	44 R-Rsq
9 P×Kt	9 B-QB4	45 Q-Kt7	45 R-Qsq
10 P-KR3	10 Castles	46 P-KB4	46 Q-Q3(E)
11 Kt-K5	11 P-QKt4(A)		
12 Kt-Kt4	12 P×P	Position after Black's 46th move.	
13 Q×BP	13 B×Kt		
14 Q×B	14 B-B4		
15 Kt-B3(B)	15 Kt-Q2		
16 Q-Q4	16 R-Ksq		
17 B-K3	17 Q-Ktsq		
18 CastlesQR	18 Q-Kt3		
19 Q-R4	19 Q-Q3		
20 Kt-Kt5	20 Q-K4		
21 P-KKt3	21 Kt-Kt3		
22 Q-Kt3	22 KR-QBsq		
23 B-B4	23 Q-K2		
24 P-Q6(c)	24 P×P		
25 Kt×QP	25 R-B4		
26 Q-R3	26 Kt-Q2		
27 Kt×B	27 Q-K3		
28 P-KKt4(D)	28 QR-QBsq		
29 P-QB3	29 R-B5		
30 R-Q6	30 Q-Ksq		
31 KR-Qsq	31 Kt-B4		
32 Q×P	32 Kt-Q6ch	47 Q-B3	47 Q-Kt3ch
33 KR×Kt	33 P×R	48 K-B2	48 Q-Kt4
34 Q-K7	34 Q-R5	49 P-Kt3(F)	49 Q-QR4
35 R×QP	35 R×B	50 K-Ktsq	50 Q-R6
36 Q-K5	36 R×Kt	51 R-Q3	51 Q×Pch
		52 K-Bsq	52 R-Ksq
		53 R-K3	53 R-Qsq

WHITE.	BLACK.	NOTES.
54 R-Q3	54 R-Ksq	(A) A very ineffective move in this position. The following variations are suggestive: (a) P-K6, 12 PxP! R-Ksq, 13 Kt-Kt4 Kt-K5, 14 Q-B3 Q-R5ch, 15 Kt-B2 KtxKt, 16 QxKt QxQBP. (b) P-QB3,
55 R-K3	55 R-Qsq	
	Drawn game.	

12 PxP Q-R4ch, 13 B-Q2 BxPch, 14 QxB QxKt.

(B) Thus White retains the Pawn with a tolerably good game.

(C) White has fully assumed the attack, which he maintains with vigour. The heroic manner in which Black saves the game is astonishing and beyond all praise.

(D) Surely RxKt would have cut short all further resistance?

(E) A very strong move, threatening R-Ktsq, QxP, and Q-Q8ch.

(F) Extremely weak. R-K4 would still win with a little care.

GAME 39.—Played at London. White, Mr. Pollock; Black, Mr. A. Burn.

Scotch Gambit.

WHITE.	BLACK.	WHITE.	BLACK.
1 P-K4	1 P-K4	20 Q-B4	20 Kt-K4
2 Kt-KB3	2 Kt-QB3	21 Q-Kt3ch(I)	21 K-Bsq(K)
3 P-Q4	3 PxP	22 RxRP	22 B-R3(L)
4 KtxP	4 P-KKt3(A)	23 R-Q5(M)	23 Kt-B5(N)
5 KtxKt(B)	5 KtPxKt	24 P-K5!(O)	24 PxP(P)
6 B-QB4(C)	6 B-KKt2	25 Kt-K4	25 QxP
7 Kt-B3	7 Kt-K2(D)	26 R-R8ch	26 K-K2
8 B-K3	8 Castles	27 Q-R4ch	27 K-K3(Q)
9 Q-Q2	9 R-Ksq	28 R-R6ch	28 KxR
10 CastlesQR(E)	10 P-QR4	29 Kt-B3ch	29 K-B4
11 P-KR4	11 P-R5	30 Kt-R4ch	30 K-Kt5(R)
12 P-R5	12 P-R6	31 BxKt(S)	31 BxB
13 RPxP	13 PxPch	32 P-R3ch(T)	32 K-Kt4!
14 K-Ktsq	14 KtxP(F)	33 Kt-B3ch	33 K-B4
15 B-Q4(G)	15 Kt-K4	34 R-KB6	34 Q-Q2!
16 B-Kt3	16 P-Q3	35 R-Q6(U)	35 QxR(V)
17 P-B4	17 Kt-Kt5	36 Kt-K4ch	36 K-Kt4
18 BxB	18 KxB	37 KtxQch	37 PxKt
19 P-B5(H)	19 Q-B3		and wins easily.

NOTES.

(A) This defence is unsatisfactory if properly met. It seeks to bring about a position of the Three Knights' game.

(B) The best duty for the Knight, as the doubled Pawns are troublesome to Black's game.

(C) White may also play 6 Q-Q4 Q-B3, 7 P-K5 Q-K3, 8 B-K3 Kt-K2, 9 B-B4 Kt-Q4, 10 Castles B-Kt2, &c., or 6 B-K3 B-Kt2, 7 P-QB3 Kt-B3.

(D) The proper post for the Knight in this opening is KB3, but in this instance it cannot be played there this move. The best defence is 7 P-Q3, followed by Kt-KB3.

(E) Quite sound. White has now a very fine game.

(F) On viewing the position after this race of Rooks Pawns the Black King will be found to be the chief sufferer in position.

(G) Threatening, by the exchange of Bishops, to make Black's position defenceless.

(H) Threatening to win at once by 20 Q-B4 and, if then Kt-K4, by 21 RxPch KxR, 22 R-Rsqch K-Ktsq, 23 Q-R6.

(I) RxP, followed by Q-Kt3 is unsound, as the Knight can go to Kt3.

(K) If K-Rsq mate in eight moves.

(L) With the intention of creating a defence by B-B5, a move which would also promise to attack, if not met with care.

(M) White plays brilliantly, but incorrectly here. He ought to have played QR-Rsq, threatening QR-R6, and he could not fail to win the game. R-Q5 has two points, it threatens RxKt, and it defies the QB Pawn, but forgets that Black has at least two defences.

(N) Mr. Burn conducts this difficult game with unvarying "sang froid" and defensive skill.

(O) The Rook at Q5 was in imminent danger, for the White Knight could not move, on pain of mate.

(P) If 24 QxBP, 25 R-R8ch and wins the Queen. If 24 RxP, 25 RxR KtxR (QxR would cost a Rook, and if 25 PxR, 26 Kt-K4 QxBP, 27 R-R8ch with the text attack below but with equal pieces), 26 Kt-K4 QxP, 27 R-R8ch, &c.

(Q) If 27 P-B3, 28 Q-R7ch QxQ, 29 RxQch K-K3, 30 R-B5 K-B4, 31 Kt-Kt3ch and wins a piece.

(R) If 30 K-Kt4 mate in three moves, if 30 K-Q4 White wins by Q-Rsq.

(S) The cart before the horse. White has a forced win by playing the Pawn first, thus 31 P-R3ch KxP (if K-Kt4 mate in two, and if K-R4 mate in three), 32 BxKt BxB (if 32 KxKt mate in eight moves, if 32 K-Kt5, 33 BxBch K-R4 [K-R6 mate in six, and if 33 Q-B5, 34 Q-Ksqch KxKt, 35 R-R4 and wins], 34 B-Q3 and will win), 33 QxB, and wins.

(T) Quite useless now.

(U) A despairing effort.

(V) Had he taken the Rook with Pawn, he would have been mated on the move; with the King only drawn at best; but with the Queen he secures the victory.

GAME 40.—The following "Gallery Finish," as Mr. Pollock called it, was played at Simpson's Divan, London, 28th April 1888. White, Mr. Pollock; Black, Amateur.

Irregular Opening.

WHITE.	BLACK.	WHITE.	BLACK.
1 P-K4	1 P-K4	10 CastlesQR	10 Kt-Q4
2 P-Q3	2 Kt-QB3	11 P-KR3	11 P-KR3
3 Kt-QB3	3 B-Kt5	12 P-KKt4	12 B-K3
4 B-Q2	4 BxKt	13 P-Kt5	13 Kt-B5
5 BxB	5 P-Q3	14 PxP	14 KtxBch
6 Kt-B3	6 P-B4	15 QxKt	15 B-Q4
7 B-K2	7 Kt-B3	16 Kt-R2	16 BxR
8 PxP	8 BxP	17 PxP	17 R-Ksq
9 Q-Q2	9 Castles	18 Q-R5	18 B-Q4

WHITE.	BLACK.	WHITE.	BLACK.
19 R-Ktsq	19 B-K3	21 Q-R8ch	21 K-B2
20 Kt-B3	20 Kt-K2	22 Kt-Kt5ch	22 K-B3

Whereat P-Kt8 becomes a Kt, giving double check, and mate next move.

GAME 41.—Played at Simpson's Divan, January 1888. White, Rev. Cyril Pearson; Black, Mr. Pollock.

Danish Gambit.

WHITE.	BLACK.	WHITE.	BLACK.
1 P-K4	1 P-K4	18 BxQBP(c)	18 Kt-B5
2 P-Q4	2 PxP	19 Q-Kt4	19 KKt-K6ch
3 P-QB3	3 PxP	20 K-B2	20 RxPch
4 B-QB4	4 Kt-KB3	21 K-B3	21 B-Kt5ch
5 KtxP	5 Kt-B3	22 K-B4	22 BxKt(D)
6 KKt-K2	6 B-B4	23 R-Ktsq	23 R-B7ch
7 B-KKt5?(A)	7 BxPch	24 K-Kt5	24 K-K2(E)
8 K-Bsq	8 B-Kt3	25 K-R6	25 RxPch
9 Kt-Q5	9 Kt-KKt5(B)	26 K-Kt7	26 PxB
10 BxQ	10 KxB	27 Q-B3	27 R-B7
11 Q-Q2	11 P-Q3	28 P-Kt3	28 P-B3(F)
12 KtxB	12 RPxKt	29 P-K5?	29 Kt-B4ch
13 Q-Kt5ch	13 Kt-K2	30 KxP	30 KtxP
14 QxP	14 R-KKtsq	31 Q-R3	31 B-Q6
15 Q-Q4	15 Kt-QB3	32 QR-Ksq	32 Kt-R3ch
16 Q-Q2	16 QKt-K4		and wins. (G)
17 B-Q5	17 P-QB3		

NOTES.

(A) Here White should have Castled.

(B) Black's first intention was to play KtxKt, and after touching the piece he saw that it would be fatal.

(C) It is but just to remark that the two players were both unknown to each other; certainly each appears to have mistaken his opponent for a "rank duffer"!

(D) Threatening mate on the move.

(E) Again threatening mate.

(F) Insidious: nothing can save White now.

(G) There is no reply if 33 QxB, to R-KR7.

GAME 42.—Played in the Handicap Tournament, Simpson's Divan, 1888. White, Mr. J. Mortimer; Black, Mr. Pollock.

Two Knights' Defence.

WHITE.	BLACK.	WHITE.	BLACK.
1 P-K4	1 P-K4	4 Kt-Kt5	4 KtxP
2 Kt-KB3	2 Kt-QB3	5 BxPch	5 K-K2
3 B-B4	3 Kt-B3	6 KtxKt(A)	6 KxB

WHITE.	BLACK.	WHITE.	BLACK.
7 P-Q4	7 P-Q4	33 Kt-K2	33 RxKt
8 Kt-Kt5ch	8 K-Ktsq	34 QxBch	34 R-Kt2
9 PxP	9 KtxP	35 QxRch	35 KxQ
10 Castles	10 P-KR3	36 P-B6ch	36 K-B2
11 Kt-K4	11 B-K3	37 Kt-B3	37 RxBP
12 Kt-Kt3	12 B-QB4(B)	38 QR-Ksq	38 Q-KKtsq
13 Q-K2	13 B-Q3	39 Kt-K2	39 P-Q5
14 P-KB4	14 B-KKt5	40 P-KKt4	40 P-B4
15 Q-Kt5	15 P-B3	41 Kt-B4	41 Q-Rsqch
16 QxKtP	16 B-B4ch	Resigns.	
17 K-Rsq	17 R-Ktsq		
18 Q-R6	18 R-Kt3		
19 Q-R5	19 Kt-Q2		
20 Q-Ksq	20 K-R2		
21 Q-B3	21 R-Ksq		
22 Q-Q3ch(c)	22 K-Rsq		
23 Kt-B3	23 R-Kt5		
24 Q-Kt6	24 Kt-B3		
25 P-QR3	25 R-Kt2		
26 Kt-R4	26 B-Q3		
27 B-Q2	27 QR-K2		
28 B-B3	28 R-Ktsq(D)		
29 P-R3	29 B-K3		
30 BxKt(E)			

(See Diagram below.)

	30 PxB
31 QxBPch	31 K-R2
32 P-B5	32 B-KB2

Position after White's 30th move.

BLACK.

WHITE.

NOTES.

(A) Somewhat inferior to either 6 P-Q4 or P-Q3.

(B) And resulting naturally in Black obtaining a superior development.

(C) A splendid instance of the effects of violating the principle not to play the Queen too early, as she is liable to be harassed by the minor pieces.

(D) A curious and deceptive situation.

(E) Fatal.

GAME 43.—Played at Simpson's Divan, June 1888. White, Mr. H. Erskine; Black, Mr. Pollock.

Muzio Gambit.

WHITE.	BLACK.	WHITE.	BLACK.
1 P-K4	1 P-K4	6 QxP	6 Q-B3
2 P-KB4	2 PxP	7 P-K5	7 QxP
3 Kt-KB3	3 P-KKt4	8 BxPch	8 KxB
4 B-B4	4 P-Kt5	9 P-Q4	9 QxPch
5 Castles	5 PxKt	10 B-K3	10 Q-B3

WHITE.	BLACK.	WHITE.	BLACK.
11 Q-Q5ch	11 K-Ksq	36 Q-Q8ch	36 K-Kt2
12 RxP(A)	12 B-R3	37 Q-K7ch	37 K-Kt3
13 RxQ	13 BxBch	38 Q-K8ch	38 K-B4
14 K-Rsq	14 KtxR	39 Q-B7ch	39 K-K5
15 Q-K5ch	15 K-B2	40 Q-QB4ch	40 K-K6
16 QxB	16 R-Ksq	41 Q-K6ch	41 K-B7
17 Q-Kt3ch	17 P-Q4	42 Q-B6ch	42 K-K8
18 Kt-B3	18 Kt-B3(B)		
19 KtxP	19 B-K3		
20 P-B4	20 Kt-QR4		
21 Q-KB3	21 BxKt		
22 PxB	22 R-KBsq		
23 R-KBsq	23 K-Kt2		
24 Q-Kt3ch	24 K-Rsq		
25 QxP	25 P-Kt3		
26 Q-K7	26 QR-Ksq		
27 QxQRP	27 KtxP		
28 RxRch	28 RxR		
29 P-KR3	29 Kt-QB5		

After many more moves the game was drawn.

Position after Black's 29th move.

(See Diagram below.)

30 P-QR4	30 Kt(B5)-K6
31 P-QKt4	31 Kt-B8
32 Q-QKt7	32 Kt-B6
33 QxKtP	33 Kt-Kt6ch
34 K-Ktsq	34 R-B8ch
35 K-R2	35 Kt(B6)-K7

NOTES.

(A) The strongest attack which White can obtain in the "Double Muzio" is by bringing out the remaining Knight as soon as possible. On the other hand Black is generally obliged to surrender his Queen for the sake of breaking the attack and he generally has a good opportunity for this, as in the present game.

(B) Too rash. P-B3 should be played.

GAME 44.—Played in the Handicap Tournament, Simpson's Divan, 1888. White, Mr. J. Mason; Black, Mr. Pollock.

Two Knights' Defence.

WHITE.	BLACK.	WHITE.	BLACK.
1 P-K4	1 P-K4	9 Q-Kt4	9 P-QB3
2 Kt-KB3	2 Kt-QB3	10 BxKt(B)	10 QPxB
3 B-B4	3 Kt-B3	11 B-Kt5	11 P-B3
4 Castles	4 KtxP	12 QR-Qsq	12 Q-K2
5 Kt-B3	5 Kt-B4(A)	13 B-Bsq	13 P-K4
6 P-Q4	6 PxP	14 Q-K2	14 B-Q2
7 KtxP	7 KtxKt	15 P-B4	15 Castles
8 QxKt	8 Kt-K3	16 Kt-K4	16 Q-K3

WHITE.	BLACK.	WHITE.	BLACK.
17 PxP	17 QxKP	41 R-K2	41 Q-Kt3
18 B-B4	18 QxP	42 P-R3	42 Q-R4
19 R-Ktsq	19 Q-Q5ch	43 B-B4	43 QxPch
20 K-Rsq	20 B-KB4	44 B-R2	44 Q-QKt6
21 Kt-Kt3	21 B-Q2	45 Q-Kt8ch	
22 P-B3	22 Q-R5		
23 QR-Qsq	23 B-QB4(c)		
24 Kt-K4	24 B-QR6		
25 R-Q4	25 Q-Kt4		
26 P-B4	26 Q-Kt3(D)		
27 R-Q3	27 P-KB4(E)		

White here proposed a draw which was accepted. (H)

Position after Black's 27th move.

(See Diagram below.)

28 Kt-Kt5(F)	28 KR-Ksq
29 Q-B3	29 B-B4
30 Kt-B7	30 B-K3
31 RxRch	31 RxR
32 KtxR	32 QxKt
33 R-Qsq	33 Q-Ktsq
34 Q-K2	34 P-KKt4(G)
35 BxP	35 BxP
36 Q-K5	36 B-Q4
37 QxPch	37 K-Ktsq
38 Q-K5ch	38 K-Rsq
39 R-Ksq	39 P-QR4
40 P-QR4	40 K-R2

NOTES.

(A) The Knight may also be retired to B3 or even to Q3, or it may be left at K5, and B-K2 played. KtxKt, however, is perfectly safe.

(B) Mr. Mason adopts a very bold and attacking policy in the present game.

(C) He might perhaps have played B-R6 at once.

(D) It is easily seen from this game how important a piece the Queen is in defending against an attack against a King Castled, especially on the Q side.

(E) There is nothing else; the Knight must of course be prevented from giving check at Q6.

(F) The game now becomes extremely interesting. It is, however, very likely that White could have won the Queen at this point. Suppose 28 P-B5 BxP, 29 R-QKt3 Q-R4, 30 KtxB QxKt, 31 Q-R6! Black would therefore have to submit to the loss of the Queen by 29 B-Kt5, 30 Kt-Q6ch BxKt, 31 RxQ, but there would still be some fight left.

(G) White of course threatened Q-K5.

(H) The manner in which both sides force a draw is rather amusing, thus, K-R3, 46 Q-R8ch B-R2, 47 B-Ktsq Q-R6ch, 48 B-R2.

GAME 45.—Played in the Handicap Tournament, British Chess Club, 1888. White, Mr. I. Gunsberg; Black, Mr. Pollock.

Four Knights' Opening.

WHITE.	BLACK.	WHITE.	BLACK.
1 P-K4	1 P-K4	25 K-Ktsq(K)	25 BxBP
2 Kt-QB3	2 Kt-KB3	26 QR-Ksq	26 R-Q3(L)
3 Kt-B3	3 Kt-B3		
4 P-QR3(A)	4 P-Q4		
5 B-Kt5	5 P-Q5		
6 Kt-K2	6 B-Q3(B)		
7 P-Q3	7 P-KR3(C)		
8 Castles	8 Castles		
9 Kt-Kt3	9 Kt-K2		
10 Kt-R4	10 P-Kt4(D)		
11 KKt-B5	11 BxKt		
12 PxB	12 Q-Bsq		
13 Q-B3	13 P-Kt5(E)		
14 Q-K2	14 KtxP		
15 KtxKt(F)	15 QxKt		
16 BxP	16 KR-Qsq		
17 P-KB3(G)	17 Q-R4		
18 Q-Q2	18 K-R2		
19 B-Kt5	19 P-K5		
20 P-KB4(H)	20 P-K6(I)		
21 Q-K2	21 P-Kt6!		
22 QxQ	22 KtxQ		
23 BxR	23 PxPch	27 B-B4	27 Kt-Kt6
24 KxP	24 RxB	Resigns. (M)	

Position after Black's 26th move.

NOTES.

(A) An artful move, which Mr. Gunsberg used to play with success about this time.

(B) Another and perhaps a better move is KtxP, recommended by Zukertort.

(C) Dr. Zukertort played here B-Q2. Black's fifth and seventh moves are, "per se," objectionable and opposed to principle. The case however is exceptional, and certainly it is a strong point to keep the White QB out of the field.

(D) White probably did not expect this rebuff. It is correct, however, Black having plenty of force to support the advance.

(E) Clearly the attack has changed hands.

(F) If 15 Kt-K4 Q-Qsq!, 16 KtxKtch QxKt, 17 QxPch K-R2, and Black still has the attack.

(G) Overlooking the force of Black's rejoinder.

(H) The alternative, P-KR4, was decidedly unsatisfactory.

(I) Much better than P-Kt6.

(K) If 25 P-KKt3 R-KKtsq, 26 R-KKtsq KtxKtP, 27 RxKt BxBP, 28 R-KKtsq RxR, 29 RxR P-K7, and wins. The best defence was 25 R-B3.

(L) Leading to a very elegant finish.

(M) If 28 RxB R-R3, or if 28 R-B3 R-R3, 29 RxKt BxR, 30 R-K2 B-B7ch, 31 RxB R-R8ch, 32 KxR PxR, and wins.

GAME 46.—Played in the Handicap Tournament, British Chess Club, 1888. White, Mr. Pollock; Black, Mr. H. E. Bird.

Sicilian Defence.

WHITE.	BLACK.	WHITE.	BLACK.
1 P-K4	1 P-QB4	27 Kt-B5(E)	27 B-Bsq
2 P-Q4	2 PxP	28 R-Qsq	28 B-Q2
3 Kt-KB3	3 Kt-QB3	29 B-K6	29 BxB
4 KtxP	4 P-KKt3	30 KtxBch	30 K-B3
5 KtxKt	5 KtPxKt(A)	31 KtxR	31 RxKt
6 Q-Q4	6 P-B3(B)	32 P-B4	32 P-B4
7 Kt-B3	7 B-KKt2	33 R-Q5	33 RxP
8 B-QB4	8 Q-Kt3	34 RxBP	
9 Q-Q3	9 Kt-R3		
10 Castles	10 Kt-Kt5(C)	and wins.	
11 Q-Kt3	11 P-Q3		
12 P-KR3	12 Kt-K4	Position after White's 15th move.	
13 B-Kt3	13 B-QR3		
14 B-K3	14 Q-Kt2		
15 P-B4(D)			
(See Diagram below.)			
	15 BxR		
16 PxKt	16 B-QR3		
17 PxQP	17 R-Qsq		
18 B-B5	18 PxP		
19 BxQP	19 B-Bsq		
20 P-K5	20 BxB		
21 PxB	21 K-Bsq		
22 Kt-K4	22 Q-Kt3ch		
23 K-Rsq	23 Q-Q5		
24 R-Ksq	24 K-Kt2		
25 P-B3	25 Q-K4		
26 QxQ	26 PxQ		

NOTES.

(A) It has been found in practice that Black can recapture with KtP without disadvantage. Taking with QP gives White a little attack.

(B) Preferable would be Kt-B3, and if 7 P-K5 Kt-R4.

(C) Not good, as White's reply obviates at once Q-B2 and Kt-K4.

(D) The sacrifice of the exchange makes the game very interesting.

(E) White has now a little the best of the bargain.

GAME 47.—Played in the Handicap Tournament, Simpson's Divan, 1888. White, Mr. Pollock; Black, Mr. H. E. Bird.

Four Knights' Opening.

WHITE.	BLACK.	WHITE.	BLACK.
1 P-K4	1 P-K4	3 Kt-B3	3 Kt-B3
2 Kt-KB3	2 Kt-QB3	4 B-Kt5	4 B-B4(A)

WHITE.	BLACK.	WHITE.	BLACK.
5 KtxP	5 KtxKt	33 K-Kt2	33 BxR
6 P-Q4	6 B-Kt5	34 RxB	34 Q-K7ch
7 PxKt	7 KtxP	35 Q-B2	35 QxKP
8 Castles(B)	8 BxKt(c)	36 Q-B3ch	36 K-Ktsq
9 PxB	9 KtxQBP	37 Q-B8ch	37 K-Kt2
10 Q-Kt4	10 Q-K2(D)		
11 B-Kt5(E)	11 Q-K3		
12 Q-Kt4	12 KtxB		
13 QxKt	13 P-QKt3		
14 P-KB4	14 B-Kt2		
15 QR-Qsq	15 Q-QB3		
16 Q-K2	16 P-KR3		
17 B-R4	17 Q-K5		
18 Q-Kt4	18 P-KKt4		
19 KR-Ksq	19 Q-B3		
20 PxP	20 CastlesQR(F)		
21 P-Kt6	21 QR-Ktsq		
22 P-Kt7	22 R-R2		
23 B-B6	23 P-KR4		
24 Q-R3	24 R-R3		
25 R-K3	25 R-Kt3		
26 R-Q2	26 Q-Kt4		
27 P-Kt3(G)	27 Q-B3		
28 KR-Q3	28 Q-B4ch		
29 K-Bsq	29 B-R3	38 Q-B3ch(H)	38 K-Ktsq
30 QxPch	30 K-Kt2	39 R-Q5	39 QxP(Kt2)
31 QxKBP	31 RxBch	40 RxP	40 Q-B6(I)
32 QxR	32 Q-K6	41 QxQ	Resigns.

Position after Black's 37th move.

NOTES.

(A) Inferior to B-Kt5.

(B) Q-Q4 is the usual move, but the text move may be made without danger.

(C) If KtxKt, 9 PxKt BxP, White may obtain the advantage by 10 Q-Kt4, while 10 R-Ktsq would also be good play.

(D) Taking the Bishop is clearly out of the question.

(E) He could also take the Knight's Pawn, exchanging Queens if Q-Bsq, with a capital game.

(F) Both sides are evidently bent on attack. Owing, however, to the Bishops being on opposite colours little real progress can be made, and, as it turns out, but not before some very animated discussions, Black eventually loses by trying to force a win out of a drawn position.

(G) White defends with commendable caution.

(H) If QxR Black forces a draw by checking with Q at K7 and K8 or KKt5 accordingly.

(I) Although reputed as more or less reckless in play, it scarcely ever has occurred to Mr. Bird to make a blunder of this magnitude. The game, however, should, with a little care, be won in the end by White.

GAME 48.—Played in the Handicap Tournament, Simpson's Divan, 1888. White, Mr. J. H. Zukertort; Black, Mr. Pollock.

Two Knights' Defence.

WHITE.	BLACK.	WHITE.	BLACK.
1 P-K4	1 P-K4	24 B-QB4	24 Kt-Qsq
2 Kt-KB3	2 Kt-QB3	25 Q-R5	25 R-Kt3
3 B-B4	3 Kt-B3	26 P-Q5	26 P-B4(F)
4 Kt-Kt5	4 P-Q4	27 P-Q6	27 QxKP(G)
5 PxP	5 Kt-QR4	28 Q-Kt6ch	28 K-Rsq
6 B-Kt5ch	6 P-B3	29 BxRP	29 R-Kt2
7 PxP	7 PxP	30 B-B4	Resigns. (H)
8 B-K2	8 P-KR3		
9 Kt-KB3	9 P-K5		
10 Kt-K5	10 Q-B2		
11 P-Q4	11 B-Q3		
12 P-KB4	12 Castles(A)		
13 Castles	13 P-B4		
14 P-B3	14 R-Ktsq(B)		
15 K-Rsq	15 PxP		
16 PxP	16 Kt-Q4		
17 Kt-QB3(c)	17 KtxKt		
18 PxKt	18 BxKt(D)		
19 BPxB	19 QxBP		
20 B-Q2	20 Q-QR6		
21 R-Bsq(E)			
(See Diagram below.)			
	21 Kt-Kt2		
22 R-B3	22 Q-K2		
23 R-KKt3	23 K-R2		

Position after White's 21st move.

NOTES.

(A) If PxP en pass, 13 KtxP at KB3 B-KKt5, 14 Castles BxKt, 15 BxB BxPch, 16 K-Rsq, with the better game, and a likelihood of recovering the extra Pawn again.

(B) B-Kt2, with a view to occupying the centre files by QR-Qsq, &c., would be more to the point.

(c) It will be seen how important was White's 15th move.

(D) An unpleasant necessity, if the QBP is to be taken. If QxP, 19 B-Q2 Q moves, 20 BxKt QxB, 21 Kt-B6, winning the exchange.

(E) It is not difficult to see that White will be able to at once prosecute an overwhelming attack on the weak K side. The text move threatens "en passant" to win the exchange by Q-Ksq Kt-Kt2, B-QKt4.

(F) If R-Kt3, 27 P-Q6 Q-Ksq, 28 RxP! KRxR, 29 QxRch K-Rsq, 30 BxR, and wins. The text move is of course desperation.

(G) If Q-Ksq, 28 RxPch and mates next move. If Q-Q2, 28 Q-Kt6ch or BxRP wins.

(H) A beautifully played game on the part of Dr. Zukertort.

GAME 49.—Played in the Handicap Tournament, Simpson's Divan, 1888. White, Mr. Pollock; Black, Mr. F. J. Lee.

French Defence.

WHITE.	BLACK.	WHITE.	BLACK.
1 P-K4	1 P-K3	25 R-K3	
2 Kt-QB3	2 P-Q4		
3 Kt-B3	3 Kt-KB3		
4 P-K5	4 KKt-Q2		
5 P-QKt3(A)	5 P-QR3		
6 B-Kt2	6 P-QB4		
7 B-Q3	7 B-K2		
8 Castles	8 Castles		
9 Q-K2	9 Kt-QB3		
10 QR-Ksq	10 Kt-Kt5		
11 P-QR3(B)	11 KtxB		
12 QxKt	12 P-QKt4		
13 Kt-K2	13 Kt-Kt3		
14 Kt-Kt3	14 B-Q2		
15 K-Rsq	15 P-QR4		
16 Kt-Ktsq	16 P-R5		
17 Kt-R3	17 PxP		
18 PxP(c)	18 P-B5		
19 Q-K3	19 PxP		
20 P-B4	20 P-Kt3(D)		
21 P-B5	21 KPxP	25	25 R-R5(I)
22 Q-R6(E)	22 B-K3(F)	26 P-K6 !(K)	26 R-KKt5(L)
23 RxP(G)	23 BxR(H)	27 Kt-Kt5(M)	27 RxKt
24 KtxB	24 PxKt	28 R-R3(N)	Resigns.

Position after White's 25th move.

NOTES.

(A) Quite an unusual method of treating the French Defence.

(B) White's position on the Queen's side would be safer with this Pawn unmoved. It is, however, necessary to dislodge the Knight in order to mass the forces for the attack on the other wing.

(C) Here White has to capture from the centre, while the RP is left weak.

(D) P-B4 is essential to a correct defence.

(E) This is a most important point. White should have played 22 B-Q4 (attacking the Knight) whereby Black's QP would be fixed, thus frustrating P-Q5, which at the last moment in the actual game might have turned the tables. The time used in this move of the Bishop was actually used in White's 25th move, which led to a startling finish only owing to Black missing his way.

(F) Of course P-K6 was threatened.

(G) Threatening to continue with R-R5.

(H) Not PxR, on account of Kt-R5.

(I) See note (E). The correct defence is K-Rsq! after which the game should, with a little care, result decisively in Black's favour. After the text move White wins by force.

(K) Not 26 R-Kt3ch R-Kt5, 26 P-K6 P-Q5!

(L) Obviously P-Q5 now would shut out the Rook, and White would win at once by R-Kt3ch. Black will now have no time for P-Q5.

(M) Utterly unexpected and a problem-like conclusion.

(N) Mate is forced in three moves. The winner of this game was presented by the late Mr. F. H. Lewis, a most generous patron of Chess, with a special "brilliancy prize" of £1, which was awarded to him at a dinner held at Simpson's to celebrate the tournament.

GAME 50.—Played in the Handicap Tournament, Simpson's Divan, 1888. White, Mr. O. C. Muller; Black, Mr. Pollock.

Philidor's Defence.

WHITE.	BLACK.	WHITE.	BLACK.
1 P-K4	1 P-K4	24 B-Q6	24 Kt-Ksq
2 Kt-KB3	2 P-Q3	25 PxP	25 RxB
3 P-Q4	3 PxP	26 QxR	26 KtxQ
4 KtxP	4 Kt-KB3	27 PxR	27 KtxB
5 Kt-QB3	5 B-K2(A)	28 RxKt	28 Q-Rsq
6 B-QB4	6 Castles	Resigns.	
7 Castles	7 P-QR3(B)		
8 P-QR4	8 KtxP(C)		
9 KtxKt	9 P-Q4		
10 B-Q3	10 PxKt		
11 BxP	11 Kt-Q2		
12 P-QB3	12 B-B3		
13 B-K3	13 Kt-B4		
14 B-B2	14 Kt-K3		
15 Q-Q3(D)	15 P-KKt3		
16 QR-Qsq	16 Kt-Kt2		
17 Q-B4	17 B-Q2		
18 KR-Ksq	18 Q-Bsq		
19 B-B4	19 P-B4		
20 Kt-Kt3	20 P-Kt3		
21 B-K4	21 R-R2		

(See Diagram below.)

| 22 P-R5(E) | 22 B-QKt4 |
| 23 Q-Q5 | 23 R-Qsq |

Position after Black's 21st move.

NOTES.

(A) According to some highly interesting statistics compiled by a correspondent in the "New York Sun," from 1,500 match and tournament games, Philidor's Defence was played but little over once in one hundred games, less frequently than any one of the 17 openings considered, and yet was second to the Two Knights' Defence only as the hardest defence to beat. By far the most frequently played openings were the Ruy Lopez, QP opening, and French Defence. The present form of the "Philidor" is a safe one, and rather better than playing Kt-QB3 early.

(B This might mean a general advance on the Q side by P-QKt4, P-QB4, &c., but White forestalls it.

(C) As usual, Black improves his game by this capture, which is a consequence of the opponent's sixth move, which was hardly his best.

(D) White could exchange, leaving four Bishops on the field, but he certainly would have no advantage.

(E) The position has worked itself up in a curious manner and is most difficult. But here White, thinking no doubt to gain a decisive advantage, falls right into a trap and loses the game forthwith. Compare Diagram.

GAME 51.—Played in the Bradford International Congress. White, Mr. C. v. Bardeleben; Black, Mr. Pollock.

Irregular Opening.

WHITE.	BLACK.	WHITE.	BLACK.
1 P-Q4	1 P-KB4	26 K-Qsq	26 B-Q6(I)
2 Kt-QB3(A)	2 P-Q4	27 B-Q6(K)	27 QxB
3 B-B4	3 P-K3	28 Q-K5(L)	28 QxQ
4 P-K3	4 Kt-KB3	29 PxQ	29 KRxP
5 Kt-B3	5 B-Kt5	30 RxP	30 QRxP
6 P-QR3(B)	6 BxKtch	31 R-Kt8ch	31 K-Q2
7 PxB	7 Kt-K5!	Resigns.	
8 Kt-Q2(C)	8 KtxQBP		
9 Q-R5ch	9 P-Kt3		
10 Q-R6	10 Q-K2		
11 P-KR4(D)	11 R-Ktsq		
12 Kt-B3	12 Kt-K5		
13 B-Q3	13 Kt-QB3		
14 BxKt	14 BPxB		
15 Kt-K5	15 KtxKt		
16 BxKt	16 B-Q2!		
17 Q-Kt5(E)	17 Q-B2(F)		
(See Diagram below.)			
18 R-QKtsq	18 R-KBsq		
19 Q-Kt3	19 B-B3		
20 BxP(G)	20 Q-Q2!		
21 P-R5	21 P-KKt4		
22 B-K5	22 B-Kt4(H)		
23 QxP	23 B-R3		
24 B-B4	24 R-Bsq		
25 R-Kt2	25 Q-B3		

Position after Black's 17th move.

NOTES.

(A) We prefer 2 P-QB4 previous to the sortie of the QKt.

(B) White not having prevented, with 5 P-QR3, his QKt being pinned, should now have played 6 B-Q3, as Black's continuation is obvious.

(C) The best under the circumstances. He must now try to make a counter demonstration, the Queen's side being compromised. If 8 P-QB3, then P-B3, followed effectively by Q-R5ch; and if 8 Q-Q3, P-Kt3, followed by B-R3 would win.

(D) White should have tried to bring his King into safety by 11 B-Q3, and 12 Castles, instead of weakening his King's position too.

(E) If 17 BxP, then 17 B-Kt4, thus preventing White from Castling.

(F) Obviously Black does not exchange Queens, which would be in favour of White. In any case he might hope for a draw, the Bishops being of opposite colour.

(G) A last resource would have been to Castle, with chances for a draw. Under ordinary circumstances Herr v Bardeleben might have done so, but he, no doubt, played up to his score.

(H) This cuts off the retreat of the King, which Mr. Pollock aimed at for the last few moves.

(I) This pretty move decides the game.

(K) Quite useless, he might as well resign.

(L) If 28 PxB Q-B3 would win.

GAME 52.—Played in the International Tournament, Bradford, 1888. White, Rev. J. Owen; Black, Mr. Pollock.

Irregular Opening.

WHITE.	BLACK.	WHITE.	BLACK.
1 Kt-KB3	1 P-KB4	24 KtxBP	24 R-K2
2 P-Q4	2 Kt-KB3	25 Kt-K6	25 Q-Kt5
3 P-K3	3 P-K3	26 QR-Bsq	26 R-R3
4 B-Q3	4 P-QKt3	27 R-KB2	27 R-R6(c)
5 Castles	5 B-Kt2	28 Kt-Kt5	28 R-R4
6 P-B4	6 B-K2	29 B-Qsq	Resigns.
7 Kt-B3	7 Castles		
8 P-Q5	8 Kt-R3		
9 P-QR3	9 Kt-B4		
10 B-B2	10 Q-Ksq(A)		
11 Kt-Q4	11 Q-Kt3		
(See Diagram below.)			
12 P-B3(B)	12 Q-R4		
13 P-QKt4	13 Kt-R3		
14 PxP	14 B-Q3		
15 P-KKt3	15 PxP		
16 KtxKP	16 R-B2		
17 Kt-Q5	17 KtxKt		
18 PxKt	18 R-Ksq		
19 B-Kt3	19 Kt-Ktsq		
20 B-Kt2	20 Kt-Q2		
21 P-B4	21 Q-Kt3		
22 Q-Q3	22 Kt-B3		
23 BxKt	23 RxB		

Position after Black's 11th move.

NOTES.

(A) QKt-K5 would be more advantageous here or on the next move.

(B) For in defending the King's side White is preparing to drive the adverse QKt out of play again, as well as thereby threatening to win one of the centre Pawns.

(C) After RxKt, 28 PxR QxPch, 29 K-Bsq, Black would have nothing left.

GAME 53.—Played in the International Tournament, Bradford, 1888. White, Capt. G. H. Mackenzie; Black, Mr. Pollock.

Irregular Opening.

WHITE.	BLACK.	WHITE.	BLACK.
1 Kt-KB3	1 P-Q3	24 KR-Bsq	24 R-KB2
2 P-Q4	2 B-Kt5	25 P-QR4	25 K-Qsq
3 P-K3	3 Kt-Q2	26 Q-Kt6ch	26 RxQ
4 P-B4	4 P-K4	27 BxRch	27 K-Ksq
5 Kt-B3	5 P-KB3(A)	28 Kt-K3	28 Kt-Q2
6 B-K2	6 Kt-K2	29 P-R5	29 P-Q4
7 Q-Kt3	7 P-QKt3(B)	30 KPxP	Resigns.
8 Castles	8 Kt-B3		
9 Q-Kt5	9 Kt-R4		
10 P-Kt4	10 Kt-Kt2		
11 Q-B6	11 Q-Bsq		
12 PxP	12 BPxP		
13 Kt-Q5	13 K-Qsq		
14 P-K4	14 P-KR3		
15 Kt-Q4	15 BxB		
16 KtxB	16 P-KKt4(C)		
17 KKt-B3	17 R-R2		
18 B-K3	18 P-QR4		
19 P-KR3			
(See Diagram below.)			
	19 P-R5(D)		
20 KtxRP	20 Kt-Ktsq		
21 Q-Kt5	21 R-R3(E)		
22 KKtxKtP	22 P-B3		
23 KtxQ	23 KxKt		

Position after White's 19th move.

NOTES.

(A) A novel method of opening certainly. The text move seems at least unnecessary, and Kt-K2 preferable.

(B) R-QKtsq is the proper reply. Black however is bent on upsetting all the canons of opening, and devises a (suicidal) scheme to lure the White Queen to destruction.

(C) To prevent P-KB4.

(D) The idea of still ensnaring the Queen, while himself under attack, is unsound. R-R3 at once is a better move, or possibly Kt-Ktsq.

(E) White threatened KtxKtP.

GAME 54.—Played in the International Tournament, Bradford, 1888. White, Mr. J. H. Blackburne; Black, Mr. Pollock.

Ruy Lopez.

WHITE.	BLACK.	WHITE.	BLACK.
1 P-K4	1 P-K4	3 B-Kt5	3 P-QR3
2 Kt-KB3	2 Kt-QB3	4 B-R4	4 Kt-B3

WHITE.	BLACK.	WHITE.	BLACK.
5 Q-K2(A)	5 P-QKt4	30 PxKt	30 Q-R2
6 B-Kt3	6 B-B4	31 Q-R6ch	31 K-Ksq
7 P-B3	7 Castles	32 P-B7ch	32 K-Q2
8 Castles	8 P-Q4	33 P-B8(Kt)ch	33 BxKt
9 P-Q3	9 B-KKt5(B)	34 QxB	34 R-K2
10 B-Kt5	10 Kt-K2	35 R-B7	35 K-K3
11 QKt-Q2	11 P-Q5(C)	36 RxRch	36 QxR
12 P-KR3	12 BxKt	37 QxQch	Resigns.
13 KtxB	13 Kt-Kt3		
14 QR-Bsq(D)	14 PxP		
15 PxP	15 P-R3		
16 Kt-R4(E)	16 KtxKt ?		
17 BxKt	17 B-R6(F)		
18 QR-Qsq	18 P-B4		
19 P-KB4	19 Q-Kt3		
20 PxP	20 Kt-Q2		
21 B-Q5	21 QR-Ksq		
22 RxP(G)			

(See Diagram below.)

	22 RxR
23 BxRch	23 KxB
24 Q-R5ch	24 P-Kt3
25 QxRP	25 R-K3
26 R-Bsqch	26 K-Ktsq
27 B-B6	27 P-B5ch(H)
28 P-Q4	28 KtxB
29 QxPch	29 K-Bsq

Position after White's 22nd move.

NOTES.

(A) A sound move, somewhat favoured by Blackburne.

(B) PxP, followed by Q-K2, is safer.

(C) The necessity for such a move, where his game should be developing, ought not to arise. Black must be conceded to have the worst of the opening.

(D) Further increasing his lead.

(E) This seems to have been unexpected, but it is a little doubtful whether it is quite sound, as after PxB, 17 KtxKt R-Ksq, Black's position is improved, and it becomes necessary for White to see after the safety of his Kt, which will be threatened by Q-Q2 and K-R2.

(F) Some sort of attempt at a diversion, but quite purposeless. His best course was now B-K2.

(G) A fine stroke of play.

(H) There is no escape from the vice-like grip.

GAME 55.—Played in the International Tournament, Bradford, 1888. White, Mr. E. Thorold; Black, Mr. Pollock.

Irregular Opening.

WHITE.	BLACK.	WHITE.	BLACK.
1 Kt-KB3	1 P-Q4	40 R-B8ch	40 K-Kt3
2 P-Q4	2 B-Kt5	41 B-K4ch	41 K-Kt2
3 B-B4	3 BxKt	42 R-B5	42 R-R4
4 KPxB(A)	4 P-K3	43 B-Q3	43 P-QKt5
5 B-Q3	5 B-Q3	44 P-QB4	44 P-R5
6 Q-Q2	6 Kt-QB3	45 R-R5	45 P-R6
7 P-B3	7 Kt-B3	46 P-Kt3	46 K-B3
8 Castles	8 Kt-KR4(B)	47 B-K4	47 R-Ktsq
9 BxB	9 QxB	48 R-R6	48 QR-KRsq
10 Kt-R3	10 P-QR3	49 RxPch	49 K-K2
11 P-KKt3	11 CastlesKR	50 P-B5	50 RxPch
12 Q-Kt5	12 P-KKt3	51 K-Kt4	51 R-R7
13 P-KB4	13 K-Kt2	52 R-QR6	52 R-Qsq
14 QR-Ksq	14 Q-Qsq	53 P-Q5	53 RxRP
15 Q-Kt4(c)	15 Kt-B3		
16 Q-R3	16 Q-Q3		
17 Kt-B2	17 Kt-K2		
18 R-K5	18 Kt-Q2		
19 Kt-K3(D)	19 KtxR		
20 BPxKt	20 Q-Qsq		
21 P-KKt4	21 P-KB4		
22 PxP e.p. ch	22 RxP		
23 P-Kt5	23 R-B2		
24 QxKP	24 Q-Q3		
25 QxQ	25 PxQ		
26 B-B2	26 QR-KBsq		
27 B-Kt3	27 R-B5		
28 P-KR3	28 P-R3		
29 PxPch	29 KxP		
30 KtxP	30 KtxKt		
31 BxKt	31 P-KKt4		
32 P-B3	32 R-QKtsq(E)		
33 R-Ksq	33 K-Kt3		
34 R-K7	34 P-Kt4	54 K-B5(F)	54 R-R7
35 R-QR7	35 R-Kt3	55 P-Q6ch	55 K-Bsq
36 R-R8	36 R-KB3	56 P-B6	56 R-R2
37 R-Kt8ch	37 K-B4	57 P-B7	57 R-B2ch
38 K-B2	38 P-R4	58 K-Kt4	58 R-Bsq
39 K-Kt3	39 R-KR3	59 R-R8	Resigns.

Position after Black's 53rd move.

NOTES.

(A) Taking with KtP is generally preferred in similar positions. It is better to double Pawns "towards" the centre than "from" it.

(B) Black has now the better game.

(C) The exchange of Queens would give Black the best of the ending, on account of White's doubled Pawns.

(D) Bold indeed, but almost justifiable in the close state of the game, and in face of P-QB4, by which Black would have obtained an improved position.

(E) Black ought to have been a little more conservative with his Pawns, for his opponent has now a full equivalent for the loss of the exchange.

(F) Mr. Thorold plays the latter part of the game exceedingly well.

GAME 56.—Played in the International Tournament, Bradford, 1888. White, Mr. J. Taubenhaus; Black, Mr. Pollock.

Four Knights' Opening.

WHITE.	BLACK.
1 P-K4	1 P-K4
2 Kt-QB3	2 Kt-QB3
3 Kt-B3	3 Kt-B3
4 B-Kt5	4 B-Kt5
5 P-Q3	5 P-Q3
6 Castles	6 B-Kt5(A)
7 Kt-Q5	7 B-QB4
8 B-Kt5	8 P-QR3(B)
9 BxKtch(C)	9 PxB
10 BxKt(D)	10 PxB
11 Kt-K3	11 Q-Q2
12 P-B3	12 KR-Ktsq
13 KtxB	13 QxKt
14 Kt-Ksq(E)	14 P-KR4!
15 QxQ	15 PxQ
16 P-KKt3(F)	16 P-B4!
17 K-Kt2(G)	17 PxP
18 PxP	18 K-K2
19 Kt-Q3	19 B-Kt3
20 P-KB4	20 P-B3
21 Kt-Kt4(H)	21 P-R4
22 Kt-Q3	22 KR-KBsq
23 QR-Bsq	23 K-Q2
24 PxP	24 BPxP
25 RxR	25 RxR
26 R-Bsq	26 RxR
27 KxR	27 K-K3
28 Kt-B2	28 BxKt
29 KxB	29 P-B4
30 K-K3	

Position after White's 30th move.

BLACK.

WHITE.

WHITE.	BLACK.
	30 P-Q4(I)
31 PxPch(K)	31 KxP
32 K-Q3	32 P-B5ch
33 K-K3	33 P-R5
34 P-QR3	34 P-B3
35 K-K2	35 K-K5
36 K-B2	36 K-Q6
37 K-Kt2	37 P-K5
38 P-R4	38 PxP e.p. ch
39 KxP	39 P-K6
Resigns.	

NOTES.

(A) Not very orthodox, but admissible.

(B) This, or P-KR3, is apparently the only available move, for if B-K3 White could obtain a dangerous attack by P-Q4.

(C) If the Bishop retreats, Black will get a good game by P-QKt4 and Kt-Q5.

(D) Not necessary here nor advisable, as the doubling of the Pawns only strengthens Black's centre, thus rendering Castling unnecessary, as the King will be secure from any attack for a long time to come.

(E) White bases his hopes on having a Kt against a B for the ending, the former piece being generally very deadly to doubled Pawns. Black on the other hand trusts to his powerful Pawn centre.

(F) To guard against P-Kt6, but as that advance could not be made at once on account of 17 PxP RxP, 18 P-Q4, he would have perhaps done better with Kt-B2.

(G) If PxP R-Kt4 recovers the Pawn.

(H) Very questionable, as he cannot take the QBP, and therefore loses valuable time.

(I) The ending is most interesting. Black is practically a Pawn ahead and although it is, " per se," a badly doubled one it wins the game by gaining a move.

(K) Probably P-QKt3 would have drawn the game.

GAME 57.—Played in the International Tournament, Bradford, 1888. White, Mr. Pollock; Black, Mr. J. Mason.

Evans Gambit Declined.

WHITE.	BLACK.
1 P-K4	1 P-K4
2 Kt-KB3	2 Kt-QB3
3 B-B4	3 B-B4
4 P-QKt4	4 B-Kt3
5 P-B3	5 Kt-B3
6 P-Q3	6 P-Q3
7 B-KKt5	7 P-KR3
8 B-R4	8 P-Kt4
9 B-KKt3	9 Kt-K2
10 Q-Kt3	10 Castles(A)
11 QKt-Q2	11 Kt-Kt3
12 P-KR4	12 P-Kt5
13 P-R5	13 Kt-B5
14 BxKt	14 PxB
15 Kt-R4	15 P-B3
16 Q-B2	16 P-Q4
17 B-Kt3	17 P-R4
18 PxRP	18 BxRP
19 CastlesQR(B)	19 B-K3(c)
20 P-Q4	20 R-Bsq
21 P-K5	21 Kt-R2
22 Kt-B5(D)	22 Q-Kt4
23 Kt-Q6	23 P-QB4(E)

Position after Black's 23rd move.

WHITE.	BLACK.
24 KtxR	24 RxKt
25 P-B4	25 BPxP
26 B-R4	26 BxKtch
27 KxB	27 RxP
Resigns.	

NOTES.

(A) A bold game, such as Mason will play occasionally.

(B) This appears to be quite justifiable.

(C) If KtxRP, 20 Kt-B5 BxKt, 21 RxKt, &c.

(D) It was unaccountable that White did not select the much stronger move of Kt-Kt6, when if PxKt, 23 QxPch K-Rsq, 24 QxB Q-Kt4, 25 P-B3 PxP, 26 PxP BxP, 27 Kt-Ktsq B-Kt5, 28 QR-Ktsq and he has an excellent game.

(E) In splendid style. See diagram.

GAME 58.—Played in the International Tournament, Bradford, 1888. White, Mr. J. Mortimer; Black, Mr. Pollock.

Two Knights' Defence.

WHITE.	BLACK.	WHITE.	BLACK.
1 P-K4	1 P-K4	26 PxKt	26 BxR
2 Kt-KB3	2 Kt-QB3	27 PxB	27 Q-Kt4ch
3 B-B4	3 Kt-B3	28 K-Rsq	28 Q-B3
4 Kt-Kt5	4 P-Q4	29 Kt-B3	29 R-Q7
5 PxP	5 Kt-QR4	30 R-Bsq	30 Q-Q5
6 B-Kt5ch	6 P-B3	31 Kt-Ktsq	31 Q-Kt7
7 PxP	7 PxP	32 Kt-B3	32 R-QBsq
8 B-K2	8 P-KR3	and wins.	
9 Kt-KB3	9 P-K5		
10 Kt-K5	10 Q-B2		
11 P-KB4	11 B-Q3		
12 P-Q4	12 Castles		
13 Castles	13 P-B4		
14 P-B3	14 B-Kt2(A)		
15 B-K3(B)	15 Kt-Q4		
16 Q-Q2	16 PxP		
17 BxP(C)	17 QR-Qsq		
18 Q-Ksq	18 KtxKBP		
19 RxKt	19 BxKt		
20 BxB	20 QxB		
21 R-Bsq	21 P-K6		
22 Q-Kt3	22 Q-K2		
23 P-Kt4	23 Kt-B3		
24 R-B3	24 KR-Ksq		
(See Diagram below.)			
25 Q-Ksq(D)	25 KtxP		

Position after Black's 24th move.

NOTES.

(A) See notes to Game 48, Zukertort v Pollock.
(B) 15 Kt-Q2 seems much more satisfactory.
(C) Even worse than PxP. Black obtains far too good a game.
(D) The delay in developing the Q side proves fatal. See diagram.

GAME 59.—Played at the Nottingham Congress, 1888. White, Mr. Pollock; Black, Mr. E. Schallopp.

Evans Gambit.

WHITE.	BLACK.	WHITE.	BLACK.
1 P-K4	1 P-K4	6 Castles	6 Kt-B3(A)
2 Kt-KB3	2 Kt-QB3	7 P-Q4	7 KtxKP
3 B-B4	3 B-B4	8 R-Ksq	8 Kt-Q3(B)
4 P-QKt4	4 BxKtP	9 B-KKt5	9 Kt-K2
5 P-B3	5 B-R4	10 KtxP	10 Castles

WHITE.	BLACK.	WHITE.	BLACK.
11 BxKt	11 QxB	21 R-Qsq	21 B-KB3
12 KtxBP	12 QxRch	22 R-Ksq	22 K-Bsq
13 QxQ	13 KtxB	23 Kt-Q4	23 B-Q4
14 Kt-K5	14 R-Ksq	24 Q-B5	24 R-Ksq
15 Q-KBsq	15 KtxKt	25 RxRch	25 KxR
16 PxKt	16 RxP	26 Kt-Kt3	26 BxKt
17 Kt-Q2	17 P-QKt4	27 QxR	27 BxP
18 Kt-B3	18 R-QB4	28 QxPch	28 K-Qsq
19 Q-Q3	19 B-Kt2	29 Q-Q3ch	Resigns.
20 QxQP	20 BxP		

It was at the Nottingham Congress, 1888. Schallopp had his last game to play against Pollock, and if he won it he would have tied with Burn for the first prize. Pollock had the move, and offered the Evans Gambit—the last opening any other player would have chosen against Schallopp; but, strange as it may appear, Schallopp played the defence like a tyro, and had a lost game in the opening, and so jeopardised the chance of a division of the first and second prize, and Burn was first. For the sake of illustrating the incident, we give the game in question.

Black not only did not take advantage of the opportunity given him to advance 13 Kt-B5, but actually replied with a weak move, too, by advancing prematurely the QBP, thus enabling White to gain the important move 16 Kt-Q4, and to get a telling attack. The play in the middle game is forced; the QKtP can only be defended by 20 B-Q2, because of the bad position of the QKt, and White's powerful 21 Kt-B5 follows as a matter of course.

With 24 Kt-B4 Black had to give up the Pawn ahead, and had nothing left but a bad position, and to sustain a powerful attack which became irresistible with 27 P-K5, the beginning of the pretty final combination. In this form of Evans Gambit a single weak move in the defence is generally fatal.

NOTES.

(A) 6 Kt-B3 is inferior to 6 P-Q3. It gives White the opportunity for the "Richardson" variation. The only chance after 7 P-Q4 is 7 Castles. The following would be a continuation:—8 PxP KKtxP, 9 B-Q5 KtxQBP, 10 KtxKt BxKt, 11 Kt-Kt5 KtxP (if BxR, then 12 Q-R5 wins), 12 Q-B2 Kt-Kt3, 13 QxB Q-B3, 14 QxQ, and wins. The variations springing from any alteration of Black's defence turn out in favour of White.

(B) The only chance now left is 8 P-Q4. The text move brings him into hopeless trouble, and after some more moves he has to give up the Queen for R and B, with the Queen's side entirely undeveloped. Any further comment would only be "flogging a dead horse." Black had a lost game in the opening, and it took its natural course.

GAME 60.—Played at Simpson's Divan, February 1889. White, Mr. Pollock; Black, Mr. F. J. Lee.

French Defence.

WHITE.	BLACK.	WHITE.	BLACK.
1 P-K4	1 P-K3	7 Q-Kt4	7 P-KKt3
2 P-Q4	2 P-Q4	8 Kt-B3	8 Kt-QB3
3 Kt-QB3	3 Kt-KB3	9 P-QR3	9 Kt-Kt3
4 P-K5	4 KKt-Q2	10 B-Q3	10 B-Q2
5 P-B4	5 P-QB4	11 B-Q2	11 P-QR3
6 PxP	6 BxP	12 P-Kt4	12 B-K2

WHITE.	BLACK.
13 Castles KR	13 Kt-R2(A)
14 QR-Ksq	14 R-QBsq
15 Kt-Q4	15 Kt-B5
16 B-Bsq(B)	16 KtxRP
(See Diagram below.)	
17 KtxQP	17 PxKt
18 P-K6	18 PxP
19 BxPch	19 PxB
20 QxPch	20 K-Bsq
21 P-B5	21 PxP
22 R-K6(c)	Resigns.

NOTES.

(A) These manœuvres with single pieces waste valuable time, while the adversary is preparing an attack.

(B) A snare, into which Black sets his foot.

(c) A crushing "finale."

Position after Black's 16th move.

GAME 61.—Played in the International Tournament, Hastings, 1895. White, Mr. I. Gunsberg; Black, Mr. Pollock.

Vienna Opening.

WHITE.	BLACK.	WHITE.	BLACK.
1 P-K4	1 P-K4	21 KtxP	21 Kt-Q5
2 Kt-QB3	2 Kt-KB3	22 Q-K3 ?	22 R-R3
3 P-KKt3	3 B-B4	23 QR-Bsq	23 Q-Kt4(G)
4 B-Kt2	4 Castles		
5 KKt-K2	5 P-Q4(A)		
6 PxP	6 P-B3		
7 PxP	7 KtxP		
8 P-Q3	8 B-KKt5		
9 P-B3	9 B-K3		
10 P-QR3(B)	10 B-Kt3(c)		
11 B-Q2	11 P-QR4(D)		
12 Q-Bsq	12 R-Bsq		
13 Kt-Qsq	13 Kt-Q4		
14 Kt-B2	14 P-B4		
15 Castles	15 P-B5		
16 K-Rsq(E)	16 PxP		
17 PxP	17 R-B4		
18 P-QB4(F)	18 R-R4ch		
19 K-Ktsq			
(See Diagram below.)			
	19 Kt-B5		
20 BxKt	20 PxB		

Position after White's 19th move.

WHITE.	BLACK.	WHITE.	BLACK.
24 Kt-K2	24 KtxKtch	27 Q-Bsq	27 B-R6
25 QxKt	25 QxP	28 P-B5	28 BxB
26 KR-Ksq	26 R-Kt3	29 QxB	29 QxQ mate.

NOTES.

(A) This appears to be a very good move, affording rapid development.

(B) The QRP hardly needed defending. If, however, 10 B-Kt5 P-KR3, 11 BxKt PxB, 12 Q-Q2 K-R2, 13 Castles Q-R4, 14 K-Ktsq P-QKt4, with a winning attack.

(C) In order to retake with Q in case of 11 B-Kt5 and 12 BxKt, without fear of Kt-K4 subsequently. But Kt-Q4, followed by P-B4, seems much more attacking. Moreover, Black finds it expedient to make another waiting move on the Q side, i.e., P-QR4.

(D) In order to answer Kt-R4 with B-R2.

(E) The following variations will show the danger of attempting to win a second Pawn at this point: (a) 16 PxP PxP, 17 KtxP RxKt, 18 BxR Kt-Q5, 19 B-Kt5 Q-Q3, and White cannot provide against both Kt-K7ch and B-QB2. (b) 16 PxP PxP, 17 BxP RxB, 18 KtxR KtxKt, 19 QxKt Kt-Q5, 20 Q-K5 (20 K-Rsq B-B2, 21 Q-K4 B-B4, followed by Q-R5) B-QB2, 21 Q-R5 P-KKt3, 22 Q-R6 B-KB5, and wins. If 20 QR-Ksq, however, Black must be content with RxP, with a good attack.

(F) Which allows Black to win by a very pretty combination. Either 18 P-KKt4 or B-R3 is a better defence.

(G) There is no answer to this move.

GAME 62.—Played in the International Tournament, Hastings, 1895. White, Mr. Pollock; Black, Dr. S. Tarrasch.

French Defence.

WHITE.	BLACK.	WHITE.	BLACK.
1 P-K4(A)	1 P-K3	22 Kt-Kt6	22 Q-Kt4ch
2 P-K5(B)	2 P-KB3	23 QxQch	23 PxQ
3 P-Q4	3 P-QB4(C)	24 KtxR	24 Kt-Q5
4 B-Q3	4 P-B4(A)(D)	25 P-K7ch	Resigns. (M)(P)
5 P-KKt4(B)(E)	5 PxQP(C)		
6 PxP	6 Q-R4ch		
7 P-B3(D)(F)	7 QxKPch		
8 Kt-K2	8 Kt-QB3(G)		
9 Castles	9 B-B4(E)		
10 R-Ksq	10 Q-B3(H)		
11 Kt-Q2(I)	11 KPxP(F)		
12 PxP	12 B-K2(G)(K)		
13 Kt-KB3	13 K-Qsq(L)		
14 B-KKt5(M)	14 Q-B2		
15 BxBch	15 KKtxB		
16 Q-Q2(H)(N)	16 P-KR3		
17 Kt-K5	17 KtxKt(I)		

(See Diagram below.)

18 PxKt	18 P-QKt3
19 Kt-B4(K)(O)	19 B-Kt2
20 B-Kt5	20 Kt-B3
21 P-K6	21 Q-K2(L)

Position after Black's 17th move.

NOTES, from the "British Chess Magazine."

(A) Black's second and third moves seem to constitute a premature operation against White's forming a Pawn centre. The logical continuation would be 4 QBPxP, 5 Q-R5ch K-K2, 6 Kt-KB3 Q-Ksq, 7 Q-R4 Kt-B3, 8 Castles, but Black will hardly maintain the Pawn gained, while White has a capital position. A well known game (Pollock v Blackburne, London, 1886) proceeded 4 P-KKt3, 5 P-KR4 P-KB4, 6 B-KKt5 B-K2, 7 BxB QxB, 8 Kt-QR3 PxP, 9 Kt-Kt5 K-Qsq, 10 Q-Q2 Kt-QB3, 11 Kt-Q6 P-QKt3, 12 Kt-B3 P-KR3, 13 P-B3 Q-Kt2, 14 PxP KKt-K2, 15 CastlesQR, White winning after a very pretty game. In this variation, if 5 QBPxP, 6 P-R5 Q-R4ch, 7 K-Bsq QxKP, 8 PxP P-KR3, 9 Kt-KB3 Q-Q4, 10 KtxQP would have given White a winning attack (in spite of the critics of that day), for if QxKt, 11 P-Kt7 BxP, 12 B-Kt6ch, &c. Dr. Tarrasch admitted that he was acquainted with the London game.

(B) Having gained a move in the opening, White can safely act thus at once against the adverse Pawn centre.

(C) Black initiates a counter attack which must be met with the utmost care.

(D) With this move White had to take into consideration the plan of Castling, and afterwards playing R-Ksq. The QBP, which Black never has time to capture, becomes a most important factor in the attack, and the whole line of play is far superior to 7 K-Bsq, which would avoid the second check from the Queen.

(E) The difficulty experienced by the German player in finding out a satisfactory defence may be appreciated from the fact that he consumed a full hour over his first nine moves!

(F) P-Q4, the alternative, to keep the Kt from K4, would have been very hazardous indeed, as the reply 12 Kt-KB4 would attack both KP and QP.

(G) Clearly he dare not recapture, nor does B-Kt5 hold out pleasant prospects.

(H) This seizes important diagonals and unites the Rooks, besides defending the QKtP, preparatory to playing QR-Bsq and B-B4 in certain contingencies.

(I) This exchange, which indeed can hardly be avoided, plays the opponent's game, as it opens up a more important file for him than the King's.

(K) The winning move, cutting off Black's possible chances of attack by Q-Kt3ch, &c.

(L) If Q-Ksq, 22 QR-Qsq, also winning immediately.

(M) If 25 K-Ksq, 26 BxPch KxB, 27 QR-Qsq RxKt, 28 RxKtch, &c.

THE following very interesting notes to the above game were written for the "Globe," St. John, N.B., 10th April 1896, by Mr. W. H. K. Pollock.

When two strong players meet in an important single contest over the Chess board for the first time, there are several reasons why the unexpected should be expected to occur. The stronger, or the one bearing the greater repute, is less likely to be prepared for the style of the weaker than "vice versa," and is more likely to be caught off his guard. The weaker, particularly if (as in my case in the game about to be considered) he has undergone some galling reverses just previously, and is looking for more trouble, will be furnished with a nervous stimulus or goad to a strenuous cerebral effort—a stimulus such as produces what are called "inspired games," and which cannot by any effort of will be "called up" by the player. I cannot explain this "inspiration," but its effects on a man's play are usually that his moves are made with nearly twice the ease and rapidity of ordinary occasions, and he feels confident of producing something new—up to the point of mental exhaustion.

Ordinarily, however, an inspired game is brief—the brilliancy "partie" in a tournament rarely exceeds 30 moves at the resignation point. The very natural question arises: Suppose the other player is also breathed upon by the celestial afflatus and equally sits down to the board with the "conviction" that he is able to win the game. It will hardly ever happen that two players endowed with powers of originality shall, from the start of a game, be possessed of equal "form," an equally well distributed lubrication of the cephalic machinery, and the player who is "there first" will obtain a superior position, especially if opposed by a tolerably firm resistance, which a few skillful and problem-like touches will suffice to turn brilliantly into a winning advantage.

It may be interesting to mention, partly as illustrating the above remarks (although I am not going to give myself away as having been the weaker player on each occasion), that, upon my first meeting them in tournament play I have succeeded in defeating Steinitz, Pillsbury, Tarrasch, Mason, Lipschutz and Bardeleben, and amongst stars of somewhat lesser magnitude, but not lesser brilliancy, Lee, Mortimer, Hanham, Mills, Locock, Thorold, Loman, Hodges, and Albin, while drawing with Showalter and having really stubborn battles with Lasker, Zukertort, Weiss, Bird, and Mackenzie. Others I forget and am glad of it, for I have already blown my own trumpet harder than is good for my bronchitis.

Most of your readers will know Dr. Tarrasch as a short and slightly-built man of keenly intellectual, but very kindly mien, very courteous in demeanour and outwardly cool and collected over the Chess board. In some of these respects, as also in his vivacity, habit of wearing a beard and spectacles, he reminds one of the late Dr. Zukertort, but Dr. Tarrasch is by no means diminutive in stature, and I may say, with apology to comparisons, that in conversation with the latter the most timid "duffer" would be at home, and there is never any need to try to humour the great "Nuremberg medicine man."

And now for some notes to the game which I was fortunate enough to win from this great player in the Hastings tournament. I write them with many misgivings, having been asked to make them of a "psychological" and descriptive, rather than an "analytical" and sarcastic nature, which comes easier. They will be better understood, or at least the game will be more enjoyed, if the latter nature of notes be supplied by the reader's industry.

(A) My first idea was to play an attacking game of an original nature, and to be very careful not to be premature, nor to overshoot the mark. I had no notion as to what defence my opponent would be likely to adopt.

(B) I played this move not only to take my opponent, but myself, "out of the books." I had not the remotest idea that Dr. Tarrasch would work into a variation played by me before (against Blackburne in 1886). It was the stranger in that he was acquainted with that game. He either unconsciously followed the English master's false track in acting prematurely against the White centre Pawns, and recollected it later on, or else, as I fancy, his memory was misled by Steinitz's notes on the game in question in the "International Chess Magazine," and other notes of smaller calibre which erroneously declared White's attack unsound. It is a good plan to take yourself clear out of the beaten track, so long as you keep the principles in view, in order to cultivate originality.

(C) These moves are, I believe, a premature attempt to break up White's centre. Especially in a close game like the "French," the Pawn centre is the business which first occupies the minds of both players.

(D) The Blackburne game went as follows:—4 P-KKt3, 5 P-KR4 P-KB4, 6 B-Kt5 B-K2, 7 BxB QxB, 8 Kt-QR3 PxP, 9 Kt-Kt5 K-Qsq, 10 Q-Q2 Kt-QB3, 11 Kt-Q6 P-Kt3, 12 Kt-B3 P-KR3, 13 P-B3 Q-Kt2, 14 PxP KKt-K2, 15 CastlesQR K-B2. The run of the moves is pretty. Note that if 5 PxQP, 6 P-R5 Q-R4ch, 7 K-Bsq QxKP, 8 PxP P-KR3, 9 Kt-KB3 Q-Q4, 10 KtxP B-Kt2 (if QxKt, 11 P-Kt7 BxP, 12 B-Kt6ch and wins), White now recovers his Pawn with a splendid game, and this is the variation that shipwrecked the critics.

(E) The real difficulty that confronted, and I might say confused Black, was to determine whether this was a sound or unsound advance, and, if the latter, how to prove it so. As I won this game the move was "of-coursed" by the London press. Had I lost it, be sure the adverse result would both have been laid to the account of this very move, and the move itself set down as another of Mr. Pollock's ingenious but ridiculous vagaries. There is a risk in it, but I was convinced that the risk lay in my being unable to follow it up properly.

(F) The key of the position. K-Bsq is not so good. I may observe that in making the text move I purposed to follow it up as occurred, up to and including my tenth move, without which 7 P-B3 would be void of force.

(G) Dr. Tarrasch consumed a whole hour over his first nine moves (the time limit being 30 moves in the first two hours), and was at this stage plunged in a very brown study indeed. So much impressed was I with his reflecting that I had to make several excursions around the hall to watch the ceiling and the other games, in order to avoid being infected with it, and so changing my more rapid tactics into too much unprofitable analysing.

(H) He could not, even if he desired, obtain a perpetual check by PxP, followed by BxPch, &c.

(I) This is now the only difficult piece to bring into play.

(K) Recapturing would clearly lose a piece.

(L) Possibly K-Bsq might have turned out better.

(M) Hereabouts the little circle of spectators around the roped off table began to increase, although it never nearly approached the size of that which watched some other of the games in which I was engaged.

(N) Occupying important diagonals and connecting the Rooks. I had also in view the continuation of QR-Bsq and B-B4 in certain contingencies. This cannot be done at once, as Black could make for both QRP and QKtP with his Queen.

(O) The game is now virtually won.

(P) For if K-Ksq, 26 BxPch KxB, 27 QR-Qsq RxKt, 28 RxKtch K-Ksq, 29 R-Q8ch.

My opponent asked a question as to the game referred to already, and after a little analysis of the opening moves, observed, with a slight sigh—" Sehr streng attack."

He took his defeat, a serious one for him at that stage, as a perfect gentleman should, but as some of the best of us in that sorrowful " Second Battle of Hastings " did not always, although we were generally pretty quiet about it, inside the Congress Hall. I consider this by far my best game at Hastings, in spite of the help which I undoubtedly received from my antagonist, and of my better acquaintance with the exact nature of the opening than even his, that of so distinguished a master of theory.

In conclusion, I can only ask my readers to forgive any appearance of conceit in these notes, which, from their nature, must savour all too strongly of the pronoun " ego."

GAME 63.—Played in the International Tournament, Hastings, 1895. White, Mr. W. Steinitz; Black, Mr. Pollock.

Giuoco Piano.

WHITE.	BLACK.	WHITE.	BLACK.
1 P-K4	1 P-K4	10 Kt-R3	10 P-B3
2 Kt-KB3	2 Kt-QB3	11 Kt-B4	11 B-B2
3 B-B4	3 B-B4	12 Kt-K3	12 Kt-R4(E)
4 P-B3(A)	4 Q-K2(B)	13 P-KKt3	13 P-KKt3
5 P-Q4	5 B-Kt3	14 P-QKt4(F)	14 P-KB4(G)
6 P-QR4	6 P-QR4	15 Kt-Kt2(H)	15 PxQP
7 Castles	7 P-Q3	16 PxQP(I)	16 Kt-B2(K)
8 P-Q5(C)	8 Kt-Qsq	17 R-Ksq	17 Castles(L)
9 B-Q3	9 Kt-KB3(D)	18 Kt-Q4	18 Q-B3

WHITE.	BLACK.	WHITE.	BLACK.
19 Kt-Kt5	19 B-Kt3	29 Kt-R4(P)	29 Kt-B4
20 PxP	20 BxRP	30 RxP(Q)	30 KtxRch
21 B-K2	21 Kt-Kt2	31 KtxKt	31 KtxKP
22 B-Q2	22 B-Q2	32 Q-Ktsq	32 KtxBP
23 R-KBsq	23 QR-Bsq	33 Kt-K4	33 Q-Qsq
24 P-QB4	24 B-Kt3	34 QxP	34 Kt-R4
25 B-K3	25 BxB	35 Q-Kt4	35 B-Kt5
26 PxB	26 Kt-Kt4(M)	36 R-KBsq	36 B-R6
27 Kt-B3(N)		37 R-Ksq	37 R-Ktsq
		38 QxP	38 QxQ
		39 KtxQ	39 R-Kt7
		40 B-Qsq	40 R-Kt7ch
		41 K-Rsq	41 R-KB7
		42 Kt-K4	42 R(B7)xKt
		43 BxR	43 RxB
		44 P-Q6	44 R-B8ch
		45 RxR	45 BxR
		46 K-Ktsq	46 B-Q6(R)
		47 Kt-B6ch	47 K-B2
		48 KtxP	48 K-K3
		49 K-B2	49 KxP
		50 K-K3	50 B-B7
		51 P-R4	51 Kt-B5ch
		52 K-K2	52 K-Q4
		53 P-Kt4	53 K-Q5(S)
		54 Kt-B8	54 B-Q6ch
		55 K-Ksq	55 K-K6
		56 P-R5	56 PxP(T)
		57 PxP	57 B-K7
	27 P-B5!	58 Kt-Q7	58 Kt-R6
28 Q-B2(O)	28 P-B6	Resigns.	

Position after White's 27th move.

NOTES.

(A) A favourite opening with Mr. Steinitz in this tournament, in which he has beautifully demonstrated the efficiency of some new ideas contained in the last section of the "Modern Chess Instructor."

(B) Strangely enough, this valid old defence of the Berlin "Pleiades" has escaped proper notice in the work referred to. A little story comes in here: Previous to the championship match between Steinitz and Lasker, at the request of the latter I played the defence to the Giuoco in a few off-hand games with him at the Manhattan Chess Club. I adopted this old defence without success, although Lasker admitted it was new to him. But I told him that Steinitz would play it against him and beat him if he did not play the attack differently. (It is no easy matter to reply correctly to Lasker's bad moves.) Lasker good humouredly suggested that we submit the theoretical question to Showalter. However, he did "not" adopt this attack against Steinitz. The points of the defence are well shown in the present game.

(C) This is, as usual, a questionable advance.

(D) White's ninth move was in order to prevent P-KB4. Without doubt Black should now have played for the advance by P-Kt3.

(E) If PxP, 13 B-Kt5ch, followed by KtxQP. Nor can Black well Castle, on account of Kt-R4, threatening to establish a Kt at B5.

(F) Intending no doubt 15 PxBP PxP, 16 P-Kt5, when it would be difficult to prevent the posting of the White Knight at Q5.

(G) It is necessary for Black to attack, but the situation is a critical one.

(H) 15 PxQBP might have been tried as an alternative to prevent P-KB5, for if then P-B5, 16 PxQKtP, followed by B-Kt5ch and Kt-Q5.

(I) Preferable certainly seems 16 B-Kt5ch, and if B-Q2, 17 PxKBP, with the threat of KtxKP or B-KKt5 presently.

(K) In order to keep the QB out.

(L) Black has now an excellent position.

(M) Of course an attack by P-Kt4 might be on the cards, but Black prefers the safer plan of Kt-K5 and QB4, thus first securing the Queen's side.

(N) Bad, as yielding the opponent a splendid opportunity for a K side assault.

(O) If 28 PxP PxP, attacking the Knight.

(P) If the B moves, Kt-R6ch, followed by PxKtch.

(Q) If 30 KtxKt BxKt, 31 B-Q8 P-B7ch, &c.

(R) Not B-R6, on account of 47 P-Kt4.

(S) The ending is a good one for the "gallery;" either the K or P must advance with immediate effect.

(T) Unnecessary, Black has a mate in four moves here.

GAMES PLAYED AT ODDS.

GAME 64.—White, Mr. Pollock; Black, Mr. A. Rumboll, Bath.
Scotch Gambit.
Remove White's Queen's Knight.

WHITE.	BLACK.
1 P-K4	1 P-K4
2 Kt-B3	2 Kt-QB3
3 P-Q4	3 PxP
4 B-QB4	4 B-B4
5 Kt-Kt5	5 Kt-R3
6 Q-R5	6 Kt-K4
7 Kt-K6!(A)	

(See Diagram below.)

Position after White's 7th move.

	7 B-Kt5ch(B)
8 P-B3	8 Kt-Q6ch
9 BxKt	9 PxP
10 KtxKtPch	10 K-Bsq
11 BxKt	11 PxPch
12 K-K2	12 PxR(Q)
13 RxQ	13 Q-B3
14 Kt-K6ch	14 K-Ktsq
15 P-K5	15 QxKt

White mates in three moves. (C)

NOTES.

(A) This beautiful move, which wins a piece by force, is mentioned in Selkirk's "Book of Chess," but in very few, if any, more recent works in English.

(B) Producing a veritable vortex! It would have been better to play PxKt, and the game would be about even.

(C) "Ein sehr lebhaftes Spiel."

GAME 65.—White, Mr. Pollock; Black, Mr. A. Rumboll.

Irregular Opening.

Remove White's Queen's Knight.

WHITE.	BLACK.	WHITE.	BLACK.
1 P-KB4	1 P-Q4	24 Q-Bsq(H)	24 P-Kt7
2 Kt-B3	2 P-K3	25 Q-QKtsq	25 R-Kt4 ?
3 P-K3	3 P-QKt3	26 BxKtP	26 P-KR4
4 B-K2	4 B-Kt2	27 B-K2	27 R-Kt6
5 Castles	5 B-Q3	28 R-B3	28 R-Qsq
6 P-QKt3	6 Q-B3	29 Q-B2	29 Q-R5(I)
7 R-Ktsq	7 Q-R3(A)		

White mates in five moves.

8 B-Kt2	8 Kt-KB3		
9 Q-Ksq	9 Kt-K5		
10 P-KR3	10 Kt-Q2		
11 P-B4	11 CastlesKR		
12 K-R2	12 P-KKt4(B)		
13 Kt-K5	13 KtxKt		
14 PxKt	14 B-Kt5		
15 R-Qsq	15 PxP		
16 P-R3(C)	16 BxQP		
17 RxB	17 KtxR(D)		
18 QxKt	18 PxP		
19 R-B6			

Position after White's 19th move.

(See Diagram below.)

	19 Q-R5(E)		
20 B-Kt4	20 QR-Qsq		
21 Q-K2	21 BxP(F)		
22 KxB	22 K-Kt2(G)		
23 B-QB3	23 R-Q4		

NOTES.

(A) Although, curiously enough, Black has not yet moved a Knight, he has opened with spirit and manœuvred the Queen and two Bishops into menacing positions to the Castled King.

(B) Vigorously played. This advance would, however, be safer with the King housed on the other side, as White has his forces ready for concentration on this.

(C) White appears to have exchanged his dangerous position on the K side for worse troubles in the centre.

(D) P-B6 was much better. It is difficult indeed to see what White could have done in reply.

(E) A grave for a Queen! Black had here a beautiful stroke in KR-Qsq (in order in certain contingencies to liberate the Queen, via KBsq), and if then 20 QxRch RxQ, 21 RxQ R-Q7, 22 R-R5 RxKB, 23 RxPch K-Bsq, 24 B moves P-Kt7, and wins.

(F) Surely the Bishop could be put to a better use, if not a nobler death, than this.

(G) It is indeed no easy matter to see what Black is driving at.

(H) A very skillful move. Not only does it prevent Black from doubling Rooks on account of the attack on the KBP, but were White incautiously to move B-Ksq, to win the Queen, the reply P-Kt7 would turn the tables. See also White's next move.

(I) Black does not see all the dangers of the position. There is a marked contrast between his opening and ending play.

GAME 66.—Played at Simpson's Divan, London, April 1887. White, Mr. Pollock; Black, Mr. E.

Irregular Opening.

Remove White's Queen's Knight.

WHITE.	BLACK.	WHITE.	BLACK.
1 P-KB4	1 P-Q4	26 R-Kt3	26 RxQ
2 P-K3	2 Kt-KB3	27 BxRch	27 B-Kt2
3 Kt-B3	3 P-K3	28 BxB	28 Kt-K5
4 B-K2	4 B-Q3	29 R-Kt4	29 Kt-Kt4
5 Castles	5 Castles	30 B-R6	30 P-B3
6 P-QKt3	6 P-B4	31 RxP	31 R-B3
7 B-Kt2	7 Kt-B3	32 R-B8 mate.	
8 P-KR3	8 P-Q5		
9 Q-Ksq	9 B-Q2		
10 P-R3	10 R-Ksq		
11 Q-R4	11 P-K4		
12 BPxP	12 KtxP		
13 PxP	13 KtxKtch		
14 BxKt	14 B-B3		
15 PxP	15 BxPch		
16 K-Rsq	16 BxB		
17 RxB	17 Kt-K5		
18 Q-Kt4	18 B-Bsq		
19 QR-KBsq	19 Q-Kt4		
20 Q-Q7	20 R-K2		

(See Diagram below.)

21 Q-Q3	21 QxQP
22 Q-B4	22 Kt-Q3
23 Q-KR4	23 R-Bsq
24 BxP	24 R-K5
25 Q-B6	25 R-K3

Position after Black's 20th move.

GAME 67.—Played in the Handicap Tournament, City of London Chess Club, April 1887. White, Mr. —; Black, Mr. Pollock.

Remove Black's King's Bishop's Pawn.

L

WHITE.	BLACK.	WHITE.	BLACK.
1 P-K4	1 Kt-QB3	25 R-Q4	25 Kt-Q2
2 P-Q4	2 P-Q4	26 R-B4	26 RxR
3 PxP	3 QxP	27 KxR	27 R-K7
4 B-K3(A)	4 P-K4	28 P-KR4	28 RxP
5 P-QB4	5 B-Kt5ch	29 R-Ksq	29 K-Qsq
6 Kt-Q2	6 Q-K5	30 R-K3	30 R-QB7
7 P-Q5	7 B-Kt5(B)	Resigns. (I)	
8 Kt-B3(C)	8 Castles		
9 P-QR3(D)	9 Kt-Q5		
10 B-K2(E)	10 BxKtch		
11 KtxB	11 Kt-B7ch		
12 K-Bsq			

(See Diagram below).

	12 Q-B4(F)
13 BxB	13 KtxBch
14 K-Ktsq	14 KtxB
15 P-B3	15 Q-Q6(G)
16 PxKt	16 Q-K6ch
17 K-Bsq	17 R-Bsqch
18 Kt-B3	18 P-K5
19 Q-K2	19 QxQch
20 KxQ	20 PxKtch
21 PxP	21 Kt-B3
22 KR-Qsq	22 R-Ksqch
23 K-B2	23 KR-Bsq
24 K-Kt3	24 R-K6(H)

Position after White's 12th move.

NOTES.

(A) An excellent line of play is 4 Kt-KB3, and if B-Kt5, 5 Kt-B3 BxKt, 6 KtxQ BxQ, 7 KtxPch K-Q2, 8 KtxR BxP, 9 P-Q5, and White will easily extricate his imprisoned Knight, remaining with a winning game. The text move allows Black to advance the isolated KP with effect.

(B) Black plays a very forward game, and though the legitimate result should have been a draw, it was not easy to weigh the merits of the attack. White, indeed, seems to have regarded it as altogether unsound.

(C) If 8 Q-R4, Black could either play BxKtch, or as follows: Castles, 9 QxB (9) PxKt BxKt mate) QxBch, 10 PxQ KtxQ, 11 B-K2 Kt-KB3, with an excellent game.

(D) Again, if 9 Q-R4 BxKKt, 10 PxKt BxKt mate.

(E) After 10 PxB, Black would have to be content with a draw by perpetual check. He is now able to win in a remarkable manner.

(F) See diagram of this problem-like situation.

(G) This costs a Pawn, but maintains the attack.

(H) Threatening Kt-K5ch.

(I) If 31 R-K4 Kt-B4, 32 R-Q4 R-B6, winning another Pawn.

GAME 68.—Played in the Handicap Tournament, City of London Chess Club, 1887-8. White, Mr. H.; Black, Mr. Pollock.

Remove Black's King's Bishop's Pawn.

WHITE.	BLACK.
1 P-K4	1 P-Q3
2 P-Q4	2 Kt-KB3
3 Kt-QB3	3 Kt-B3(A)
4 P-Q5	4 Kt-K4
5 P-B4	5 Kt-B2
6 B-B4(B)	6 P-KKt3
7 P-KR3	7 B-Kt2
8 KKt-K2	8 Castles
9 Kt-Q4	9 Kt-R4(c)
10 P-KKt4	10 P-K4
11 PxP en pass	11 Q-R5ch
12 K-Q2	12 Kt-K4(D)
(See Diagram below.)	
13 PxKt	13 B-R3ch
14 K-Q3	14 Q-Kt6ch
15 Kt-B3	15 RxKtch
16 QxR	16 QxQch
17 K-Q4	17 P-B4ch
18 K-Q5	18 BxPch
Resigns. (E)	

Position after Black's 12th move.

NOTES.

(A) This move allows White to institute a strong attack. Black, however, has little option, unless he select a slow and cramping continuation.

(B) Effectually preventing P-K4, and perhaps even better than 6 Kt-B3.

(C) A desperate effort for breathing air, which succeeds beyond anticipation. White should probably reply with Kt-K6.

(D) See diagram of this curious position.

(E) After KxB, mate is forced in two moves.

GAME PLAYED ON THE CONTINENT.

GAME 69.—Played in the Hauptturnier, German Chess Association, Hamburg, 1885. White, Mr. Pollock; Black, Herr Doppler.

French Defence.

WHITE.	BLACK.	WHITE.	BLACK.
1 P-K4	1 P-K3	14 Kt-R3	14 BxKt
2 P-Q4	2 P-Q4	15 PxB(D)	15 B-B6(E)
3 PxP	3 PxP	16 Kt-Ktsq	16 B-R4(F)
4 Kt-KB3	4 Kt-KB3	17 P-QR3	17 Q-Q2(G)
5 B-Q3	5 B-Q3	18 P-Kt4	18 B-Qsq
6 Castles	6 Castles	19 Kt-B3	19 P-QR3(H)
7 P-QKt3(A)	7 B-KKt5	20 K-Rsq	20 R-QBsq
8 P-B4	8 P-B4	21 R-Ktsq	21 P-KKt3(I)
9 QPxP(B)	9 B-K4!	22 P-B4	22 Q-B3ch(K)
10 PxP	10 BxR	23 R-Kt2	23 QKt-Q2
11 P-Q6(c)	11 Kt-B3	24 P-Kt5	24 PxP
12 B-K2	12 R-Ksq	25 BxP	25 QxRch
13 B-K3	13 Kt-K4	26 KxQ	26 R-K3

WHITE.	BLACK.
27 B-B4	27 R-Ksq
28 Kt-Q5	28 Kt-K5
29 Q-Kt4	29 P-B4
30 Kt-K7ch	30 K-Rsq
31 B-Q4ch	31 Kt(K5)-B3
32 Q-Kt5	32 BxKt
33 PxB	33 K-Kt2
34 B-K6	34 P-R3
35 Q-R4	35 P-KKt4

(See Diagram below.)
White mates in five moves. (L)

Position after Black's 35th move.

NOTES.

(A) An idea of Steinitz's, but not to be recommended. The following moves occurred in a game between Messrs. Pollock and Skipworth (Hereford International Tournament, 1885): 7 P-QKt3 R-Ksq, 8 B-Kt2 B-KKt5, 9 P-B4 P-B3, 10 Kt-B3 QKt-Q2, 11 Q-B2 R-Bsq, 12 QR-Ksq B-Ktsq, 13 P-KR3 B-R4, 14 Kt-Qsq Kt-K5. The QB is stronger on its original diagonal than at QKt2 in this opening.

(B) Of course an oversight of the first magnitude.

(C) This game is a pretty good example of "sang froid." Having lost a Rook for two Pawns in the opening, White, instead of resigning, coolly sets to work with might and main to win the game (or of course draw it should a chance offer) by making the best moves he can find on the board, and—succeeds! (10 QxP wins the exchange.)

(D) If 15 BxB KtxBch, 16 QxKt B-K4, 17 QxP Kt-Kt5, and should win easily.

(E) If B-Kt7 White could well reply 16 Kt-Kt5.

(F) Otherwise he loses the B or submits to a draw.

(G) To make room for the Bishop.

(H) In order to prevent B-QKt5.

(I) This apparently defensive move contains a trap. If 22 B-KKt5, with a view to P-B4, BxKKt, and B-KKt4, Black wins by the reply 22 KKt-Kt5.

(K) Black in turn is treated to a trap and falls right into it.

(L) Beginning with 36 PxP.

GAMES PLAYED IN IRELAND.

GAME 70.—Played in a match of first seven games, between Mr. Pollock and Mr. W. L. Harvey, T.C.D., at the Dublin Chess Club, November 1882, the match being won by Mr. Pollock. Final score: Pollock 7, Harvey 5, Drawn 2. White, Mr. W. L. Harvey; Black, Mr. Pollock.

French Defence.

WHITE.	BLACK.	WHITE.	BLACK.
1 P-K4	1 P-K3	2 P-K5(A)	2 P-Q4

WHITE.	BLACK.
3 PxP en pass	3 BxP
4 P-Q4	4 Kt-KB3(B)
5 B-Q3	5 Castles
6 B-KKt5	6 P-KR3
7 B-R4	7 P-B4
8 PxP	8 BxBP
9 Kt-KB3	9 Kt-B3
10 P-QR3	10 P-K4
11 Kt-B3	11 P-KKt4
12 KtxKtP	12 PxKt
13 BxP	13 Q-Q5
14 Q-B3	14 Kt-KKt5
(See Diagram below.)	
15 CastlesKR(c)	15 P-B4
16 QR-Qsq	16 P-K5
17 BxP	17 PxB
18 RxQ	18 PxQ
19 R-Q5	19 PxP
20 KxP	20 KtxBP
and wins.	

Position after Black's 14th move.

NOTES.

(A) Introduced by Steinitz in the Vienna Tournament, 1882. The "Chess Monthly" considered the innovation, in common with the authorities, of questionable value.

(B) This move, followed by the Queen's Fianchetto, is preferred to Kt-QB3.

(c) CastlesQR would give White a powerful, if not a winning attack.

GAME 71.—Played in the even Tournament of the Belfast Chess Congress, September 1886. White, Mr. J. D. Chambers; Black, Mr. Pollock.

English Opening.

WHITE.	BLACK.	WHITE.	BLACK.
1 P-QB4	1 P-K4	15 P-B5	15 B-K2
2 P-K3	2 Kt-KB3	16 BxP?(E)	16 PxP
3 Kt-QB3	3 P-Q4(A)	17 PxP	17 RxKt
4 PxP	4 KtxP	18 BxKtP	18 QxB
5 Q-Kt3	5 KtxKt(B)	19 BxR	19 R-KBsq
6 KtPxKt	6 B-Q3	20 B-K2	20 Kt-B5
7 Kt-B3	7 Castles	21 P-Kt3	21 Kt-R6ch
8 P-Q3	8 Kt-B3	22 K-Kt2	22 KtxP(F)
9 B-K2	9 B-K3	23 B-B4!	23 BxB!
10 Q-B2(c)	10 P-B4	24 QxBch	24 K-Rsq
11 Castles	11 Q-B3	25 P-KR3	25 Q-Kt7!
12 B-Kt2	12 Q-R3	26 QR-Ktsq	26 Q-Q7
13 P-K4	13 Kt-K2	27 K-R2?	
14 P-B4(D)	14 Kt-Kt3	Black mates in two moves.	

NOTES.

(A) Rosenthal sanctions this method of answering the English Opening.
(B) The only effective reply.
(C) Taking the Pawn would give Black a forced attack.
(D) A powerful move, which gives the advantage to White.
(E) A mistake; he would have kept the advantage by taking with Kt.
(F) Strong, but risky-looking.

GAME 72.—Played at the Irish Chess Association, Belfast, 1886. White, Mr. A. Burn; Black, Mr. Pollock.

Irregular Opening.

WHITE.	BLACK.	WHITE.	BLACK.
1 Kt-KB3	1 P-KB4	28 R-Kt2	28 PxPch
2 P-K3	2 P-K3	29 K-Rsq	29 KxKt
3 P-Q4	3 Kt-KB3	30 RxPch	30 K-B3
4 P-B4	4 B-Kt5ch(A)	31 R-Kt2	31 Q-B6
5 QKt-Q2(B)	5 Castles	32 KxP	32 R-Rsqch
6 B-K2	6 P-QKt3	33 K-Ktsq	33 Q-Q8ch
7 Castles	7 B-Kt2	34 K-B2	34 Q-Q5ch
8 Q-B2	8 Kt-B3	35 B-K3	35 QxKtPch
9 R-Qsq	9 Q-Ksq	Resigns.	
10 Kt-Bsq	10 Kt-K5		
11 Kt-Ksq	11 Q-Kt3		
12 Kt-Q3(C)	12 KtxBP !		
13 KxKt(D)	13 KtxP		
14 KtxB(E)	14 KtxQ		
15 KtxKt	15 P-B5 !		
16 Kt-Ksq !	16 PxPch		
17 K-Ktsq(F)	17 R-B7 !		

(See Diagram below.)

18 Kt-Kt3	18 RxB !		
19 KtxR	19 Q-Kt5		
20 Kt-QB3	20 P-K7 !		
21 R-Q2	21 BxP		
22 KtxP	22 B-B3ch(G)		
23 Kt-Kt3	23 P-KR4		
24 Kt-Q3	24 P-R5		
25 Kt-K5	25 Q-R6		
26 KtxB	26 RPxKt		
27 Kt-K7ch	27 K-B2		

Position after Black's 17th move.

BLACK.

WHITE.

NOTES.

(A) This is not a useless check, as Black thereby gains a little time.
(B) If instead, 5 B-Q2, Black could exchange Bishops without disadvantage. But if 5 Kt-B3, he would gain a theoretical "pull" by BxKt, subsequently "fixing" the doubled Pawns by P-QB4.
(C) Leaving open an opportunity for a brilliant sacrifice, of which Black is not

slow to avail himself. A few days later, in the Handicap Tournament of the same meeting, the eleven first moves between the same players were precisely the same, Mr. Burn again playing White. The game then switched off as follows: 12 P-B3 Kt-Kt4, 13 K-Rsq B-Q3, 14 P-QR3 P-KR4, 15 P-QKt4 P-R5, 16 P-B5 B-K2, 17 B-Kt2 P-R6, 18 P-Kt3 Kt-Qsq, 19 Kt-Q2 QKt-B2, 20 Kt-Q3 Kt-R3, 21 R-KBsq P-B5 ? Mr. Burn won the game.

(D) If 13 KtxKt KtxQP equally. Or if 13 Kt-B4 Kt-R6ch, 14 KtxKt (14 K-Rsq KtxKt, &c.) KtxP, 15 Kt-B4 KtxQ, 16 KtxQ PxKt, 17 R-Ktsq B-B4, and wins. Again, 13 P-Q5 KtxKt (Kt-R6ch draws), 14 PxKt Kt-K8 ! (this beautiful move was overlooked by the critics), 15 RxKt BxP, and wins.

(E) The sacrifice of the Queen was by far the best resource, and indeed appears at first sight almost a sufficient one.

(F) White overlooked his opponent's continuation, which is really as pretty as the previous play. However, if 17 KxP Q-K5ch, 18 K-Q2 R-B7, 19 Kt-Kt3 Q-Q5ch, 20 Kt-Q3 RxP, and should win easily.

(G) As the sequel shows, B-Kt2ch would have been rather better.

GAME 73.—Played at the Irish Chess Association, Belfast, 1886. White, Mr. Pollock; Black, Mr. J. H. Blackburne.

Evans Gambit Declined.

WHITE.	BLACK.	WHITE.	BLACK.
1 P-K4	1 P-K4	29 Kt-K3	29 Kt-Bsq
2 Kt-KB3	2 Kt-QB3	30 Kt-B5ch	30 K-Ktsq
3 B-B4	3 B-B4	31 Q-B3	31 Kt-K3
4 P-QKt4	4 B-Kt3	32 B-B2 !	32 Q-R2
5 P-Kt5	5 Kt-R4	33 P-Kt3(k)	33 K-B2
6 B-K2(A)	6 Kt-KB3(B)	34 B-K3	34 K-Ksq
7 P-Q3	7 P-Q3	35 K-Kt2	35 QR-Ktsq
8 B-Kt5	8 P-KR3	36 K-B2	36 Kt-Kt2
9 B-R4	9 B-K3	37 P-R5	
10 Kt-B3	10 Q-K2		
11 Kt-R4	11 R-Qsq(c)	Position after White's 37th move.	
12 KtxB	12 RPxKt		
13 P-B4(D)	13 P-Kt4		
14 B-Kt3	14 Kt-Q2		
15 P-KR4	15 P-Kt5		
16 Kt-Q2	16 P-R4		
17 Q-B2	17 R-KKtsq		
18 Kt-Bsq(D)	18 Kt-Bsq		
19 P-B3	19 PxP		
20 KBxP	20 B-Kt5(E)		
21 BxB	21 RxB		
22 Kt-K3(F)	22 R-Kt3		
23 Kt-Q5(G)	23 Q-Q2		
24 Q-B2	24 Kt-R2(H)		
25 CastlesKR	25 P-KB3		
26 K-R2	26 K-B2		
27 Q-B3	27 R-KRsq(I)		
28 QxRP	28 K-Kt2		

WHITE.	BLACK.	WHITE.	BLACK.
	37 KtxKt	48 PxP	48 RxPch
38 QxKt!	38 KR-Kt2	49 K-Kt5	49 K-K2
39 QxQ	39 RxQ	50 K-R5	50 R-B6
40 R-Rsq	40 K-B2	51 B-Kt5ch	51 K-Ksq
41 K-B3	41 R-QRsq(L)	52 R-KBsq	52 QR-B2
42 QR-KKtsq	42 K-Bsq	53 K-Kt4	53 R-Q2
43 K-Kt4	43 R-Kt2ch	54 R-B6	54 P-Q4
44 K-B5	44 K-B2(M)	55 R-K6ch	55 K-Bsq
45 P-R6	45 R-R2	56 R-Bsqch	
46 P-Kt4	46 R-KKtsq	and wins.	
47 P-Kt5	47 R-Kt3		

NOTES.

(A) Introduced, I believe, by Blackburne himself many years ago. The object is shown in the sequel.

(B) Especially as this Knight is liable to a "pin" from the QB, from which it is most difficult to release him, Black should adopt the combination P-Q3, B-K3 and P-QB4. This would also frustrate the design which White carries out successfully on his 10th to 13th moves.

(C) Black plays over-tamely; Castling on the Queen's side might have been ventured.

(D) Necessary, before advancing the KBP.

(E) This was not a good move, and White's position now becomes stronger and stronger by degrees.

(F) A pretty device. If RxB, Kt-B5.

(G) A terrible position for the Knight, as Black cannot now obtain relief on the Q side by P-QB3.

(H) To prevent the loss of the exchange by Kt-B6ch.

(I) It was useless to attempt to defend the RP. If R-R3 White could continue Q-K2, R-B5, &c. The diversion which Black here devises is, however, of no avail.

(K) All this is managed neatly and in the nick of time.

(L) In desperation, to release the Kt by Kt-Kt6.

(M) The play of the King is another desperate manœuvre, this time to spread a "mating net" by doubling Rooks on KKt file.

GAME 74.—Played simultaneously at the Dublin Chess Club, Leinster Hall, 14th December 1887. White, Mr. J. Morphy; Black, Mr. Pollock.

Two Knights' Defence.

WHITE.	BLACK.	WHITE.	BLACK.
1 P-K4	1 P-K4	7 KtxR	7 KtxBP
2 Kt-KB3	2 Kt-QB3	8 RxKt	8 QxRch
3 B-B4	3 Kt-B3	9 K-Rsq	9 P-Q4
4 Kt-Kt5	4 KtxP(A)	10 BxP	10 B-KKt5
5 KtxBP(B)	5 Q-R5	11 B-B3	11 BxB
6 Castles	6 B-B4	12 PxB	12 Kt-Q5

WHITE.	BLACK.	WHITE.	BLACK.
13 Q-Ktsq(c)	13 QxBPch	16 KxQ	16 KtxPch
14 Q-Kt2	14 Q-Q8ch	17 K-Bsq	17 KtxR(d)
15 Q-Ktsq	15 QxQch	Resigns.	

NOTES.

(A) A favourite continuation of Mr. Pollock's, though well known as a dangerous one for the second player.

(B) The correct play is 5 BxPch. The text move leads to variations which are all in favour of the second player.

(C) These moves are all forced, and Black's method of attack proceeds on familiar lines.

(D) The whole of this gamelet is conducted by Black with most consummate accuracy.

GAME 75.—Played simultaneously at the Clontarf Chess Club. White, Mr. Pollock; Black, Mr. A. Stephens.

Vienna Opening.

WHITE.	BLACK.	WHITE.	BLACK.
1 P-K4	1 P-K4	20 Castles	
2 Kt-QB3	2 Kt-QB3	and wins. (G)	
3 P-B4	3 PxP		
4 Kt-B3	4 P-KKt4		
5 P-KR4	5 P-Kt5		
6 Kt-KKt5	6 Kt-R3(A)		
7 P-Q4	7 Q-B3(B)		
8 P-K5	8 KtxKP?		
9 PxKt	9 Q-B3		
10 Kt-Q5	10 B-Kt2		
11 B-Kt5	11 Q-B4(c)		
12 BxBP	12 P-QB3		
13 Kt-B7ch	13 K-Qsq		
14 P-K6!	14 R-Ksq(D)		
15 Q-Q2	15 BxP		
16 Kt-K4(E)			
(See Diagram below).			
	16 Q-K2		
17 R-Qsq(F)	17 P-Q4		
18 B-Q6	18 QxKP		
19 KtxQch	19 RxKt		

Position after White's 16th move.

BLACK.

WHITE.

NOTES.

(A) The correct move is P-KR3, compelling the sacrifice of the Knight. The mistake, however, is not in departing from the "books" here, but in departing from the "principles" on the next move.

(B) The career of the Black Queen in this game is a striking illustration of the importance of the rule not to develop that piece prematurely.

(C) Taking the Bishop would obviously cost Black his Queen.

(D) This is much better Chess, and more like Mr. Stephens.

M

(E) A very strong move, containing four or five distinct points.

(F) Curiously, 17 B-Q6 would here have won the adverse Queen the same as on the next move.

(G) Black, even thus handicapped, fought the game out, and was one of the last to succumb to the single player.

GAME 76.—A consultation game played simultaneously at the Dublin Chess Club. White, Messrs. Drury and Fitzpatrick; Black, Mr. Pollock.

Two Bishops' Game.

WHITE.	BLACK.	WHITE.	BLACK.
1 P-K4	1 P-K4	24 Kt-Kt4!	24 RxKP
2 B-B4	2 B-B4	25 KtxKt	25 RxR(F)
3 P-QB3	3 Kt-KB3	26 Kt-Q7ch(G)	26 K-K2
4 P-Q4	4 PxP	27 RxR	27 KxKt
5 PxP	5 B-Kt5ch	and wins.	
6 B-Q2	6 BxBch		
7 KtxB	7 KtxP		
8 BxPch(A)	8 KxB		
9 Q-Kt3ch	9 P-Q4		
10 KtxKt	10 R-Ksq		
11 P-B3	11 K-Bsq(B)		
12 Kt-K2	12 PxKt		
13 PxP	13 B-K3		
14 Castles ch	14 K-Ktsq		
15 P-Q5	15 B-B2		

(See Diagram below.)

16 Kt-Kt3(C)	16 Kt-Q2
17 R-B4	17 Kt-B3
18 QR-Bsq	18 Q-Q3
19 Q-QB3	19 R-K4
20 Kt-B5(D)	20 Q-Kt3ch
21 K-Rsq	21 QR-Ksq
22 Q-KKt3	22 B-Kt3
23 Kt-R6ch	23 K-Bsq(E)

Position after Black's 15th move.

NOTES.

(A) This line of play costs the allies a piece, though in a manner which is not at first obvious.

(B) If B-K3, 12 Kt-Kt3, saving the piece. Black had a still stronger move here in R-K3. The latter move, though apparently uncouth, is a very powerful one.

(C) White here misses a grand chance of recovering the piece, with a winning game, e.g.:—15 RxB KxR, 16 P-Q6ch K-Kt3, 17 Kt-B4ch K-Kt4 (if K-B3, 18 R-KBsq), 18 Q-Kt3ch K-B3, 19 R-KBsq, and wins.

(D) In spite of the oversight on their sixteenth move, they conduct their attack with spirit and determination.

(E) K-Rsq seems safer.

(F) A fine stroke of play, evidently premeditated. The position is one of a highly instructive nature.

(G) White must now still remain a piece to the bad, play as they may.

PART II.

GAMES PLAYED IN THE UNITED STATES AND CANADA.

GAME 77.—Played in the sixth American Congress, New York, 1889. White, Herr Max Weiss; Black, Mr. Pollock.

Ruy Lopez.

WHITE.	BLACK.	WHITE.	BLACK.
1 P-K4	1 P-K4	17 P-QKt4	17 BxPch
2 Kt-KB3	2 Kt-QB3	18 K-Rsq	18 Q-K8
3 B-Kt5	3 P-QR3		
4 B-R4	4 Kt-B3		
5 P-Q3(A)	5 B-B4(B)		
6 P-B3(C)	6 P-QKt4(D)		
7 B-Kt3(E)	7 P-Q4		
8 PxP(F)	8 KtxP		
9 Q-K2	9 Castles		
10 Q-K4(G)	10 B-K3		
11 KtxP(H)	11 KtxKt		
12 QxKt	12 Kt-Kt5(I)		

Position after Black's 18th move.

BLACK.

Position after Black's 12th move.

BLACK.

WHITE.

13 Castles(K)	13 KtxQP	19 P-R3	19 KtxB
14 Q-R5	14 BxB	20 RxQ	20 RxRch
15 PxB	15 R-Ksq	21 K-R2	21 B-Kt8ch
16 Kt-Q2	16 Q-K2	22 K-Kt3	22 R-K6ch
		23 K-Kt4	23 Kt-K7
		24 Kt-Bsq	24 P-Kt3
		25 Q-Q5	25 P-R4ch
		26 K-Kt5	26 K-Kt2

(See Diagram below.)

27 KtxR	27 P-B3ch
28 K-R4	28 B-B7ch
29 P-KKt3	29 BxP mate.

Position after Black's 26th move.

NOTES.

(A) The steady German attack, which makes it difficult for Black to defend his KP except by P-Q3 in reply, and this somewhat hampers his game.

(B) Morphy played thus against Anderssen, and the defence has never been "proved" unsound by analysis, while it is very often attended with success in actual play.

(C) Providing a retreat for the Bishop, as well as threatening 7 BxKt QPxB, 8 KtxP, without fear of Q-Q5.

(D) Preventing the line of play indicated.

(E) Retreating the Bishop to B2 is generally preferred.

(F) Here most masters prefer Q-K2. White, however, aims at winning the KP.

(G) Beyond a doubt this wins the Pawn, and some good authorities still think White's plan to be sound.

(H) Another course lay in 11 Kt-Kt5, in answer to which Black must not play P-KB4, which would lose by 12 KtxB PxQ, 13 KtxQ RxKt, 14 PxP. Nor would 11 Kt-B3 be sound. Black would therefore have to play P-Kt3, when after 12 KtxB PxKt, 13 Castles Q-Q3, he would certainly have an excellent game, in spite of the awkward situation of his Pawns.

(I) The first step in a most startling combination.

(K) This evades the intended complications, but in no way breaks the attack. The only move that promised hopes of safety was to take the offered piece, dangerous as it appears. The following might be the continuation: 13 PxKt BxKtPch, 14 K-Qsq (best) BxBch, 15 PxB QxPch, 16 Kt-Q2 QR-Qsq, 17 Q-K3 Q-Q2.

GAME 78.—Played in the sixth American Congress, New York, 1889. White, Mr. I. Gunsberg; Black, Mr. Pollock.

Ruy Lopez.

WHITE.	BLACK.	WHITE.	BLACK.
1 P-K4	1 P-K4	15 B-QB4	15 Castles
2 Kt-KB3	2 Kt-QB3	16 B-K3	16 KtxB
3 B-Kt5	3 P-QR3	17 PxKt	17 Kt-R4
4 B-R4	4 Kt-B3	18 BxRP	18 Q-K3
5 P-Q3	5 P-QKt4	19 B-B4	19 KtxB
6 B-Kt3	6 P-Q4	20 PxKt	20 QxBP
7 PxP	7 KtxP	21 Q-B5	21 P-KB3
8 Castles	8 B-K2	22 P-QKt3	22 Q-B3
9 R-Ksq	9 Q-Q3	23 QR-Bsq	23 P-Kt3
10 QKt-Q2	10 B-Kt5	24 Q-B3	24 P-B4
11 P-KR3	11 BxKt	25 Kt-Q2	25 Q-B6
12 QxB	12 R-Qsq	26 Kt-B4	26 P-K5
13 P-QR4	13 P-Kt5	27 Q-K2	27 B-B4
14 Kt-K4	14 Q-Q2	28 K-Rsq	28 R-Q4

WHITE.	BLACK.	WHITE.	BLACK.
29 R-Bsq	29 P-B3	49 Q-Q7ch	49 K-Bsq
30 R-B2	30 B-R2	50 Q-B8ch	50 K-B2
31 QR-Bsq	31 B-Ktsq	Drawn by perpetual check.	
32 P-Kt4	32 P-B5		
33 PxP	33 RxP		
34 Kt-K3	34 P-Kt4		
35 K-Kt2	35 Q-K4		
36 K-Rsq	36 Q-B6		
37 K-Kt2	37 Q-K4		
38 K-Rsq	38 R-B6		
39 RxR	39 PxR		
40 Q-B2	40 R-Q5		

Position after Black's 40th move.

(See Diagram below.)

41 Kt-B5	41 R-K5
42 Q-Q2	42 R-K7
43 QxPch	43 K-Bsq
44 Q-R6ch	44 K-Ktsq
45 Q-Kt5ch	45 K-Bsq
46 Q-R6ch	46 K-Ktsq
47 Q-Kt5ch	47 K-Bsq
48 Q-Q8ch	48 K-B2

GAME 79.—A bright little game played in a simultaneous display at the Baltimore Chess Association's Annual Tourney, 1890. White, Mr. Spencer; Black, Mr. Pollock.

Hamppe's Knight's Game.

WHITE.	BLACK.	WHITE.	BLACK.
1 P-K4	1 P-K4	11 P-Q5?	11 Kt-K2
2 Kt-QB3	2 Kt-KB3	12 K-Rsq	12 Kt-B4
3 P-B4	3 P-Q4	13 KKt-Q4	13 Q-R5
4 KPxP	4 PxP	14 KtxKt	14 BxKt
5 B-B4	5 B-QKt5	15 Q-Q4	15 KR-Ksq
6 Kt-B3	6 Castles	16 Q-B2	16 Kt-Kt6ch
7 Castles	7 P-B3	17 K-Ktsq	17 QR-Bsq
8 PxP	8 KtxP	18 BxP	18 KtxKtch
9 P-Q4	9 P-QR3	19 K-Rsq	19 QxQ
10 Kt-K2	10 Kt-KR4	and wins two pieces and the game.	

GAME 80.—A bright little game played at Chicago, June 1890. White, Mr. Blanchard; Black, Mr. Pollock.

Two Knights' Defence.

WHITE.	BLACK.	WHITE.	BLACK.
1 P-K4	1 P-K4	4 Kt-B3(A)	4 KtxP
2 Kt-KB3	2 Kt-QB3	5 BxPch(A)	5 KxB
3 B-B4	3 Kt-B3	6 KtxKt	6 P-Q4

	WHITE.	BLACK.
7	Kt(K4)-Kt5ch	7 K-Ktsq
8	P-Q4	8 P-KR3
9	Kt-R3	9 B-KKt5(B)
10	PxP	10 KtxP
11	Kt(R3)-Ktsq(c)	11 B-QB4
12	B-B4	12 Kt-Kt3
13	B-Kt3	13 K-R2
14	Q-Q3	14 R-Ksqch
15	K-Bsq	15 R-K5(D)
16	R-Ksq	16 Q-K2
17	QxP(E)	17 RxRch
18	KtxR	18 R-Qsq
19	Q-B4	

Position after White's 19th move.

(See Diagram below.)

Black mates in two moves.

NOTES.

(A) These moves give Black a chance to free his game through a slight counter attack.

(B) BxKt, 10 PxB PxP, 11 KtxP Q-B3 is rather preferable.

(C) For here White can improve matters by 11 Kt-B4.

(D) Insidious, as threatening B-KB4 in some cases, and also preventing Kt-K5.

(E) Black's coveted opportunity.

GAME 81.—The following fine game, played at Chicago, is a good illustration of Mr. Pollock's method of extricating himself from an uncomfortable position. White, Mr. Pollock; Black, Mr. Hermann.

Staunton's Knights' Game.

WHITE.	BLACK.	WHITE.	BLACK.
1 P-K4	1 P-K4	16 P-Q5	16 Q-R2
2 Kt-KB3	2 Kt-QB3	17 P-Kt4(c)	17 P-KR4
3 P-B3	3 Kt-B3	18 P-QR4	18 P-R5
4 P-Q4	4 P-Q3	19 B(Kt3)-B2	19 Kt-R4
5 B-QKt5	5 B-Q2	20 Q-K3	20 Kt-B5
6 Q-K2	6 Kt-QKtsq(A)	21 B-Kt5(D)	21 Q-R4
7 B-QB4	7 Q-K2	22 Kt-B3	22 Q-Kt5
8 Kt-Kt5	8 B-K3	23 Kt-Ksq	23 P-R6
9 KtxB	9 PxKt	24 P-Kt3	24 Kt-Kt7
10 Castles	10 Kt(Ktsq)-Q2	25 QxRP	25 KtxKt
11 P-B4	11 Castles	26 B-B6!(E)	26 PxB
12 B-Q3	12 PxBP		
13 BxP	13 P-K4	(See Diagram below.)	
14 B-Kt3(B)	14 P-KR3	and White mates in five moves.	
15 Kt-Q2	15 P-KKt4		

NOTES.

(A) Starting a little counter attack that turns White's attack into a defence.

(B) If 14 PxP, White loses the attack entirely.

(C) The attack on both wings becomes interesting.

(D) Preparing his surprise party.

(E) Which now comes off with great success.

GAME 82.—The following brief game, played at Brooklyn, 1891, is notable for its peculiar finish. White, Mr. Pollock; Black, Mr. Bonn.

Allgaier Opening.

WHITE.	BLACK.
1 P-K4	1 P-K4
2 P-KB4	2 PxP
3 Kt-KB3	3 P-KKt4
4 P-KR4	4 P-Kt5
5 Kt-Kt5	5 P-Q4
6 PxP	6 QxP
7 Kt-QB3	7 Q-Qsq
8 P-Q4	8 B-Q3
9 B-B4	9 Kt-KR3
10 Castles	10 Castles
11 QBxP	11 Kt-B3
12 Kt-Q5	12 BxB
13 RxB	13 B-B4
14 Q-Q2	14 P-Kt3
15 QR-KBsq	15 Kt-R4
16 B-Q3	16 BxB
17 Kt-B6ch	17 K-Kt2
18 Q-Bsq	18 R-Rsq
19 QKtxRP	19 P-KB4
20 RxBP	20 Q-Q3

Position after Black's 26th move.

Position after Black's 20th move.

and White mates in three moves.

GAME 83.—During Mr. Gunsberg's visit to Baltimore, in February 1891, Mr. H. S. Habersham gave a prize for a single-handed duel between Mr. Gunsberg and Mr. Pollock, with the following result. White, Mr. Pollock; Black, Mr. Gunsberg. A second game resulted in a victory for Mr. Gunsberg.

Hamppe's Knights' Game.

WHITE.	BLACK.	WHITE.	BLACK.
1 P-K4	1 P-K4	2 Kt-QB3	2 Kt-KB3

WHITE.	BLACK.
3 P-B4	3 P-Q4
4 PxKP	4 KtxP
5 Kt-B3	5 Kt-B3(A)
6 B-Kt5	6 B-QKt5
7 Q-K2	7 BxKt
8 KtPxB	8 Castles
9 Castles	9 Q-K2
10 P-QR4	10 R-Ksq
11 B-R3	11 Q-K3
12 P-B4	12 Kt-Q3(B)
13 QBxKt	

(See Diagram below.)

	13 QxB(c)
14 PxQ	14 RxQ
15 PxQP	Resigns.

Position after White's 13th move.

NOTES.

(A) B-K2 is perhaps the safety reply.
(B) Kt-B3 may be a better resource.
(C) Hallucination! Black must, however, suffer some loss. If 13 PxB, 14 Kt-Kt5 Q-Kt3! (if QxP, 15 Q-R5, &c.), 15 KtxBP PxBP, 16 RxP, &c.

GAME 84.—An intensely interesting combat, played in the Lexington Congress, 1891. White, Mr. Louis Nedemann; Black, Mr. Pollock.

Staunton's Knights' Game.

WHITE.	BLACK.	WHITE.	BLACK.
1 P-K4	1 P-K4	19 BxB	19 RxB
2 Kt-KB3	2 Kt-QB3	20 Kt-Kt4(A)	20 QxPch
3 P-B3	3 Kt-B3	21 K-Ktsq	21 P-Q6
4 P-Q4	4 KtxKP	22 P-QR3	22 Q-B7ch
5 P-Q5	5 B-B4	23 K-R2	23 B-Q3(B)
6 PxKt	6 BxPch	24 Kt-K3	24 Q-B4
7 K-K2	7 KtPxP	25 Q-Kt4	25 R-B5
8 Q-R4	8 P-KB4	26 Q-K6ch	26 K-Rsq
9 QKt-Q2	9 B-Kt3	27 Kt-Kt4	27 R-R5
10 KtxKt	10 PxKt	28 Kt-K3(c)	28 P-Q7!
11 QxKP	11 Castles	29 BxP	29 RxPch
12 K-Qsq	12 P-Q4	30 PxR	30 QxPch
13 QxKP	13 B-Kt5	31 K-Ktsq	31 R-Ktsqch
14 Q-Kt3	14 Q-Q2	32 K-B2	32 R-Kt7ch
15 B-Q3	15 P-Q5	33 K-Qsq	33 QxRch
16 P-B4	16 B-QB4	34 K-K2	34 Q-R3ch
17 K-B2	17 B-B4	35 Kt-B4(D)	35 R-Ktsq
18 Kt-K5	18 Q-K3	36 R-KBsq	36 P-B4

WHITE.	BLACK.
37 R-B4	37 Q-Kt4
38 R-K4	38 BxP
39 B-B3(E)	39 R-Ktsq!
40 R-Kt4	40 Q-Ktsq
41 P-Kt3	41 B-Kt8
42 Kt-K5	42 Q-Kt4ch
43 R-B4	43 R-Ksq(F)
44 Q-B7	44 B-Q5
45 K-B3	45 Q-Kt2ch
46 K-Kt4	46 Q-K5ch
47 K-R3	47 Q-R8ch
48 K-Kt4	48 Q-K5ch
49 K-R3(G)	49 QxKt
50 RxP	50 Q-K5
51 R-B5	51 Q-R8ch
52 K-Kt4	52 R-K5ch
53 R-B4	53 P-R4ch
54 K-Kt5	54 R-K4ch
55 R-B5	55 B-K6ch
56 K-Kt6	56 Q-B3ch
Resigns.	

Position, if 57 KxP.

BLACK.

WHITE.

Whereupon Black would mate in eleven moves. (H)

NOTES.

(A) Fearing the loss of a piece by B-Q3.

(B) B-B7 had its points also.

(C) Neither party had any idea of drawing tactics. Throughout the game White could force a draw by 28 Kt-R6. Black's reply could not well be delayed on account of 29 R-Qsq. White calculates the ensuing variation most accurately.

(D) Not so good as interposing the Q (!).

(E) Menacing mate in three. His next move also threatens a speedy issue.

(F) A most peculiar position! If now 44 Kt-B7ch K-Ktsq, 45 Kt-R6ch K-Bsq, and wins.

(G) Most ingenious, there is but one reply.

(H) "Miron," the Chess Editor of the "New York Clipper," sends the following solution of above, and says, "there is a printer's error, which I think I have corrected." 57 Q-R3ch, 58 K-Kt4 R-K5ch, 59 K-B3 Q-R8ch, 60 K-K2 B-Q5ch, 61 K-Q3 Q-Kt8ch, 62 K-B4 B-K4ch, 63 K-Q5 Q-Kt2ch, the other four play themselves. The most amusing specimen I ever came across of a King trying to cuddle up to a R and B in hopes of getting one of them: and the performances of the Q in ordering him "out of that!" reminds me of the story of the Irish Soldier, who, single-handed and alone, brought in three prisoners. Asked how he managed it, Pat replied, "Faith and I surrounded thim."

GAME 85.—Played in the Brooklyn Club Championship Tourney, 19th March 1892. White, Mr. Pollock; Black, Mr. A. J. Souweine.

Evans Gambit.

WHITE.	BLACK.	WHITE.	BLACK.
1 P-K4	1 P-K4	2 Kt-KB3	2 Kt-QB3

WHITE.	BLACK.	WHITE.	BLACK.
3 B-B4	3 B-B4	20 Q-Kt5ch	20 K-Qsq
4 P-QKt4	4 BxKtP	White mates in two moves.	
5 P-B3	5 B-B4		
6 Castles	6 P-Q3		
7 P-Q4	7 PxP		
8 PxP	8 B-Kt3		
9 Kt-B3	9 Kt-B3(A)		
10 P-K5			

(See Diagram below.)

Position after White's 10th move.

	10 PxP(B)
11 B-R3	11 Kt-QR4
12 R-Ksq	12 KtxB
13 Q-R4ch	13 P-B3
14 QxKt	14 B-K3
15 RxP	15 Q-Q2
16 RxB(c)	16 PxR(D)
17 Kt-K5	17 Q-Bsq
18 R-Ksq	18 Kt-Q4(E)
19 KtxKt	19 BPxKt

NOTES.

(A) A radical error in the Evans when the centre Pawns have been exchanged. The Knight should not be deployed until measures have been taken, either by Kt-R4 or B-Kt5, to prevent the co-operation of White's KKt and B against the KBP.

(B) If P-Q4, 11 PxKt PxB, 12 R-Ksqch K-Bsq, 13 B-R3ch K-Ktsq, 14 P-Q5, with a powerful attack.

(C) Necessary, to prevent Black from Castles QR. Had he played Q-Bsq it would have been useless.

(D) Clearly if QxR, 17 R-Ksq follows.

(E) Fatal. Black overlooked the ensuing mate. The game could hardly be saved, however, for if B-B2 (to prevent 19 Kt-Kt5) might continue, 19 KtxP, and if P-QR3 either 19 KtxP or Kt-R4.

GAME 86.—A fine defence played in Brooklyn Chess Club Tourney, 1892. White, Mr. Eugene Delmar; Black, Mr. Pollock.

Dutch Opening.

WHITE.	BLACK.	WHITE.	BLACK.
1 P-Q4	1 P-KB4	9 P-B3	9 P-B4
2 P-K3	2 Kt-KB3	10 P-QR3	10 Kt-B3
3 P-QB4	3 P-K3	11 R-Ktsq	11 Kt-KR4(B)
4 B-Q3	4 B-Kt5ch	12 P-QKt4	12 PxQP
5 B-Q2(A)	5 BxBch	13 PxP	13 Q-Kt4
6 KtxB	6 Castles	14 P-B4	14 Q-R3
7 Kt-K2	7 P-QKt3	15 R-B2	15 Kt-K2
8 Castles	8 B-Kt2	16 Kt-KBsq	16 Kt-Kt3

WHITE.	BLACK.
17 Q-Q2	17 Kt-B3

(See Diagram below.)

WHITE.	BLACK.
18 P-R3(c)	18 Kt-R5
19 Q-K3(d)	19 QR-Ksq
20 Kt(K2)-Kt3	20 K-Rsq
21 P-R4	21 R-KKtsq
22 P-R5	22 P-KKt4
23 PxKKtP	23 RxP
24 KR-Kt2(e)	24 QR-KKtsq
25 PxP	25 PxP
26 Q-K5(f)	26 BxP
27 K-R2	27 BxP
28 K-Rsq	28 BxKt
29 BxB	29 RxKt
Resigns.	

Position after Black's 17th move.

BLACK.

WHITE.

NOTES.

(A) Kt-Q2 is preferable. The loss of his QB hampers White's subsequent endeavours to form a Pawn centre, owing to the weakness of his Black squares.

(B) Initiating a vigorous attack.

(c) He could not well help making this weakening move, as Kt-Kt5 is threatened.

(D) Guarding against BxKtP, followed by Kt-B6ch, if RxB.

(E) After doubling his Rooks Black would have threatened RxKt, temporarily sacrificing Q, failing the precaution in text.

(F) Falling into the very trap avoided at 19.

GAME 87.—A skirmish with Showalter. White, Mr. J. W. Showalter; Black, Mr. Pollock.

Two Knights' Defence.

WHITE.	BLACK.	WHITE.	BLACK.
1 P-K4	1 P-K4	15 Q-R5ch(d)	15 K-Ktsq(e)
2 Kt-KB3	2 Kt-QB3	16 PxP	16 R-K5
3 B-B4	3 Kt-B3	17 P-KR3	17 Q-K2
4 P-Q4	4 PxP	18 B-K3	18 RxB
5 Kt-Kt5	5 Kt-K4	19 PxR	19 QxPch
6 QxP(a)	6 KtxB	20 K-Rsq	20 Q-Kt6
7 QxKt(b)	7 P-Q4	21 RxB	21 QxR
8 PxP	8 KtxP(b)	22 PxP	22 BxKtP
9 Castles	9 B-K2	23 Kt-B3(f)	23 Q-Kt6
10 R-Qsq	10 P-QB3	24 R-QKtsq(g)	24 R-Ksq
11 Q-K2	11 Castles	Resigns.	
12 KtxRP(c)	12 KxKt		
13 P-QB4	13 B-Q3		
14 PxKt	14 R-Ksq		

He loses a piece or is mated. Quite a little study.

NOTES.

(A) An attack introduced by Showalter in 1891; pronounced excellent by Steinitz.

(B) Much better than the more obvious QxP, to which White replies 9 Q-K2ch.

(C) Sacrificing development for material.

(D) If 15 Q-Q3ch K-Ktsq, 16 PxP R-K8ch, 17 RxR BxPch, winning the Q for R and B.

(E) With this move Black at least equalises the position; White's 17th being forced, on account of the attack on two spots.

(F) Slow Stick! thou com'st too late!

(G) Fatal! The Q should have been played.

GAME 88.—During the first quarter of 1893 Mr. Pollock took a considerable circuit of the American Chess centres, having no less than eighteen formal appointments at Buffalo, New York, for the week 13th-18th March. One game ran thus. White, Mr. Pollock; Black, Mr. T. N. Wilcox.

Sicilian Defence.

WHITE.	BLACK.	WHITE.	BLACK.
1 P-K4	1 P-QB4	8 B-KB4	8 P-B3(B)
2 P-Q4	2 PxP	9 Kt-Q6ch	9 K-Q2
3 Kt-KB3	3 Kt-QB3	10 B-Kt5ch	10 Kt-B3
4 KtxP	4 KtxKt	11 PxP	11 Q-R4ch
5 QxKt	5 P-K3	12 P-B3	12 QxB
6 Kt-B3	6 Kt-K2	13 PxKtch	13 QxP
7 Kt-Kt5	7 P-Q4(A)	14 Kt-B7ch, and wins.	

NOTES.

(A) He ought certainly to have played Kt-B3, careless of the check at Q6.

(B) A strange position so early.

GAME 89.—An uncommonly beautiful, though not quite original game, which occurred in a "simultaneous" of twenty-four games at Washington, 1893. White, Mr. Pollock; Black, Mr. W. H. Gwyer jun.

King's Knight's Gambit.

WHITE.	BLACK.	WHITE.	BLACK.
1 P-K4	1 P-K4	(See Diagram below.)	
2 P-KB4	2 PxP		13 Kt-KR3(B)
3 Kt-KB3	3 P-KKt4	14 PxPch	14 K-Bsq(C)
4 B-B4	4 B-Kt2	15 BxP!	15 Kt-Q2
5 P-Q4	5 P-Q3	16 Castles	16 KtxP
6 P-KR4	6 P-KR3	17 R-Q6(D)	17 PxB
7 PxP	7 PxP	18 R-Kt6	18 QxR(E)
8 RxR	8 BxR	19 QxQ	19 QKt-K4
9 Kt-B3	9 P-QB3(A)	20 Q-R5	20 B-Kt5
10 Kt-K5	10 PxKt	21 Q-R4	21 B-Kt2
11 Q-R5	11 Q-B3	22 B-K2	22 P-B6
12 PxP	12 Q-Kt2	23 PxP	23 BxP
13 P-K6			

WHITE.	BLACK.
24 BxB	24 KtxB

Drawn game. (F)

NOTES.

(A) Kt-QB3 is better play.

(B) Or Kt-B3, 14 PxPch, and Black must be careful not to play K-Bsq, on account of BxP, mating if either Q or B be taken.

(C) Clearly if KtxP, 15 BxKtch would allow White to regain the piece sacrificed.

(D) Another interesting situation.

(E) Black plays for the most part with great judgment. Here if Q-K4, 19 R-Kt8ch.

(F) Hereabouts White preferred a draw, as it seemed impossible to find anything to win with. The draw was refused, to Black's subsequent regret, after a long fight.

Position after White's 13th move.

GAME 90.—The following [was one of the games played in a blindfold exhibition, 8th April 1893. White, Mr. Pollock (blindfold).

Giuoco Piano.

WHITE.	BLACK.	WHITE.	BLACK.
1 P-K4	1 P-K4	19 KtxB	19 QxKt
2 Kt-KB3	2 Kt-QB3	20 P-K5	20 PxP
3 B-B4	3 B-B4	21 BxP	21 Q-KR5(c)
4 Castles	4 P-Q3	22 B-B3	22 B-Bsq
5 P-B3	5 Kt-B3	23 B-Ktsq	23 Kt-K5
6 P-Q4	6 PxP	24 BxKt(D)	24 RxB
7 PxP	7 B-Kt3	25 RxR	25 QxR
8 Kt-B3	8 Castles	26 R-Ksq	26 Q-B3
9 P-KR3	9 P-KR3	27 Q-K3	27 Q-Q3
10 B-K3	10 P-R3(A)	28 Q-Kt5	28 Q-KKt3
11 Q-Q2	11 Q-K2	29 Q-R4	29 Q-Q3(E)
12 QR-Ksq	12 B-Q2	30 R-K3	30 B-B4
13 B-Q3	13 QR-Ksq	31 R-Kt3	31 B-Kt3
14 BxKRP	14 KtxQP(B)	32 P-B4	32 Q-Q4
15 KtxKt	15 BxKt	33 R-Kt5	33 Q-K5
16 B-KKt5	16 P-R4	34 Q-Kt3	34 K-R2 ?
17 Kt-K2	17 Q-K4	35 P-B5	35 BxP ?
18 B-KB4	18 Q-QB4	36 RxPch	Resigns.

NOTES.

(A) KtxKP seems to be the proper continuation here.

(B) PxB would be very dangerous, on account of QxRP, threatening Kt-KKt5, with Kt-Q5 and P-K5.

(c) Of course if RxB, 22 B-R7ch wins the Queen.

(d) There seems to be more in 24 Q-Q4.

(e) A little aimless on both sides, perhaps, but while White was handicapped by having to conduct four other games sans voir, Black had, according to the rules, to make his move instantly when it came to his turn to play.

GAME 91.—Played in the Handicap Tournament, New York State Chess Association Midsummer Congress, Staten Island, New York, August 1893. White, Mr. J. M. Hanham; Black, Mr. Pollock.

Irregular Opening.

WHITE.	BLACK.	WHITE.	BLACK.
1 P-QR3	1 P-K4	25 Q-Kt2	25 KtxBP
2 P-K3	2 P-Q4	26 RxKt	26 BxR
3 P-Q4	3 Kt-QB3	27 QxB	27 QxKt
4 Kt-KB3	4 P-K5	28 B-Kt2	28 R-B7
5 KKt-Q2	5 P-B4	29 R-B2	29 RxKB
6 P-QB4	6 PxP	30 RxR	30 R-Q8ch
7 KtxBP(A)	7 Kt-B3	Resigns.	
8 Kt-B3	8 B-K3		
9 B-K2	9 B-K2		
10 Q-B2	10 Castles		
11 Castles	11 Q-Ksq(B)		
12 P-QKt4	12 Q-Kt3		
13 P-Kt5	13 Kt-Qsq		
14 Kt-K5	14 Q-R3		
15 P-B4	15 Kt-B2		
16 KtxKt	16 BxKt		
17 Kt-Qsq	17 B-Q3		
18 P-QR4	18 K-Rsq		
19 Kt-B2	19 QR-Bsq		
20 Kt-R3	20 P-B4(c)		

(See Diagram below.)

21 Kt-Kt5	21 B-KKtsq
22 PxP	22 BxQBP
23 Q-Q2	23 Kt-Q4
24 R-R3	24 KR-Qsq

Position after Black's 20th move.

BLACK.

WHITE.

NOTES.

(A) Most players would prefer BxP.

B) Black has undeniably the more promising position and properly masses his forces against White's inadequately guarded King's side.

(c) The scene of conflict has shifted to the centre, against which Black has a powerful attack.

GAME 92.—Played in the Staten Island Congress, 1893. White, Mr. Pollock (Albany C.C.); Black, Mr. Halpern (City C.C.).

French Defence.

WHITE.	BLACK.	WHITE.	BLACK.
1 P-K4	1 P-K3	14 Q-R2	14 Castles (F)
2 Q-K2(A)	2 P-Q4	15 P-B4	15 Kt-B3
3 PxP	3 QxP	16 P-R5	16 Kt-Bsq
4 Kt-QB3	4 Q-Qsq	17 QR-Ktsq	17 P-QKt3
5 Kt-B3	5 Kt-KB3	18 KR-Ksq	18 PxP
6 P-Q4	6 Kt-B3	19 R-Kt5	19 Kt-Kt5
7 Q-B4(B)	7 B-Kt5(c)	20 RxKt	20 PxR
8 B-Q2	8 BxKt ?	21 Q-R5	
9 PxB	9 B-Q2	Adjourned. (G)	
10 B-Q3	10 Q-K2		
11 CastlesKR	11 Kt-Q4(D)		
12 Q-Kt3	12 Kt-Kt3		
13 P-QR4(E)	13 Kt-R4		

The game was scored by White by default, Mr. Halpern being unable to attend on the following morning.

NOTES.

(A) A novelty which will bear inspection. The object is shown in the sequel.

(B) If 7 B-K3 Black might reply Kt-KKt5.

(C) Doubtful; if, however, Kt-QR4 White could play the Q to her third.

(D) Threatening to force a favourable exchange of Queens by Kt-R4.

(E) For Black intended Kt-QR4, followed by Kt-B5.

(F) If KtxRP, 15 Kt-K5 P-QKt4, 16 KtxB QxKt, 17 P-QB4, winning a piece, while BxRP more obviously loses by 15 P-QB4 at once.

(G) White's spirited sacrifice promises an attack on either wing. 22 BxPch is immediately threatened. If P-QB4, 22 PxP (menacing P-B6) B-B3, 23 Kt-K5, at least recovering the material. Or P-KB4, 22 BxKtP Kt-Q3, 23 QxBP, &c.

GAME 93.—Played at the New York State Chess Association Meeting, April 1893. White, Mr. Frere; Black, Mr. Pollock.

Ruy Lopez.

WHITE.	BLACK.	WHITE.	BLACK.
1 P-K4	1 P-K4	17 Kt-K4	17 P-B5
2 Kt-KB3	2 Kt-QB3	18 B-B2	18 P-B3
3 B-Kt5	3 Kt-R4	19 PxP	19 KtxP
4 P-Q4	4 P-QR3	20 Kt-Q6	20 B-QR3
5 B-Q3	5 PxP	21 QR-Ktsq	21 Kt-Ksq
6 KtxP	6 P-KKt3	22 KR-Qsq	22 Kt-B2
7 B-Q2	7 P-QB4	23 P-QKt3(c)	
8 Kt-KB3	8 B-Kt2	(See Diagram below.)	
9 B-B3	9 Kt-KB3		
10 Castles	10 P-QKt4		23 P-B6
11 P-K5	11 Kt-R4	24 P-QKt4	24 Kt-K3
12 BxKt	12 QxB	25 R-Kt3	25 RxKt !
13 Q-Q2(A)	13 QxQ	26 PxR	26 Kt-Q5
14 QKtxQ	14 Castles	27 RxKt	27 BxR
15 P-B4(B)	15 R-Ktsq	28 K-Bsq	28 R-Kt3
16 PxP	16 PxP	29 Kt-K4	29 R-QB3

WHITE.	BLACK.
30 K-K2	30 P-Q4
31 K-Q3	31 R-B5
32 KtxP	32 B-Bsq
33 K-Q2	33 BxP
34 KtxQP	34 B-R6
35 B-Q3	35 R-Q5
36 Kt-B7	36 B-Q2
37 K-B3	37 R-R5
38 BxQKtP	38 B-KB4
39 K-Q2	39 RxP
40 B-K2	40 P-R4
41 P-Kt5	41 P-R5
42 P-Kt6	42 BxP
43 RxB	43 P-R6
44 R-Kt8ch(D)	44 K-R2
45 Kt-K6	45 BxKt
46 R-Ktsq	46 B-B5
Resigns. (E)	

Position after White's 23rd move.

NOTES.

(A) The exchange of Queens is forced; White threatens P-KKt4.

(B) Mr. Pollock said later that the following continuation would have given White an advantage: 15 Kt-Kt3 P-B5, 16 B-K4 R-R2, 17 Kt-B5, &c.

(C) Very ingeniously played; Black cannot change to advantage, and P-B6 leaves it at White's mercy.

(D) Mr. Frere was pressed for time and moved hastily. He could have won by R-B6, followed by R-Bsq.

(E) If 47 R-Ksq BxB, 48 RxB RxRch, and the Pawn Queens.

GAME 94.—Played in an Impromptu Tournament, at New York City, October 1893. White, Mr. Pollock; Black, Mr. G. H. D. Gossip.

Evans Gambit Declined.

WHITE.	BLACK.	WHITE.	BLACK.
1 P-K4	1 P-K4	14 B-Kt2	14 P-Q5
2 Kt-KB3	2 Kt-QB3	15 Kt-Qsq(A)	15 Kt-Q2
3 B-B4	3 B-B4	16 Q-Kt3(B)	16 P-B3
4 P-QKt4	4 B-Kt3	17 P-B3	17 Kt-Kt6
5 P-Kt5	5 Kt-R4	18 R-Ktsq	18 BPxP
6 B-K2	6 P-Q3	19 BPxP	19 Q-B7
7 Castles	7 Kt-KB3	20 Kt-B3	20 P-Kt5
8 Kt-B3	8 B-K3	21 B-Qsq	21 QxQP
9 P-Q3	9 P-B3	22 B-K2	22 Q-B7
10 P-QR4	10 Q-B2	23 B-Qsq	23 Q-Q6
11 B-R3	11 CastlesKR	24 B-K2	24 Q-B7
12 Q-Q2	12 KR-Qsq	Drawn game. (C)	
13 Q-Kt5	13 P-Q4		

NOTES.

(A) Is not this a wonderful Evans? KB and QKt are both in a fix.

(B) This move is a mystery, the R on Qsq could not shoot diagonally, and the Q should not have been afraid of it. It threatened to take QP.

(C) The Bishop attacks the Queen perpetually, and the game was agreed to count half a point to each. See Diagram.

Position after Black's 24th move.

GAME 95.—Played in the Impromptu Tournament, 1893. White Mr. Pollock; Black, Mr. H. N. Pillsbury.

Irregular Opening.

	WHITE.		BLACK.		WHITE.		BLACK.
1	P-K4	1	P-K4	26	P-B7	26	K-Kt2
2	P-Q3	2	B-B4	27	QR-Ktsq	27	K-Bsq
3	Kt-KB3	3	P-Q3	28	Q-K3	28	KtxP
4	Kt-B3	4	Kt-K2	29	R-R4	29	P-Q4
5	P-Q4	5	PxP	30	R-B4	30	Q-K3
6	KtxP	6	QKt-B3	31	Q-Q4	31	R-Qsq
7	B-K3	7	BxKt	32	R-B6	32	Q-K2
8	BxB	8	Castles	33	BxP	33	RxB
9	B-K3	9	P-B4	34	R(B6)xB	34	PxR
10	Q-Q2	10	PxP	35	QxR	35	P-K6
11	Castles	11	B-B4	36	Q-B3	36	PxP
12	B-K2	12	Q-Q2	37	QxBP	37	K-Kt2
13	P-KR3	13	QR-Ksq	38	R-Ksq	38	Q-Q2
14	P-KKt4	14	B-Kt3	39	Q-B3	39	Kt-Q3
15	P-KR4	15	Kt-Bsq	40	Q-B3ch	40	K-B2
16	P-R5	16	B-B2	41	R-Rsq	41	K-K2
17	P-Kt5	17	P-KKt3	42	Q-Kt7ch	42	K-Qsq
18	PxP	18	BxKtP	43	R-R8ch	43	Kt-Ksq
19	B-B4ch	19	K-Rsq	44	QxP	44	Q-K2
20	Kt-Q5	20	Kt-Kt3	45	Q-Q3ch	45	K-Bsq
21	BxKt	21	RPxB	46	P-B3	46	Q-K8ch
22	Kt-B6	22	RxKt	47	K-B2	47	Q-K4
23	PxR	23	Q-B4	48	Q-R3ch	48	K-Qsq
24	Q-B3	24	Kt-K4	49	Q-R4ch	49	K-Bsq
25	B-Kt3	25	R-QBsq	50	Q-Kt4ch	50	K-Qsq

Position after White's 52nd move.

WHITE.	BLACK.
51 Q-Q4ch	51 QxQ
52 PxQ	

(See Diagram below.)

White won after 81 moves.

GAME 96.—Played in the Handicap Tournament, Café Bondy, 49 Bowery, New York, 1893. White, Mr. Pollock; Black, Mr. M. Lissner.

Two Knights' Defence.

WHITE.	BLACK.	WHITE.	BLACK.
1 P-K4	1 P-K4	22 BxB	22 KtxB
2 Kt-KB3	2 Kt-QB3	23 P-Q4	23 Kt-QB3
3 B-B4	3 Kt-B3	24 K-K2	24 Kt-B5ch
4 Q-K2	4 B-B4	and White wins.	
5 Kt-Kt5	5 Castles(A)		
6 KtxBP	6 Q-K2(B)		
7 KtxPch	7 P-Q4		
8 PxP(C)			
(See Diagram below.)			
	8 BxPch !		
9 K-Qsq	9 KtxKt		
10 P-Q6ch	10 KtxB		
11 PxQ	11 B-Kt5		
12 PxR(Q)ch	12 RxQ		
13 QxQB	13 KtxQ		
14 P-KR3	14 Kt-B3		
15 R-Bsq(D)	15 B-Kt3		
16 P-QKt3	16 Kt-Q3		
17 B-Kt2	17 Kt-R4		
18 RxRch	18 KxR		
19 B-K5	19 Kt-B2		
20 B-R2	20 B-Q5		
21 P-B3	21 B-K4		

Position after White's 8th move.

NOTES.

(A) This costs the exchange. Black might play instead Kt-Q5, and if 6 BxPch K-Bsq, 7 Q-B4 Q-K2, threatening to win a piece by P-KR3.

(B) A most extraordinary step for a player of experience. But it does not compare for strangeness with what is to follow. (Best here is RxKt, 7 BxRch KxB, 8 Q-B4ch P-Q4, 9 QxB Kt-Q5, with some little attack for the exchange).

(C) See diagram. Many a good player would resign the game at this point, in Black's situation. He has lost three Pawns, and his Queen and Knight are both in danger. Also, either Q or KtxKt loses the Q. But problem composers have strange fancies, and seven moves later, aided by a not very obvious slip on the part of the first player, Mr. Lissner missed a chance of gaining a distinct if not a winning advantage.

(D) Here is the slip referred to. Black in reply might have played Kt-KR4, recovering the exchange and Pawn, with a winning game.

GAMES PLAYED AT ODDS.

GAME 97.—A dainty bit at odds of Rook, Pawn, and move. White, Amateur; Black, Mr. Pollock.

Remove Black's Queen's Rook and King's Bishop's Pawn.

WHITE.	BLACK.	WHITE.	BLACK.
1 P-K4	1 P-Q3	10 KtxP	10 B-Kt5
2 Kt-KB3	2 Kt-QB3	11 Q-Kt3	11 P-R5
3 B-Kt5	3 P-K4	12 Q-K3	12 B-R3
4 BxKtch	4 PxB	13 Kt-Kt5	13 R-Ktsq
5 Castles	5 P-Kt4!	14 Kt-K6	14 BxQ
6 P-KR3	6 P-KR4	15 KtxQ	15 B-Kt3
7 P-Q3	7 P-Kt5	16 KtxP	16 B-Q5
8 Kt-Kt5	8 PxP	17 B-K3	
9 Q-B3	9 Kt-B3	Black mates in three moves.	

GAME 98.—A brilliant from the Baltimore Chess Association Handicap Tournament, 27th December 1890. White, Mr. Pollock; Black, Mr. J. W. Dallam.

French Defence.

Remove White's Queen's Rook.

WHITE.	BLACK.	WHITE.	BLACK.
1 P-K4	1 P-K3	13 Kt-K4!!!	13 PxKt
2 P-Q4(A)	2 P-Q4	14 BxB	14 Q-B4
3 Kt-QB3	3 P-QB4	15 Q-Q2	15 Kt-B2
4 B-KB4(B)	4 Q-Kt3	16 B-K5ch	16 K-Bsq
5 Kt-Kt5	5 Kt-QR3	17 Q-B3	17 QxB
6 KPxP	6 KPxP	18 QxQ	18 KtxB
7 Kt-KB3	7 B-Q2	19 PxKt	19 P-B3
8 P-QR4	8 BxKt	20 Q-QB5ch	20 K-Qsq
9 BxBch	9 K-Qsq	21 R-Qsqch	21 K-Ksq
10 Kt-Kt5	10 Kt-R3	22 Q-B7	22 K-Bsq
11 Castles	11 B-Q3(C)	23 R-Q8ch	Resigns.
12 PxP(D)	12 QxP		

Notes.

(A) The old masters when conceding odds of QR or Kt used to play 2 P-KB4 or if 2 P-Q4, then 3 P-K5; safer lines of attack.

(B) PxQP gains a Pawn, but leaves the game too open and easy at such odds.

(C) Black should have played 11 Kt-B2.

(D) Very strong, whichever way Black retakes.

(E) Losing the Queen, on pain of some elegant checkmates. But if K-Bsq, or Q-K3, White would win by R-Qsq.

GAME 99.—A brilliant and unsound gamelet from the Baltimore Chess Association Handicap Tournament. White, Mr. Pollock; Black, Mr. D. Kemper.

Remove White's Queen's Rook.

WHITE.	BLACK.
1 P-K4	1 P-K4
2 P-KB4	2 PxP
3 B-B4	3 P-KKt4
4 Kt-KB3	4 P-KR3
5 Kt-K5	5 R-R2
6 Castles	6 Kt-KB3
7 BxPch	7 RxB
8 KtxR	8 KxKt
9 P-K5	9 Kt-Ktsq
10 Q-R5ch	10 K-Kt2
11 P-QKt4	11 B-K2
12 B-Kt2	12 Kt-QB3
13 P-KR4	13 KtxKtP?
14 PxP	14 BxP
15 RxP	15 BxR

Position after Black's 15th move.

White mates in eight moves.!!

GAME 100.—A well played and brilliantly terminated game at odds of Kt from Baltimore Chess Association Handicap Tournament, with a recognised strong player, with whom Mr. Pollock felt called upon to be wary. White, Mr. Pollock; Black, Mr. Uhthoff.

Irregular Opening.

Remove White's Queen's Knight.

WHITE.	BLACK.	WHITE.	BLACK.
1 P-KB4	1 P-KB4	8 P-B4	8 Kt-Kt3
2 Kt-B3	2 Kt-KB3	9 B-K2	9 P-KR4
3 P-K3	3 P-K3	10 Castles	10 R-R3
4 P-QKt3	4 Kt-B3	11 Kt-Kt5	11 P-Kt3
5 B-Kt2	5 B-K2	12 Q-Ksq	12 B-Bsq
6 R-Bsq	6 Kt-QKt5	13 P-Q3	13 P-R4
7 P-QR3	7 QKt-Q4	14 B-KB3	14 B-Kt2

WHITE.	BLACK.	WHITE.	BLACK.
15 P-K4	15 Q-K2	21 PxKt	21 R-KR2
16 P-B5	16 Kt-R2	22 KR-Bsq	22 Q-Qsq
17 BxB	17 QxB	23 PxP	23 KtPxP
18 PxKt	18 QBPxP	24 P-Kt6	24 R-Rsq
19 Q-K3	19 Q-K2	25 P-Kt7	25 K-Ktsq
20 R-B7	20 KtxKt	26 QxPch or BxPch and mates.	

GAME 101.—White, Mr. Pollock; Black, Mr. Uhthoff.

Centre Gambit.

Remove White's King's Knight.

WHITE.	BLACK.	WHITE.	BLACK.
1 P-K4	1 P-K4	24 PxR(Q)ch	24 K-B2
2 P-Q4	2 P-Q3	25 R-KBsq	25 Q-Q5
3 B-QB4	3 Kt-KB3	26 P-QKt4	26 K-Kt3
4 Castles	4 B-K2	27 P-KR3	27 Q-B6
5 P-B4(A)	5 PxQP	28 Q-KB5	28 P-Kt3 (Oh!)
6 P-K5	6 PxP	29 Q mates.	
7 PxP	7 Kt-Q4		
8 Q-B3	8 B-K3		
9 Kt-Q2(A)	9 P-QB3		
10 Kt-K4	10 Kt-Q2		
11 Q-KKt3	11 Q-Kt3		
12 B-KKt5	12 CastlesQR		
13 BxB	13 KtxB		
14 RxP(B)	14 P-Q6ch		
15 K-Rsq	15 BxB		
16 Kt-Q6ch	16 K-Ktsq		
17 KtxB	17 Q-B4		
18 PxP(c)	18 Kt-KKt3?		
19 P-K6ch	19 QKt-K4		
20 P-K7	20 RxP(D)		
(See Diagram below.)			
21 KtxKt	21 KtxKt		
22 R-B8ch	22 RxR		
23 QxKtch	23 QxQ		

Position after Black's 20th move.

NOTES.

(A) The opening is clearly in White's disfavour.

(B) Thinking the gain of the exchange, by BxB, Kt-Q6 and Kt-B7 an insufficient advantage, White hazards a plunge into the unknown.

(C) It would be unsafe to exchange one horse for two, on account of his aggressive Pawn. K-Rsq is somewhat preferable to Black's reply.

(D) Unwise, as White somewhat elegantly proves. The game ought now to be drawn.

GAME 102.—White, Mr. Pollock; Black, Mr. J. Henrichs.
King's Knight's Opening.
Remove White's Queen's Knight.

WHITE.	BLACK.	WHITE.	BLACK.
1 P-K4	1 P-K4	14 P-Q3	14 Q-B6
2 Kt-KB3	2 Kt-QB3	15 B-K3	15 Kt-Q4
3 B-B4	3 P-Q3	16 R-Ksq	16 R-KBsq
4 P-B3	4 B-Kt5	17 BxP	17 Kt-B5
5 Q-Kt3	5 Q-Q2	18 R-Kt3	18 Q-R8ch
6 BxPch	6 QxB	19 R-Ktsq	19 QxP
7 QxP	7 K-Q2(A)	20 P-B3	20 Kt-R6
8 QxR	8 BxKt	21 R-K2	21 RxPch (D)
9 PxB	9 QxBP	22 K-Ksq	22 Q-B5
10 R-KKtsq	10 QxKPch	23 R-K4	23 Q-B8ch
11 K-Bsq(B)	11 KKt-K2	24 K-K2	24 KtxRch
12 Q-Kt7(c)	12 P-Kt3	25 BxKt	25 Q-B8ch
13 Q-Kt5	13 B-Kt2	Resigns.	

This game admirably illustrates the point that there is a pitch or force against which even a Pollock cannot give heavy odds.—"Miron."

NOTES.

(A) Very well played this, and all the game.

(B) White cannot escape the draw by "perpetual" if 11 K-Qsq Q-B6ch, 12 K-B2 Kt-Q5ch. Still 11 K-Qsq is safer than the text move.

(c) We prefer 12 P-Kt4.

(D) This powerful stroke wins by force.

GAME 103.—An interesting encounter from the annual Handicap Tournament of the Baltimore Chess Association, 1891. White, Mr. A. Maas; Black, Mr. Pollock.
Remove Black's Queen's Rook.

WHITE.	BLACK.	WHITE.	BLACK.
1 P-Q4	1 P-KB4	14 R-KKtsq	14 Q-Rsq
2 Kt-KB3	2 Kt-KB3	15 B-Kt2	15 P-K4
3 P-B4	3 P-K3	16 B-K2	16 Q-Ktsq!
4 P-QR3	4 P-QKt3	17 Q-Q2	17 R-B2
5 P-K3	5 B-Kt2	18 Castles	18 P-Q4
6 Kt-B3	6 P-QR3	19 Q-Kt5	19 P-Q5(A)
7 B-Q3	7 B-Q3	20 QR-Ksq	20 P-Q3
8 P-R3	8 Kt-B3	21 P-KR4	21 P-QR4
9 P-QKt4	9 Castles	22 P-R5	22 PxP
10 P-K4	10 PxP	23 P-R6(B)	23 P(Kt5)xP
11 KtxP	11 KtxQP!	24 BxRP	24 Q-Rsq
12 KtxB	12 KtxKtch	25 K-Kt2	25 Q-R4
13 PxKt	13 PxKt	26 R-QBsq	26 B-B3

WHITE.	BLACK.
27 BxP(c)	
(See Diagram below.)	
	27 R-R2
28 QxPch	28 RxQ
29 RxRch	29 K-Rsq
30 R-KB7	30 Kt-Ktsq
31 B-B8	31 KtxP
32 BxKt	32 Q-Kt5ch
33 K-R2	

Drawn by perpetual check.

Position after White's 27th move.

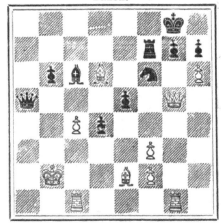

NOTES.

(A) Black's defensive measures tell somewhat, but he has a precarious and uphill game.

(B) One too far! Up to this White has played excellently.

(C) The climax! White now most cleverly effects a draw, albeit driven thereto.

GAME 104.—A very curious game played in the Baltimore Chess Association's Winter Handicap Tournament, 1890. White, Mr. H. S. Habershom; Black, Mr. Pollock.

French Defence.
Remove Black's King's Knight.

WHITE.	BLACK.
1 P-K4	1 P-K3
2 Kt-KB3	2 P-QKt3
3 B-B4	3 B-Kt2
4 Kt-B3	4 B-Kt5
5 P-Q3(A)	5 P-Q4
6 PxP	6 PxP
7 Q-K2ch	7 K-Bsq
8 B-Kt3	8 P-Q5
9 P-QR3	9 B-R4
10 Q-K5	10 PxKt
11 Castles	11 Kt-B3
12 Q-KB5	12 Q-B3
13 Q-Q7	13 R-Ksq
14 B-Kt5	14 Q-Kt3
15 QR-Ksq	15 P-B3
16 Kt-R4	16 Q-R4
17 P-Kt4	17 Kt-K4(B)
18 RxKt	18 RxR
19 BxP(c)	

Position after White's 19th move.

The move sealed at adjournment; but Mr. Habershom did not return to finish. It ought to lose the game.

NOTES.

(A) Leading to the loss of a piece, in the winning of which, however, Black has to put up with a very awkward position.

(B) A very remarkable, and, we may say, even beautiful resource.

(C) The final position is a fine one, and White had, we think, some prospect of a draw.

GAME 105.—Played in a match between Messrs. Schofield and Pollock. White, Mr. Schofield; Black, Mr. Pollock.

Remove Black's King's Bishop's Pawn.

WHITE.	BLACK.	WHITE.	BLACK.
1 P-K4	1 P-Q3	18 Q-Kt3	18 K-Rsq
2 Kt-KB3	2 Kt-KB3	19 B-Kt5	19 B-KB3
3 Kt-B3	3 P-K4	20 BxB	20 PxB
4 P-Q4	4 PxP	21 Q-R4	21 R-B2
5 KtxP	5 Kt-B3	22 R-B3	22 P-B3
6 B-QKt5	6 B-Q2	23 Kt-B4	23 P-B5
7 Castles	7 B-K2	24 R-Kt3	24 Q-Kt3ch
8 KtxKt	8 PxKt	25 K-Rsq	25 R-Qsq
9 B-R4	9 Q-Ktsq	26 Q-R6	26 Q-B7
10 Q-K2	10 Kt-Kt5	27 R-Kt4	27 R-KKtsq
11 P-KR3	11 Kt-K4	28 Kt-Kt6ch	28 RxKt
12 B-Kt3	12 P-B4	29 PxR	29 R-Kt2
13 P-B4	13 Kt-B3	30 R-B4	30 Q-K6
14 Kt-Q5	14 Kt-Q5	31 R-R4	31 Q-B7
15 Q-B2	15 KtxB	32 PxBP	
16 RPxKt	16 B-Qsq	After a few more moves Black	
17 P-B5	17 Castles	resigned.	

GAME 106.—White, Mr. Pollock; Black, Mr. Torsch.

Remove White's Queen's Knight.

WHITE.	BLACK.	WHITE.	BLACK.
1 P-KB4	1 P-K3	15 KR-Ktsq	15 P-K4
2 P-K3	2 P-Q4	16 B-R7	16 K-Q2
3 Kt-B3	3 Kt-QB3	17 P-R3	17 R-QRsq
4 P-QKt3	4 B-Q3	18 B-B5	18 Kt-R3
5 B-Kt2	5 Kt-B3	19 Kt-R4(c)	19 Q-B2
6 B-Kt5	6 P-QR3	20 P-R4	20 QR-Ksq
7 BxKtch(A)	7 PxB	21 P-B5	21 P-K5
8 Castles	8 B-Kt2	22 BxB	22 KxB
9 Q-Ksq	9 Q-K2	23 P-Kt5	23 RPxP
10 P-QR3	10 CastlesQR	24 PxP	24 PxP
11 P-QKt4	11 P-KR4	25 QxKtP	25 B-B3
12 Q-K2	12 Kt-Kt5(B)	26 Q-Kt4ch(D)	26 K-Q2(E)
13 BxP	13 KR-Ktsq	27 R-R7	27 Q-Kt2
14 B-Q4	14 P-B3	28 Q-Kt6	28 R-QBsq

WHITE.	BLACK.
29 P-B4	29 KtxP
30 PxP	30 BxP
31 Q-Kt5ch	31 K-K3
32 KR-Rsq	32 KtxKt
33 KR-R6ch	33 K-K4
34 P-Kt4	

(See Diagram below.)

	34 Kt-B6ch(F)
35 K-B2	35 PxP
36 PxP	36 QxP
37 Q-Kt2ch	37 Kt-Q5
38 QxKtch and mates next move.	

Position after White's 34th move.

NOTES.

(A) Not commendable, but the object is to save time and bring up the Rooks rapidly to attack on the King's side, should Black Castle there.

(B) The sacrifice of the P was intentional, and should yield Black some attack.

(C) The moved sealed at the adjournment.

(D) Both sides singularly overlooked that White could have won here by 26. R-R6; if Q-Q2, 27 P-Q4 or Q-Kt4ch.

(E) If K-K4 mate follows in two.

(F) An unfortunate and curiously disastrous slip. He had only to play PxP and the day was won.

GAME 107.—A remarkably neat game, played in the Bowery Tournament, September 1893. White, Mr. Loeb; Black, Mr. Pollock.

Remove Black's King's Bishop's Pawn.

WHITE.	BLACK.
1 P-K4	1 Kt-QB3
2 P-Q4	2 P-K4
3 PxP	3 KtxP
4 Q-R5ch	4 Kt-Kt3
5 B-QB4	5 Kt-B3
6 Q-K2	6 Kt-K4
7 B-Kt3	7 B-B4
8 P-KB4(A)	8 Kt-B3(best)
9 P-K5(B)	9 Kt-Q5!
10 Q-B4	10 Q-K2
11 Kt-K2	11 P-Q4
12 Q-Q3	12 KtxKt(C)

(See Diagram below.)

13 QxKt(D)	13 B-KKt5
14 Q-Q3	14 Kt-K5
15 BxP(E)	15 Q-R5ch
16 P-Kt3	

Black mates in two moves.

Position after Black's 12th move.

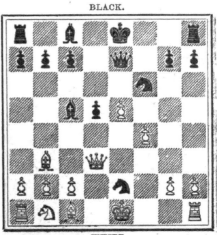

NOTES.

(A) White misjudges the position in undertaking an immediate attack.

(B) 9 Q-B4 threatening mate, the B, and P-K5, all of which things Black's forced reply obviates.

(C) If B-B4, 13 Q-Qsq Kt×Kt, 14 P×Kt, and Black loses a piece.

(D) Here if 13 P×Kt Kt×Bch, 14 P×Q Kt×Qch, 15 P×Kt P-B3, with an excellent game.

(E) Losing off-hand. White calculates seemingly on either Kt-B7 or CastlesQR as replies, neither of which would avail much.

POLLOCK-MOEHLE MATCH.

A HOT CONTEST, CINCINNATI, JUNE 1890.

SCENE: A close Chess room over Kammaron's saloon, Cincinnati. Time: midsummer. Temperature: ninety degrees. Stakes: 100 dols. Terms: seven games up, to be played at the rate of not less than two games a day.

Charlie Moehle, familiar of the famous automaton "Ajeeb," opened game 1 with a slashing attack. Pollock lashed out his two Knights on second and third moves, played 4 P-Q4, gave up a Pawn on his ninth move, won it back on his sixteenth, tripped on his nineteenth, and fell on his thirty-second.

Lemon squash, cucumbers, and ice-water having been served, game 2, another two Knights' defence, opened by Pollock, rolled off the real like smoke. The "Ajeeb" man quickly went down. Score: 1 all.

Game 3.—Moehle struck out with an Evans, Pollock went down. Score: Moehle 2, Pollock 1.

Game 4.—A short Sicilian, Pollock revived, Moehle overpowered. Stop-clocks disregarded, no time to look at them. Score: 2 all.

Games 5 and 6.—Pollock's coat off, mosquitos bad, play rapid, Pollock won. Score: Pollock 4, Moehle 2.

Game 7.—Players mop down, Moehle's coat and vest off, more ice-water and melons, game drawn, draw not counted.

Game 8.—Opened by Pollock, who was met with a Petroff counter attack. Pollock knocked out of time. Score: Pollock 4, Moehle 3.

Game 9.—The Celtic blood of the ex-champion of Ireland up; more clothes off; Moehle knocked to pieces. From that out the score —close, like the room, the temperature, and the French defence, which was next played—kept rising in Pollock's favour. It was 5 to 4, 6 to 5, 6 to 6, and finally a Staunton of 18 moves sent Moehle's sponge flying, and Pollock was declared the winner by 7 to 6.

GAME 108.—First of the match, scored by Mr. Moehle, after some very pretty play on both sides. White, Mr. C. Moehle; Black, Mr. Pollock.

Two Knights' Defence.

WHITE.	BLACK.	WHITE.	BLACK.
1 P-K4	1 P-K4	25 K-R2	25 B-B3
2 Kt-KB3	2 Kt-QB3	26 P-Kt4	26 R-Qsq(f)
3 B-B4	3 Kt-B3	27 PxB	27 R-Q7ch
4 P-Q3	4 P-Q4	28 R-B2	28 PxP
5 PxP	5 KtxP	29 Q-R4	29 PxKt
6 Castles	6 B-K2	30 Q-Kt5ch	30 K-Bsq
7 Q-K2	7 B-KKt5	31 RxR	31 Q-Kt3
8 P-B3	8 Castles	32 R-Q8ch	Resigns.
9 P-KR3	9 B-R4(a)		
10 P-KKt4	10 B-Kt3		
11 KtxP	11 KtxKt		
12 QxKt	12 Kt-Kt3		
13 Q-Kt3(b)	13 KtxB		
14 PxKt	14 B-Q3		
15 P-B4(c)	15 B-Q6		
16 R-Ksq	16 BxQBP		
17 B-K3	17 R-Ksq		
18 Kt-Q2	18 B-Q4		
19 Kt-B3			

(See Diagram below.)

	19 P-KKt4(d)
20 Kt-Q4	20 R-K5
21 R-KBsq	21 Q-Ksq
22 Kt-B5	22 RxB(e)
23 KtxR	23 B-B4
24 QR-Ksq	24 Q-K5

Position after White's 19th move.

NOTES.

(A) The sacrifice of the Pawn in this position is unusual, and not a bad idea.

(B) Best; for if 13 P-Kt3 BxP, 14 R-Qsq KtxB, 15 PxKt B-Q3, &c.

(C) After this Black ingeniously regains the Pawn, with the better game. However, if 15 B-B4 BxB, 16 QxB Q-Q6, or R-Ksq, and we prefer Black's position.

(D) Who would say unsound of this? Yet White almost proves it so.

(E) And this! Curiously if PxP, 23 Q-R4.

(F) Hoping to draw. Black's attack is broken; if B retreats P-Kt5, if BxP Q-B3.

GAME 109.—Tenth of the match, by which Mr. Moehle captured half of the Kinzbach brilliancy prize. White, Mr. Pollock; Black, Mr. Moehle.

Two Knights' Defence.

WHITE.	BLACK.	WHITE.	BLACK.
1 P-K4	1 P-K4	5 PxP	5 Kt-QR4
2 Kt-KB3	2 Kt-QB3	6 B-Kt5ch	6 P-B3
3 B-B4	3 Kt-B3	7 PxP	7 PxP
4 Kt-Kt5	4 P-Q4	8 B-K2	8 P-KR3

WHITE.	BLACK.	WHITE.	BLACK.
9 Kt-KR3(A)	9 BxKt	32 PxR	32 R-Ktsq
10 PxB	10 Q-Q4	33 R-Ktsq	33 R-Kt4
11 B-B3	11 P-K5	34 P-R6	34 R-R4
12 B-Kt2	12 Q-K4	35 R-QKt1	35 QxQP
13 Q-K2	13 B-Q3(B)	36 R-Kt8ch	36 K-R2
14 Kt-B3	14 CastlesKR	Resigns.	
15 P-Kt3(c)	15 Kt-Q4		
16 B-Kt2	16 Kt-KB5		
17 Q-Bsq	17 P-KB4		
18 Castles(D)	18 Q-K2		
(See Diagram below.)			
19 R-Ktsq(E)	19 B-R6		
20 Q-R6(F)	20 Q-B4		
21 B-Bsq	21 KR-Ktsq		
22 Kt-R4	22 Q-K4(G)		
23 P-QB3	23 BxBch		
24 KxB	24 Q-Q4(H)		
25 P-B4	25 Q-K4ch		
26 K-R3(I)	26 Kt-K3 !		
27 P-B5	27 Kt-Q5 !		
28 R-Bsq	28 Kt-Kt4ch		
29 BxKt	29 RxB		
30 P-Kt4(K)	30 Q-Q5		
31 QxKt	31 RxQ		

Position after Black's 18th move.

NOTES.

(A) Steinitz's novelty. Instructor, p. 94.

(B) We prefer Castles, (if) 14 Kt-B3 B-B4, 15 KtxP KtxKt, 16 BxKt KR-Ksq, 17 P-Q3 P-B4, 18 B-B3 Q-B3.

(C) Steinitz gives 15 P-Q3. The text move is sound.

(D) The position is not without its dangers. For instance, if 18 Kt-Qsq Black might reply Kt-Q6ch.

(E) A most critical question—Is not "this" the time to play Q-R6 instead of a move later? We give a diagram of this important position.

(F) Mr. Moehle condemns this move, and considers White's best to be 20 BxB.

(G) An admirable move, followed up in masterly style.

(H) To prevent White posting B at QB4.

(I) If 26 K-Ktsq KtxKtP, 27 PxKt RxPch, 28 K-B2 R-R6. Or 28 K-R2 QR-Ktsq.

(K) A fatal error, though it is very hard to escape the effects of Q-Q5, which Black threatens in any case, now that his Knight is defended. 30 Kt-Kt6 looks like a resource, as Black cannot sacrifice with advantage. He might, however, reply R-Qsq !

GAME 110.—Eleventh of the match, in which "Ajeeb" was automatonised through getting mixed up in a rather complicated opening. White, Mr. Moehle; Black, Mr. Pollock.

Scotch Gambit.

WHITE.	BLACK.	WHITE.	BLACK.
1 P-K4	1 P-K4	10 BxKt(A)	10 PxQ
2 Kt-KB3	2 Kt-QB3	11 BxQ	11 KxB
3 P-Q4	3 PxP	12 P-QR3	12 B-R4!
4 KtxP	4 Kt-B3	13 P-QKt4	13 PxKt
5 Kt-QB3	5 B-Kt5	14 PxB	14 P-Q5
6 KtxKt	6 KtPxKt	15 R-QKtsq	15 B-K3
7 Q-Q4	7 Q-K2	16 R-Kt4	16 P-QB4
8 P-B3	8 P-Q4	17 R-Kt7ch	17 K-Q3
9 B-KKt5	9 P-B4	18 P-R6	18 KR-QKtsq
		19 P-B4	19 RxR
		20 PxR	20 R-QKtsq
		21 B-R6	21 B-Q2
		22 K-K2(B)	22 B-B3
		23 K-Q3	23 BxKtP(c)
		24 BxB	24 RxB
		25 K-B4	25 R-Kt7
		26 R-QBsq	26 P-QR4(D)
		27 P-QR4	27 R-Kt5ch
		28 K-Q3	28 RxP
		29 R-QKtsq	29 R-Kt5
		30 R-QRsq	30 P-R5
		31 P-Kt4	31 P-Kt4(E)
		32 PxP	32 K-K4
		33 R-KBsq	33 P-B5ch
		34 K-K2	34 KxP
		35 RxP	35 P-Q6ch
		36 PxP	36 PxPch
		Resigns.	

Position after Black's 9th move.

NOTES.

(A) Bad for White's end game. The "given" is 10 B-Kt5ch K-Bsq (not a simple position, v.1. Gunsberg once lost a tourney game to Blackburne through playing B-Q2 here, which costs a Pawn), 11 Q-Q3! PxP (Black must do better than PxP; would P-B5 or R-QKtsq meet the case?), 12 PxP QxPch, 13 QxQ KtxQ, 14 B-B6, and should win.

(B) Castling might be a little better, but play as he may, Black's superior Pawn position must eventually carry the day.

(C) If RxP, 24 P-K5ch! K-Q4, 25 BxR BxB, 26 K-K2, and should win.

(D) In order to play P-R5 and R-R7, for if R-R7 at once, 27 K-Kt3.

(E) White was unable to prevent Black from breaking up his rank of infantry and so occupying Q4 or K4 with King, for the final Pawn advance.

GAME 111.—Mr. Pollock was pre-eminently a player most constantly in pursuit of ideas in actual play. It has cost him many a game, it has also now and then rewarded him with unrivalled beauties. On almost every move of every game he endeavoured to get totally free from routine, and to impart novelty and problematic criticality. In doing this he frequently managed to make the position conform to one of his favourite ideals, and then came a great masterpiece. An instance of this is afforded in the following game, which obtained the brilliancy prize awarded by Mr. Kinsbach. White, Mr. Pollock; Black, Mr. Moehle.

WHITE.	BLACK.
1 P-K4	1 P-K4
2 Kt-QB3	2 Kt-KB3
3 P-B4	3 P-Q4
4 BPxP	4 KtxP
5 Kt-B3	5 B-QB4
6 Q-K2	6 KtxKt
7 KtPxKt	7 Castles
8 P-Q4	8 B-K2
9 P-Kt3	9 P-QB4
10 B-KKt2	10 PxP
11 PxP	11 B-Kt5ch
12 B-Q2	12 BxBch
13 QxB	13 B-K3
14 CastlesKR	14 Kt-B3

(See Diagram.)

Position after Black's 14th move.

At this juncture Mr. Pollock, peering long and deeply into the future, became convinced that the further pursuit of one idea—namely that of "raking" the long White diagonal with his King's Bishop, aided by Pawns, Rooks, Knight, and Queen —would be fruitless, whereas the pursuit of another—that of posting his Bishop at Queen's third—would be rich in possibility. Accordingly he played 15 R-B2, and when his opponent replied R-Bsq he simply added 16 B-Bsq. Then came Kt-R4, 17 B-Q3 Kt-B5, 18 Q-B4, all pursuing the new idea.

Moehle began to realise the danger of the design, and advanced P-KR3, whereupon Pollock doubled his Rooks by playing 19 QR-KBsq, and induced his opponent to advance P-B3, as shown in the next diagram:—

Position after Black's 19th move.

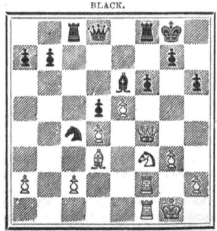

Another idea visits Mr. Pollock at this crisis. Before Black disturbs his Bishop from Q3 by Kt-Kt7, &c., he must, even if it be at some sacrifice, effect a breach in the stronghold of the adverse King. How? By 20 Kt-R4! (intending if P-KKt4, 21 Q-Bsq! PxKt, 22 QxRP, &c., or if 20 PxP, 21 QxRch QxQ, 22 RxQch RxR, 23 B-R7ch KxB, 24 RxR and wins). Black, having no better retaliation, makes assault on the base Rook by B-R6, whereupon Pollock's ideal lights the way, and he places his (21) Kt at B5!

If Pollock's Kt be taken, his Q retaking gains the desired entrance; if not, then the further ingenuity of his ideal develops.

Black sees that 21 PxP would allow 22 KtxPch, and wins, and that 21 P-KKt4 could not prevent Q-B3 and Q-R5 or B4, with fatal result.

POLLOCK-DELMAR MATCH.

NEW YORK STATE ASSOCIATION MEETING, 1891.

(Kindly contributed by Mr. H. J. Rogers, Albany, New York.)

THE chief interest of the meeting centered in the contest between Mr. Eugene Delmar, the New York champion, and Mr. Pollock, of Baltimore, the Maryland champion. The match was well contested, replete with interesting positions, and the conclusion of every game viewed by an eager and excited crowd.

The condition of the match was nine games to be played, the contestant having the best score at the conclusion to be the winner.

GAME 112.—First of the match, played at Skaneateles, New York, 20th July 1891. White, Mr. Pollock; Black, Mr. Delmar.

Vienna Opening.

WHITE.	BLACK.	WHITE.	BLACK.
1 P-K4	1 P-K4	31 B-K3	31 P-Kt5
2 Kt-QB3	2 B-B4	32 P-B4(I)	
3 P-B4	3 P-Q3		
4 Kt-B3	4 B-KKt5		
5 B-B4	5 Kt-QB3		
6 B-Kt5(A)	6 P-QR3(B)		
7 BxKtch	7 PxB		
8 P-Q3	8 Kt-K2		
9 Kt-K2	9 Kt-Kt3		
10 PxP	10 PxP(c)		
11 Kt-Kt3	11 Kt-R5		
12 Q-K2	12 Castles		
13 P-KR3(D)	13 BxKt		
14 PxB	14 P-B4(E)		
15 PxP	15 KtxP(B4)		
16 KtxKt	16 RxKt		
17 Q-K4	17 Q-KBsq		
18 K-K2	18 R-Qsq		
19 P-B3	19 R-Ksq		
20 R-Bsq	20 K-Rsq		
21 B-Q2(F)	21 Q-B2		
22 QR-Ksq	22 R-KBsq		32 R-R7ch
23 P-Kt3(G)	23 B-Kt3	33 K-Q3	33 P-Kt6
24 K-Qsq	24 RxP	34 P-B5	34 B-R2
25 RxR	25 QxRch	35 K-K4	35 K-Kt2
26 QxQ	26 RxQ	36 K-B3(K)	36 K-B2
27 RxP	27 P-R3	37 KxP	37 R-QKt7
28 P-Q4	28 RxRP	38 BxP	38 RxPch
29 K-K2	29 P-Kt4(H)	39 K-B4	39 R-Kt5
30 P-R4	30 P-QR4	40 K-K4	40 RxRP

Position after White's 32nd move.

41 B-Kt5	41 R-Kt5	44 B-Q6(L)	44 K-B3
42 B-Q8	42 P-R5	45 R-B5ch	45 K-K3
43 BxP	43 P-R6	46 R-K5ch	46 K-B3
		47 R-B5ch	47 K-K3

Position after Black's 43rd move.

BLACK.

[chessboard diagram]

WHITE.

48 R-R5	48 R-R5
49 R-R6ch	49 K-Q2
50 K-K5	50 P-R7
51 R-R7ch	51 K-Bsq
52 R-B7ch	52 K-Qsq
53 K-K6	53 P-R8(Q)
54 R-Q7ch	54 K-Bsq
55 R-B7ch	55 K-Ktsq
56 RxPch	56 K-Kt2
57 R-B7ch	57 K-R3
58 P-Q5	58 R-K5ch
59 K-Q7	59 Q-R5ch
60 P-B6	60 R-K7
61 B-K7	61 Q-Kt5ch
62 K-Q8	62 Q-Ktsqch
63 K-Q7	63 QxPch
64 B-Q6	

Black mates in two moves.

NOTES.

(A) Serious loss of time. The right play is 6 PxP PxP (or 6 KtxP, 7 B-K2, &c.), 7 P-Q3, and if Kt-Q5, 8 BxPch K-Bsq (or 8 KxB, 9 KtxPch, and should win), 9 KtxKt BxQ, 10 Kt-K6ch, and ought to win.

(B) KKt-K2 was preferable.

(C) We believe that Black might have given up the Pawn and instituted a strong attack by 10 Kt-R5, with the probable continuation 11 KtxKt QxKtch, 12 P-Kt3 Q-R6, 13 P-Q4 Q-Kt7, 14 KR-Ktsq QxRch, and wins.

(D) B-Q2, with a view of Castling, was more likely to relieve him.

(E) Not so strong as Q-B3, followed, if the Rook defended the Pawn, by Q-Kt3 or Q-K3.

(F) We see no clear reason why White on this or the next move does not capture the QBP.

(G) Now 23 QxBP would have been dangerous, on account of the rejoinder P-K5.

(H) Premature. He ought to have played R-R8, with the view of attacking at QKt8, which would have had the important effect of driving back the adverse King, as White had hardly anything better than K-Q3, and then to defend at QB2.

(I) A powerful stroke that comes in at the right time after ingenious preparations.

(K) The sealed move, the game having been adjourned after Black's previous move. White could have won easily now by 36 R-K7ch K-Kt3, 37 RxP B-Ktsq, 38 RxPch K-Kt2, 39 R-QKt6, &c.

(L) White's game is gone, and the rest is a struggle against fate.

GAME 113.—Second of the match, 20th and 21st July 1891. White, Mr. Delmar; Black, Mr. Pollock.

Ruy Lopez.

WHITE.	BLACK.	WHITE.	BLACK.
1 P-K4	1 P-K4	46 Q-K8ch	46 R-Bsq
2 Kt-KB3	2 Kt-QB3	47 Q-K7	47 R-B2
3 B-Kt5	3 P-QR3	48 Q-K3(M)	48 Q-R4
4 B-R4	4 Kt-B3	49 Q-K8ch	49 K-R2
5 P-Q3	5 B-B4	50 Q-R8ch	50 K-Kt3
6 Kt-B3(A)	6 Castles	51 QxQch	51 KxQ
7 Castles	7 P-QKt4	52 Kt-Q6	52 R-K2(N)
8 B-Kt3	8 B-Kt2(B)	53 B-K5(O)	53 K-Kt5(P)
9 B-Kt5(C)	9 B-K2		
10 Kt-K2	10 Kt-KR4		
11 B-K3	11 K-Rsq		
12 B-Q5	12 B-Q3		
13 Kt-Kt5	13 Q-B3		
14 P-QR4	14 Kt-B5		
15 Kt-KB3	15 P-Kt4		
16 P-B3	16 P-KKt5		
17 Kt-Ksq	17 KtxB		
18 PxKt	18 Kt-K2		
19 P-QB4(D)	19 P-B4(E)		
20 Kt-Kt3	20 Q-Kt3		
21 P-B4	21 P-B4		
22 Q-K2(F)	22 KtPxBP		
23 QPxP	23 P-K5		
24 P-Kt3	24 P-QR4		
25 B-Bsq	25 K-Ktsq		
26 B-Kt2	26 Q-R3		
27 Q-Q2	27 Kt-Kt3		
28 Kt-K2	28 R-R3		
29 P-Kt3(G)	29 Kt-K4		
30 Kt-QB3	30 Kt-B6ch		
31 KtxKt	31 KtPxKt		
32 Kt-Kt5	32 B-K2		
33 QR-Ksq	33 Q-R6(H)		
34 RxBP(I)			

(See Diagram below.)

	34 PxR		
35 RxB	35 R-KKt3		
36 Q-KB2	36 Q-Kt5		
37 Q-K3(K)	37 P-R4		
38 Q-K5	38 R(Kt3)-KB3		
39 R-K8	39 RxR(L)		
40 QxRch	40 R-Bsq		
41 Q-K7	41 P-R5		
42 K-B2	42 PxPch		
43 PxP	43 R-B2		
44 Q-K8ch	44 R-Bsq		
45 Q-K7	45 R-B2		

Position after Black's 53rd move.

Position after White's 34th move.

WHITE.	BLACK.	WHITE.	BLACK.
54 KtxB	54 R-R2	61 KtxP	61 P-B8(Q)
55 KtxBP	55 R-R7ch	62 Kt-K5ch	62 KxKtP
56 K-K3	56 R-K7ch	63 P-Q6	63 QxPch
57 K-Q3	57 R-K8	64 K-Q5	64 Q-K5ch
58 B-Q4	58 R-Q8ch	65 K-K6	65 K-B5
59 K-K3	59 RxB(Q)	Resigns.	
60 KxR	60 P-B7		

NOTES.

(A) If 6 BxKt QPx3, 7 KtxP BxPch, 8 KxB Q-Q5ch, recovering the Pawn with the superior game, but P-QB3 is preferable.

(B) A mode of development for this Bishop which was first introduced by Paulsen in a similar position, but is now rarely adopted by Masters.

(C) B-K3 or Kt-K2 was better adapted to assist his development.

(D) White has cleverly counterbalanced the adverse attack on the K side, as well as the superiority of the two Bishops, by his pressure on the other wing, and he obtains much the better game by this advance.

(E) Black is forced to block his Queen's Bishop thus, for he cannot afford to allow the opponent the advance of P-B5, followed by P-Q6, which would have formed a strong chain of Pawns for White that must have ultimately given the latter a telling advantage.

(F) Better than 22 PxKP BxKP, 23 BxP P-Q3, followed by P-B5, with a strong attack.

(G) Ill-advised, and overlooking the adverse fine sally. 29 Q-B3 would have given him free hand for further operations on the Q wing, as clearly Black could not answer 29 KtxP, on account of 30 KtxKt BxKt, 31 RxB and Black could not retake since mate is impending by Q-Kt7. White would thus have gained time for manœuvring KKt to QKt5 via QB2 and QR3.

(H) Impetuously throwing away his advantage, which he could have easily maintained by the preliminary precaution of 33 R-KB2.

(I) Highly ingenious and strong enough for a draw at least.

(K) We believe that White could have won here by 37 RxQP B-Bsq, 38 R-K7 P-R4, 39 R-K3, &c.

(L) Best, as White threatened QxR.

(M) In rejecting a draw he exercises good judgment, for it appears that he had a won game in the ending, though he was the exchange behind.

(N) Black makes the most of a bad case and he succeeds with his desperate ingenuity.

(O) If he had realised his danger he would not have grudged the adverse Rook the open file. 53 B-B6, which was pointed out by Mr. Gilberg, would have won the game without much difficulty.

(P) Exceedingly fine and decisive.

(Q) Black's conduct of the ending belongs to the masterpieces of play in positions of a similar description.

GAME 114.—Third of the match, 21st July 1891. White, Mr. Pollock; Black, Mr. Delmar.

From's Gambit.

WHITE.	BLACK.	WHITE.	BLACK.
1 P-KB4	1 P-K4	37 Kt-K4	37 B-K2
2 P-K4(A)	2 B-B4	38 Kt-KB3	38 P-Q6(I)
3 Kt-KB3	3 P-Q3	39 B-Ksq	39 B-Qsq
4 P-B3	4 Kt-QB3(B)	40 B-Q2	40 R(R3)-R4
5 P-Q4	5 PxQP	41 Kt-Kt3	41 R(R4)-B4
6 PxP	6 B-Kt3	42 KtxR	42 RxKt
7 B-Kt5	7 B-Q2	43 Q-R8	43 R-Q4
8 Castles	8 KKt-K2	44 R-Kt8	44 B-K2
9 Kt-B3	9 Castles	45 P-QKt4	45 BxP(K)
10 K-Rsq	10 B-Kt5	46 BxB	46 PxB
11 B-K3	11 P-Q4(C)	47 R-R8	47 R-KR4(L)
12 BxKt	12 PxB	48 P-B5(M)	
13 P-K5	13 Kt-B4		
14 B-B2	14 Q-Q2		
15 Kt-K2(D)	15 QR-Ksq		
16 Kt(K2)-Ktsq	16 R-K3		
17 P-QR4	17 R-R3		
18 Q-Ksq(E)	18 P-R4		
19 P-R3	19 Kt-K2		
20 R-R3	20 B-KB4		
21 Kt-Q2	21 Kt-Kt3		
22 R-KB3	22 Q-K2		
23 Q-K3	23 R-Qsq		
24 R-Kt3(F)	24 P-B4		
25 PxP	25 P-Q5		
26 Q-Kt3	26 BxBP		
27 R-Kt5	27 B-K3		
28 Q-KB3	28 B-Q4		
29 Q-Kt4	29 P-KB3		
30 PxP	30 PxP		
31 R-Ksq	31 Q-Kt2(G)		
32 RxB(H)	32 RxR		
33 R-K8ch	33 Kt-Bsq		
34 Q-B8	34 Q-Q2		48 K-Kt2(N)
35 Q-Kt8	35 K-B2	49 PxKt(O)	49 Q-K2(P)
36 R-B8	36 Kt-K3	50 Q-Kt8ch	50 K-R3
		51 Q-B7	Resigns.

Position after White's 48th move.

NOTES.

(A) It is quite safe to accept From's Gambit by 2 PxP, though Black obtains some temporary attack after 2 P-Q3, 3 PxP BxP, 4 Kt-KB3 Kt-KB3, which, however, ought not to last long by proper play on the other side. The next move transforms the position into one of a regular King's Gambit.

(B) 4 B-KKt5 is the authorised defence.

(C) Injudicious, as the doubled Pawn which the opponent promptly forms in reply ought to have hampered his game all along up to the ending, and White had, therefore, a manifest advantage after the reduction of forces.

(D) More to the point, for operations against the adverse Queen's side, was Kt-QR4, followed soon by R-QBsq.

(E) Parrying a neat thrust which his shrewd opponent had designed. If 18 P-R5 BxP, and White dare not recapture with the Bishop on account of the terrible rejoinder Kt-Kt5 mate, while White's Knight is obviously pinned.

(F) His game deteriorates after this ill-judged move. It was high time to stop the dangerous advance of the QBP, which the adversary was evidently preparing. 24 R-QBsq was sufficient for the purpose, for if then 24 P-QB4, 25 PxP P-Q5, 26 Q-R3, &c.

(G) Black has played exceedingly well after his release on the 24th move, but here he might have more effectively simplified matters by 31 Q-Q2, for if 32 QxQ RxQ, 33 R-B5 Kt-K2, and wins. Or, if 32 R-B5 B-K3, 33 RxB QxR, and White dare not take the Bishop, as he would lose the Queen, his KRP being pinned.

(H) Not as good a resource as 32 R-K8ch RxR, 33 RxB, winning also a Pawn with a good position, considering that Black's R at R3 could not easily get into play

(I) Delmar afterwards pointed out the following combination: 38 KtxP, 39 RxP RxPch, 40 K-Ktsq or Kt-R2 Q-Kt5, and should win.

(K) PxP was undoubtedly superior.

(L) The climax of indecision and, in fact, little short of a blunder, considering the standing of the two players. 47 K-Kt2, 48 Q-Kt8ch K-R3, a line of play pointed out by Mr. Rose, would have made the King safe and he could then win easily.

(M) The surprise is certainly ingenious, but a player of Delmar's strength ought to have forseen it. Compare diagram.

(N) The Kt had no sensible move without leaving a mate open by Q-B8ch, and if 48 RxBP, 49 Q-Kt8ch K-K2, 50 RxPch, and after capturing the Queen he also wins the Rook by Q-R7ch.

(O) [Mr. Gilberg points out that White overlooked mate in two moves by 49 Q-Kt8ch K-R3, 50 Q-Kt6 mate.—Ed.]

(P) Nothing was good, if 49 QxKP, 50 Q-B8ch K-Kt3, 51 R-Kt8ch K-B4, 52 Kt-Q4ch, winning the Queen.

GAME 115.—Fourth of the match, 22nd July 1891. White, Mr. Delmar; Black, Mr. Pollock.

English Opening.

WHITE.	BLACK.	WHITE.	BLACK.
1 P-K4	1 P-K4	18 B-KR6	18 KR-Ksq
2 Kt-KB3	2 Kt-QB3	19 Kt-Kt5	19 Q-Q2
3 P-B3	3 Kt-B3(A)	20 P-KKt4	20 P-Q5(E)
4 P-Q4	4 KtxKP	21 B-B4ch(F)	
5 P-Q5	5 B-B4(B)	(See Diagram below.)	
6 PxKt	6 BxPch		21 K-Rsq(G)
7 K-K2	7 KtPxP	22 Kt-B7ch	22 K-Ktsq
8 Q-R4	8 P-KB4	23 KtxRch	Resigns.
9 QKt-Q2	9 B-Kt3(C)		
10 KtxKt	10 PxKt		
11 QxKP	11 Castles		
12 Kt-Kt5	12 P-Kt3		
13 K-Qsq	13 P-Q4		
14 Q-KR4(D)	14 Q-K2		
15 B-K2	15 B-KB4		
16 R-Bsq	16 QR-Qsq		
17 Kt-B3	17 Q-K3		

NOTES.

(A) We consider this opening favourable for the second player if Black here adopts 3 P-Q4. The text move only leads to an even game.

(B) Too hazardous for a match game. Kt-QKtsq, as played by Weiss against Tschigorin in the Sixth American Chess Congress, is the proper move.

(C) Both parties played according to book up to this, which is new. Usually the game proceeds 9 Castles, 10 KtxKt PxKt, 11 KxB PxKt, 12 P-KKt3, &c.

(D) 14 QxKP B-Kt5ch, 15 B-K2 R-Ksq, 16 QxRch QxQ, 17 BxB, with three pieces against the Queen, was also safe.

(E) Desperate and fatal, but the only other alternative, 20 B-K3, 21 R-B6, left also little hope of retrieving fortunes.

(F) White grasps the winning opportunity vigorously. See diagram.

(G) If 21 B-K3, 22 R-B8ch RxR, 23 BxBch, and wins.

Position after White's 21st move.

GAME 116.—Fifth of the match, 22nd and 23rd July 1891. White, Mr. Pollock; Black, Mr. Delmar.

Four Knights' Game.

WHITE.	BLACK.	WHITE.	BLACK.
1 P-K4	1 P-K4	26 R-KR4	26 K-Kt2
2 Kt-KB3	2 Kt-QB3	27 P-B4	27 Kt-K4
3 Kt-B3	3 Kt-B3	28 K-Q2(F)	28 B-K3
4 P-Q4	4 PxP	29 PxP	29 BxP
5 KtxP	5 B-Kt5	30 R-QKt4	30 KtxB
6 KtxKt	6 KtPxKt	31 R-Kt7ch	31 K-R3
7 B-Q3(A)	7 P-Q4	32 PxKt	32 P-R3
8 PxP	8 PxP	33 K-K3	33 BxP
9 Castles	9 Castles	34 K-B4	34 B-B8
10 B-KKt5	10 BxKt(B)	35 R-KB7	35 P-Kt4ch
11 PxB	11 Q-Q3(C)	36 K-B5	36 BxPch
12 Q-B3	12 B-Kt5	37 KxP	37 K-R4(G)
13 Q-Kt3	13 QxQ	38 P-R3	38 R-Ksq
14 BPxQ(D)	14 Kt-Q2	39 R-KKt7	39 B-Kt3
15 B-KB4	15 P-QB3	40 R-Kt7	40 R-Qsq
16 QR-Ktsq	16 KR-Ksq	41 B-K5	41 R-Bsqch
17 KR-Ksq	17 B-K3	42 K-Kt7	42 R-Ksq
18 B-Q6	18 Kt-Kt3	43 B-B6	43 R-K6
19 B-R6	19 B-Q2	44 R-Kt6(H)	44 RxP
20 K-B2	20 RxR	45 RxRP	45 RxP
21 KxR	21 B-Bsq	46 RxP	46 R-Q6(I)
22 B-Q3	22 P-B3	47 P-R6	47 R-Q2ch
23 R-Kt4	23 K-B2	48 K-B8	48 B-K5
24 P-QR4(E)	24 P-Kt3	49 R-B5	49 P-R3
25 P-R5	25 Kt-Q2	50 R-R5	50 K-Kt3

WHITE.	BLACK.
51 B-K7	51 R-R2
52 B-B5	52 R-Rsqch
53 K-K7	53 P-Kt5
54 B-K3	54 B-B3
55 P-R7	55 R-Ksqch
56 K-Q6	56 B-B6(K)
57 B-B4	57 R-KBsq
58 B-K5	58 P-R4
59 K-K6	59 P-R5
60 R-Kt5	60 R-Ksqch
61 K-Q7	61 R-KBsq(L)
62 K-K6	62 R-Ksqch
63 K-Q7	63 R-KKtsq
64 K-K7	64 B-B3
65 R-Kt6	65 K-B4
66 B-Kt8	66 B-Kt7(M)
67 R-B6ch	Resigns. (N)

Position after White's 67th move.

NOTES.

(A) The usual continuation is here 7 Q-Q4.

(B) This exchange is disadvantageous, for the strength of White's two Bishops outweighs the slight drawback of the doubled Pawn on the latter's Queen's side. Moreover, White can hardly be stopped from advancing P-QB4 at a later stage, with at least an equal game.

(C) P-QB3 was now imperative.

(D) RPxQ was much superior.

(E) If he attempted the capture of the KRP, he would have been blocked in by P-KKt3.

(F) We believe that White could now have obtained a superior game by 28 BxKt PxB, 29 PxP PxP, 30 R-QKt4, threatening P-QB4, with a view of entering with the Bishop at K4.

(G) Necessary, as White threatened P-KKt4, followed by P-KR4, and it would have been fatal for his game if he had given time for those two moves, which confine him in a mating net.

(H) White has pursued a dangerous plan, for Black's combined two passed Pawns, which can now be formed, are certainly stronger than White's isolated QRP.

(I) Quite contrary to general ending maxims. The Rook ought to have attacked the hostile Pawn in the rear by R-QR6, and the hostile Pawn could then hardly become dangerous, while his own Pawns could march on freely, after a few precautions.

(K) B-Rsq was the easiest way of avoiding all danger, and of gaining time for the advance of his own Pawns.

(L) As pointed out by Mr. Gilberg, Black could have drawn at least here and two moves later, retaining good winning prospects by 61 RxB, 62 RxR P-R6. On examination we find that this line of play leads to a sure win for Black; who can now retreat the B to Rsq, and the advance of his Pawns cannot be stopped.

(M) An extraordinary error, B-Rsq was now the only move and good enough for a sure draw, with winning chances. Most likely it would have led to an ending with Rook and Bishop against Rook, as White would have had to sacrifice his Bishop for the two advancing Pawns.

(N) The position is a very curious one. If 67 K-Kt4, 68 B-B4ch, and mates next move by R-R6. Black therefore has no other move than 67 K-K5, whereupon White Queens, with a check.

GAME 117.—Sixth of the match, 23rd July 1891. White, Mr. Delmar; Black, Mr. Pollock.

Ruy Lopez.

WHITE.	BLACK.	WHITE.	BLACK.
1 P-K4	1 P-K4	22 R-Qsq	22 Kt-Q5
2 Kt-KB3	2 Kt-QB3	23 K-Bsq(c)	23 Q-Q2(D)
3 B-Kt5	3 P-QR3	24 P-QKt4	24 P-Kt3
4 B-R4	4 Kt-B3	25 PxP	25 PxP
5 Castles	5 B-K2	26 P-KR4	26 Q-B3(E)
6 P-Q4(A)	6 PxP	27 P-B3	27 Kt-B7
7 P-K5	7 Kt-K5	28 R-K2	28 P-B5(F)
8 KtxP	8 Castles	29 Kt-K4	29 Kt-Kt5
9 R-Ksq	9 Kt-B4	30 Q-Q2	30 Kt-Q6
10 BxKt	10 QPxB	31 Q-B3(G)	31 BxKt(H)
11 Kt-QB3	11 Kt-K3	32 RxB	32 Kt-K4
12 Kt-B5	12 B-Kt4	33 B-B4	33 Q-R5
13 Q-Kt4	13 Kt-Q5(B)	34 R-Q2	34 Kt-Q2
		35 RxP	35 Q-Kt4
		36 K-B2	36 R-Ksq
		37 BxP	37 Q-Kt8
		38 Q-Bsq	38 Q-B4
		39 B-Kt3	39 R-KKtsq
		40 B-B4	40 Kt-K4
		41 BxKt	41 PxB(I)
		42 Q-B3	42 KR-KKt2
		43 K-Ktsq	43 Q-Kt8ch
		44 Q-Bsq	44 Q-Kt3ch
		45 K-Rsq	45 Q-K6
		46 R-K4	46 Q-R3
		47 Q-Kt2	47 Q-QB3
		48 RxP	48 Q-B5
		49 R-K4	49 Q-KB8ch
		50 K-R2	50 P-R3
		51 R-KKt4(K)	

Position after Black's 13th move.

BLACK.

WHITE.

14 BxB	14 BxKt
15 Q-R4	15 P-B3
16 PxP	16 PxP
17 B-R6	17 R-B2
18 QR-Qsq	18 P-B4
19 R-K3	19 K-Rsq
20 QR-Ksq	20 B-Kt3
21 Q-B4	21 KtxP

(See Diagram below.)

51 Q-K8
52 R-Q7   52 P-KR4
53 QRxR   Resigns.

NOTES.

(A) P-Q3 gives a more retentive attack.

(B) A fine novelty. In conjunction with his 15th move, it obtains the superiority for his side.

(c) A necessary preparation for his next move, and, as will be seen, he calculates very deeply in taking that precaution; the following beautiful continuation might have arisen: 23 P-QKt4 PxP, 24 RxKt PxKt, 25 RxQch RxR, and now White has, obviously, no time to capture the QBP, whose advance will win in a few moves, whereas, after the text move, which provides an exit for his King, he will be in no danger at this juncture.

(D) Q-QBsq was by far superior.

(E) A useless speculation for an attack on the K side. Q-KB4 was the right play.

(F) This Pawn is only more weakened than before its further advance.

(G) Threatening RxKt.

(H) If 31 Kt-K4, 32 KtxP, &c.

(I) He could have made a better fight for a draw by retaking with the Queen, and he could then stand exchanging pieces, as his King would afford protection for his Pawns in the ending. His weak KP now becomes the mark of attack and must soon fall, which practically ends the game.

(K) There is no escape from the effect of this powerful blow. See diagram.

Position after White's 51st move.

GAME 118.—Seventh of the match, 23rd and 24th July 1891. White, Mr. Pollock; Black, Mr. Delmar.

French Defence.

WHITE.	BLACK.	WHITE.	BLACK.
1 P-K4	1 P-K3	21 P-KB4	21 Q-Q2
2 P-Q4	2 P-Q4	22 R-Q2	22 Q-R6
3 Kt-Q2(A)	3 P-QB4	23 QR-Qsq	23 R-B3
4 KKt-B3(B)	4 Kt-KB3	24 Kt-Bsq	24 KKtxP(G)
5 P-K5	5 KKt-Q2		(See Diagram below.)
6 P-B3	6 Kt-QB3	25 PxKt	25 R-Kt3ch
7 B-Q3	7 B-K2	26 R-Kt2	26 BxP
8 Castles	8 Castles	27 BxB(H)	27 KtxB
9 R-Ksq	9 R-Ksq	28 RxR	28 PxR
10 Kt-Bsq	10 P-B4	29 R-Q4(I)	29 Q-B6(K)
11 PxP en pass	11 BxP	30 P-KR3	30 R-K4
12 Q-B2(C)	12 Kt-Bsq(D)	31 P-KR4	31 Kt-R6ch(L)
13 PxP	13 P-K4	32 K-R2	32 QxKt
14 B-B5	14 P-K5	33 Q-Kt2	33 QxQch
15 BxB	15 RxB	34 KxQ	34 Kt-B5ch
16 Kt(B3)-Q2	16 Kt-K4	35 K-Kt3	35 Kt-K3
17 Kt-QKt3(E)	17 Kt-Q6	36 R-R4	36 KtxP
18 R-Qsq	18 Kt-Kt3	37 RxP	37 R-B4
19 B-K3	19 B-K4	38 Kt-K2	38 R-B6ch
20 P-Kt3(F)	20 B-Ktsq		

WHITE.	BLACK.	WHITE.	BLACK.
39 K-Kt4	39 K-R2	62 K-Kt2	62 P-Q7
40 Kt-Q4	40 R-B7	63 RxPch	63 K-R3
41 P-Kt4	41 Kt-Q6	Resigns.	
42 Kt-K6	42 K-R3		
43 R-R8	43 Kt-K4ch		
44 K-Kt3	44 R-B6ch		
45 K-Kt2	45 K-R4		
46 R-Q8	46 Kt-B5		
47 Kt-Q4	47 Kt-K6ch		
48 K-R2	48 R-B5		
49 K-Kt3	49 R-Kt5ch		
50 K-B2	50 Kt-Q8ch		
51 K-K2	51 KtxPch		
52 K-Q2	52 R-Kt6		
53 Kt-K6	53 KxP		
54 R-Q7	54 P-QKt4		
55 RxKtP	55 KtxP		
56 Kt-B4	56 P-Kt4		
57 Kt-K6	57 P-Q5		
58 R-R7ch	58 K-Kt5		
59 R-KKt7	59 K-R4		
60 K-K2	60 P-Q6ch		
61 K-B2	61 R-B6ch		

Position after Black's 24th move.

NOTES.

(A) Dr. Tarrasch introduced this remarkable novelty at the Manchester Tournament.

(B) 4 QPxP BxP, 5 Kt-Kt3 would have at least effected the isolation of the QP with the superior game for White.

(C) This excellent move much augments White's superiority of position.

(D) This loses a Pawn, but Black obtains a strong attack. It was anyhow his best resource, for 12 P-KR3 would have allowed White to get a strong hold of the adverse position by the reply B-Kt6, and if 12 P-KKt3, 13 BxP with a fine attack.

(E) Best. If 17 P-QKt4 Kt-Q6, 18 R-Qsq KtxQKtP, winning at least the exchange.

(F) This is weak. Here and later on White ought to have sacrificed the Rook for the Knight, gaining another extra Pawn with an excellent attack on a third Pawn on the Q side, which he could still more strengthen by B-Q4 and Kt-K3.

(G) A very fine sacrifice and quite sound. See diagram.

(H) If 27 KtxKt BxBch, 28 KtxB QxKtch, 29 Kt-B2 RxRch, 30 KxR Q-B6ch, followed by P-K6 with a winning game. Or, if 27 RxR BxBch, 28 KtxB QxKtch, 29 K-Rsq Kt-B7ch, and wins.

(I) It is difficult to find anything good, but this is evidently bad.

(K) Delmar afterwards pointed out that he could have won here straight off by 29 Q-Kt5ch, 30 Kt-Kt3 Q-B6, &c.

(L) 31 Q-Kt5ch, followed by R-R4, would have won soon with heavy forces on the board, which most likely would have led to a more elegant termination. The line of play chosen gives White an opportunity of exchanging Queens, and the ending which follows hardly requires further explanation, for some pretty situations which arise during its progress will be easily appreciated.

GAME 119.—Eighth of the match, played 24th July 1891. White, Mr. Delmar; Black, Mr. Pollock.

Sicilian Defence.

WHITE.	BLACK.	WHITE.	BLACK.
1 P-K4	1 P-QB4	29 QxR	29 QxP(K)
2 Kt-QB3	2 P-K3	30 Q-R5ch	30 K-Kt2
3 Kt-B3	3 P-QKt3	31 R-R3	31 QxBPch(L)
4 P-Q4	4 P-QR3	32 K-Ktsq	32 Q-K5ch
5 P-Q5	5 B-Kt2	33 QR-Q3	33 Kt-B3
6 B-KB4	6 Kt-K2	34 Q-Kt5ch	34 K-B2
7 B-K2	7 Kt-Kt3	35 KR-K3	35 Q-QB5
8 B-Kt3	8 Q-Bsq	36 P-R5	36 P-Kt5
9 P-KR4	9 Kt-K2	37 Q-Kt6ch	37 K-Bsq
10 Kt-R4	10 Q-Qsq	38 R-KB3	38 Q-R5
11 P-B4	11 Kt-Ktsq(A)	39 P-KKt3	39 Q-R8ch
12 PxP(B)	12 BPxP(C)	40 K-R2	Resigns.
13 Kt-Kt5	13 B-K2		
14 B-R5ch	14 P-Kt3		
15 KtxRP(D)	15 BxKP(E)		
16 Q-Kt4(F)			

(See Diagram below.)

	16 RxKt
17 QxB	17 RxB
18 QxPch	18 K-Bsq
19 QxR	19 Kt-QB3
20 CastlesQR	20 P-Kt4(G)
21 KtxP	21 Q-R4
22 KtxQPch	22 K-Kt2
23 B-K5ch(H)	23 KtxB
24 QxKtch	24 K-R2
25 Q-K4ch	25 K-Kt2
26 Kt-K5	26 R-KBsq(I)
27 Q-Kt6ch	27 K-Rsq
28 Kt-B7ch	28 RxKt

Position after White's 16th move.

NOTES.

(A) Black appeared overweighted by the odds against which he had to fight, in the circumstance that his opponent was a game ahead, and had only one more to win, or two to draw, to come off victor in the series. His play bore the mark of that depression which not infrequently overtakes Chess experts as the result of anxiety and overwork. He has wasted no less than four moves with his KKt, and two with his Q, and these two pieces have now to go home to their original squares.

(B) The initiation of a masterly planned attack.

(C) If 12 QPxP, 13 QxQch, followed by KtxKtP.

(D) Alike elegant and correct.

(E) If 15 RxKt, 16 BxPch R-B2, 17 Q-R5, and wins. Of course if 15 PxB, 16 QxRP mate.

(F) White's game is now won. See diagram of this fine position.

(G) The attempt of a counter attack against such superior force, and in such a position, could not possess much vitality.

(H) For quicker winning purposes 23 Kt-K5 KtxKt, 24 BxKtch, followed by R-Q7, was much superior.

(I) White threatened mate in two moves by Q-Kt6ch, followed by Kt-B7ch, or Q-B7ch.

(K) Black gains only a short reprieve by this counter demonstration.

(L) If 31 Q-R8ch, 32 K-Q2, and the King soon escapes pursuit from checks.

As the ninth game could not affect the result it was decided to close the match at the end of the eighth game, and Mr. Delmar was declared the winner.

POLLOCK-SHOWALTER MATCH.

PLAYED AT GEORGETOWN, KENTUCKY.

GAME 120.—First of the match, played 31st July 1891. White, Mr. J. W. Showalter; Black, Mr. Pollock.

WHITE.	BLACK.	WHITE.	BLACK.
1 P-K4	1 P-K4	33 R-R2ch	33 K-Kt6
2 P-KB4	2 PxP	34 RxP	34 KtxP
3 B-B4	3 P-KB4	35 P-B3	35 Kt-B6
4 P-K5	4 Q-R5ch		
5 K-Bsq	5 P-B6		
6 P-Q4	6 PxPch		
7 KxP	7 Kt-QB3		
8 Kt-KB3	8 Q-Kt5ch		
9 K-B2	9 B-K2		
10 P-KR4	10 P-Q3		
11 B-KKt5	11 BxB		
12 PxB	12 P-B5		
13 R-Ktsq	13 Q-R4		
14 P-K6	14 KKt-K2		
15 Kt-B3	15 P-QKt3		
16 Kt-K2	16 R-Bsq		
17 Q-Q2	17 P-Q4		
18 B-Kt5	18 BxP		
19 KtxP	19 Q-B2		
20 KtxB	20 QxKtch		
21 K-Ksq	21 Q-K5ch		
22 Q-K2	22 Q-R5ch		
23 K-Qsq	23 R-B7	36 K-B2	36 R-K7ch
24 Q-K5	24 K-B2	37 K-Kt3	37 Kt-Q7ch
25 BxKt	25 KtxB	38 K-Kt4	38 Kt-K5
26 QxBPch	26 KxKt	39 P-Kt3	39 P-R4ch
27 R-Ksqch	27 K-B4	40 K-Kt5	40 KtxPch
28 Q-B7ch	28 K-Kt5	41 KxP	41 P-Q5
29 R-Ktsqch	29 K-R6	42 RxP	42 P-Q6
30 R-Rsqch	30 K-Kt6	43 R-Q7	43 R-K6
31 QxRch	31 KxQ	44 P-Kt6	
32 RxQ	32 R-Ksq	and wins on the 48th move.	

Position after Black's 35th move.

GAME 121.—Second of the match, played 31st July-1st August. White, Mr. Pollock; Black, Mr. Showalter.

WHITE.	BLACK.	WHITE.	BLACK.
1 P-K4	1 P-K4	12 BxBch	12 QxB
2 Kt-KB3	2 Kt-QB3	13 Q-Kt3	13 Castles
3 P-B3	3 P-Q4	14 B-K3	14 Kt-R4
4 Q-R4	4 P-B3	15 Kt-Kt5	15 P-QR3
5 B-Kt5	5 Kt-K2	16 P-QR4	16 Kt-R5
6 PxP	6 QxP	17 KR-Bsq	17 KtxPch
7 Castles	7 B-Q2	18 K-Rsq	18 B-Q3
8 P-Q4	8 PxP	19 KtxP	19 BxKt
9 PxP	9 Kt-K4	20 B-B4	20 KtxQP
10 Kt-B3	10 KtxKtch	Resigns.	
11 PxKt	11 Q-KB4		

The third game was not preserved.

GAME 122.—Fourth of the match. White, Mr. Pollock; Black, Mr. Showalter.

WHITE.	BLACK.	WHITE.	BLACK.
1 P-K4	1 P-K4	15 QR-Ktsq	15 Q-R4
2 Kt-KB3	2 Kt-QB3	16 QxQ	16 KtxQ
3 B-B4	3 Kt-B3	17 Kt-B5	17 CastlesKR
4 P-Q4	4 PxP	18 KtxB	18 PxKt
5 Castles	5 KtxP	19 RxP	19 QR-Ksq
6 R-Ksq	6 P-Q4	20 QR-Ksq	20 RxR
7 BxP	7 QxB	21 RxR	21 R-Qsq
8 Kt-B3	8 Q-KR4	22 K-Bsq	22 Kt-B3
9 KtxKt	9 B-K3	23 K-K2	23 P-KR3
10 B-Kt5	10 B-QKt5	24 Kt-K5	24 KtxKt
11 P-B3	11 PxP	25 RxKt	25 K-B2
12 PxP	12 B-K2	26 K-K3	
13 BxB	13 KtxB	Drawn game.	
14 Q-R4ch	14 Kt-B3		

GAME 123.—Fifth of the match. White, Mr. Showalter; Black, Mr. Pollock.

WHITE.	BLACK.	WHITE.	BLACK.
1 P-K4	1 P-K4	9 KtxKt	9 PxKt
2 P-KB4	2 P-Q4	10 QxP	10 Q-Q2
3 Kt-KB3	3 QPxP	11 B-K2	11 R-Ksq
4 KtxP	4 B-QB4	12 Q-B4	12 Q-K2
5 B-B4	5 Kt-KR3	13 P-Q4	13 B-QKt5
6 Kt-QB3	6 Q-Q5	14 B-Q2	14 BxKt
7 R-Bsq	7 Castles	15 PxB	15 P-R4
8 Q-K2	8 Kt-B3	16 Q-Q3	16 B-B4

WHITE.	BLACK.	WHITE.	BLACK.
17 Q-B4	17 BxP	19 K-Ksq	19 Kt-Q3
18 K-B2	18 Kt-B4	Resigns.	

GAME 124.—Sixth of the match. White, Mr. Pollock; Black, Mr. Showalter.

Ruy Lopez.

WHITE.	BLACK.	WHITE.	BLACK.
1 P-K4	1 P-K4	22 KtxBch	22 RxKt
2 Kt-KB3	2 Kt-QB3	23 Q-Kt5ch	23 K-B2
3 B-Kt5	3 Kt-B3	24 Q-R5ch	24 K-K3
4 Castles	4 KtxP	25 Q-Kt4ch	25 K-B2
5 P-Q4	5 B-K2	Drawn game.	
6 Q-K2	6 Kt-Q3		
7 BxKt	7 KtPxB		
8 PxP	8 Kt-Kt2		
9 Kt-Q4	9 Castles		
10 Kt-QB3	10 Kt-B4		
11 R-Qsq	11 Q-Ksq		
12 Kt-B5	12 B-Qsq(A)		
13 P-QKt4	13 Kt-K3		
14 R-Q3	14 P-B3		
15 R-Kt3	15 PxP		
16 KtxP(B)	16 KtxKt		
17 B-R6	17 R-B2		
18 Q-R5	18 B-B3		
19 Kt-K4	19 Q-K2		
20 BxKt			
(See Diagram below.)			
	20 RxB(c)		
21 R-KB3	21 R-Kt3(D)		

Position after White's 20th move.

NOTES.

(A) Hardly time for this. White might play 13 Q-Kt4 at once, instead of the weak text move.

(B) Unsound, though very tempting.

(c) If BxB, 21 Kt-Kt5.

(D) Allows White a curious draw; the proper move was 21 B-Kt4.

GAME 125.—Seventh of the match. White, Mr. Showalter; Black, Mr. Pollock.

King's Gambit Declined.

WHITE.	BLACK.	WHITE.	BLACK.
1 P-K4	1 P-K4	4 Kt-KB3	4 P-Q4
2 P-KB4	2 Kt-KB3	5 P-Q3	5 Kt-B4
3 PxP(A)	3 KtxP	6 P-Q4	6 Kt-K3

WHITE.	BLACK.	WHITE.	BLACK.
7 B-Q3	7 P-QB4		33 P-Q7(G)
8 P-B3	8 Kt-B3	34 P-KR4	34 BxKt(H)
9 Castles(B)	9 PxP	35 PxB	35 Q-KB8ch
10 PxP	10 KtxQP	36 K-R2	36 Q-B7ch
11 KtxKt	11 KtxKt	37 K-R3	37 QxBPch
12 Q-R4ch	12 Kt-B3	38 K-R2	38 K-Ktsq(I)
13 Q-KB4	13 B-B4ch	39 BxQP	39 Q-B7ch
14 K-Rsq	14 B-K3	40 K-R3	40 QxB
15 Kt-Q2	15 Q-B2	41 QxP	41 Q-K6ch
16 Kt-B3	16 CastlesQR(C)	42 K-Kt4	42 QxP
17 Q-QR4	17 P-KR3(D)	43 P-R5	43 B-B2
18 B-Q2	18 K-Ktsq	44 P-R6	44 P-R3
19 P-QKt4	19 B-Kt3	45 Q-Kt8	45 Q-Kt6ch
20 KR-Bsq	20 Q-Q2(E)	46 K-B5	46 Q-B5ch
21 P-Kt5	21 Kt-K2	47 K-Kt6	47 Q-K5ch
22 B-Kt4	22 R-QBsq	48 K-B7	48 Q-B4ch
23 B-Q6ch	23 K-Rsq	49 K-K8	49 Q-B3
24 Q-R3	24 RxRch	50 Q-Kt7	50 Kt-Q3ch
25 RxR	25 R-QBsq		
26 RxRch	26 KtxR		
27 B-B8(F)	27 B-KB4		
28 BxP	28 B-K5		
29 B-K2	29 P-Q5		
30 BxP	30 P-Q6		
31 B-Qsq	31 QxP		
32 Q-B8	32 Q-B5		
33 B-Kt3			

Position after White's 33rd move.

Position after Black's 50th move.

51 K-Q7	51 Q-Qsqch
52 K-K6	52 Q-Ksqch
53 Q-K7	53 QxQch
54 KxQ	54 Kt-B4ch
55 K-B6	55 KtxP
56 B-K6	56 B-B5
57 P-R4	57 K-B2
Resigns.	

NOTES.

(A) 3 Kt-QB3, converting the opening into a common type of the "Vienna," is also a good continuation.

(B) Losing a Pawn unnecessarily.

(C) Castling on the K side would be quite as good.

(D) This "country" move was hardly called for.

(E) Threatening 21 Kt×P, 22 B-QKt5 Q-Q3, 23 B-KB4 P-B3, &c.

(F) Taking advantage of the country move.

(G) A resource unforseen by White. It appears to win offhand, but Mr. Showalter contrives to give a great deal of trouble yet.

(H) If B×Q mate follows in four moves.

(I) Nothing apparently comes of any further checks at present.

GAME 126.—Eighth of the match. White, Mr. Pollock; Black, Mr. Showalter.

WHITE.	BLACK.	WHITE.	BLACK.
1 P-K4	1 P-K4	33 Kt×P	33 R-R5
2 Kt-KB3	2 Kt-QB3	34 P-KKt4	34 R-R7
3 P-B3	3 P-Q4	35 K-K2	35 K-Q5
4 Q-R4	4 P-B3	36 K-B3	36 R-R8
5 B-Kt5	5 Kt-K2	37 Kt-K4	37 R-QKt8
6 P×P	6 Q×P	38 P-Kt4	38 K-K4
7 Castles	7 B-Q2	39 P-R3	39 R-Kt6
8 P-Q4	8 P×P	40 Kt×P	40 R×RP
9 P×P	9 Kt-K4		
10 B×Bch	10 Q×B		
11 Q×Qch	11 Kt×Q		
12 Kt-B3	12 Castles		
13 B-B4	13 Kt-QKt3		
14 QR-Bsq	14 QKt-Q4		
15 B-Kt3	15 Kt-B4		
16 KR-Ksq	16 Kt×B		
17 RP×Kt	17 B-Kt5		
18 Kt×Kt	18 B×R		
19 Kt-K7ch	19 K-Q2		
20 R×B	20 KR-Ksq		

Position after Black's 40th move.

(See Diagram below.)

21 Kt-B5	21 R×Rch
22 Kt×R	22 P-KKt4
23 P-KKt4	23 K-B3
24 K-Bsq	24 K-Q4
25 K-K2	25 R-Ksqch
26 K-Q2	26 R-KRsq
27 Kt-B2	27 P-KR4
28 KKt-K3ch	28 K-B3
29 Kt-K7ch	29 K-Kt4
30 P×P	30 R×P
31 Kt(K7)-Q5	31 P-QB4
32 P×P	32 K×P

41 Kt-B7ch	41 K-B3
42 Kt-Q8	42 R-Kt6
43 Kt×P	43 K-Kt3
44 Kt-R5	44 R×P
45 Kt-B6	45 R-R5
46 Kt-B4	46 K-Kt4

Position after Black's 20th move.

WHITE.	BLACK.
47 Kt(B6)-R5	47 R-R7
48 K-Kt3	48 RxP
49 KxR	49 KxP
50 Kt-K3ch	50 K-Kt4
51 K-Kt3	51 K-B3
52 K-B4	52 K-Kt3
53 Kt-Kt4	53 P-R3

Drawn game.

Showalter won the match by 6½ to 5½, the two games United States Chess Association Lexington Meeting being reckoned in.

POLLOCK-GOSSIP MATCH.

THE following games are selected from the Pollock-Gossip contest. The match was played under the auspices, and at the rooms of the Montreal Chess Club, and considerable interest was displayed in this contest between the two well-known Masters who had made Montreal their home for the time being. The games were played at the rate of three a week—on Tuesdays, Thursdays, and Saturdays—the first to win seven games to be the victor. Mr. Pollock opened the ball with a game in which he gave a taste of the very best of his quality.

GAME 127.—The first of the match, played on Saturday, 15th December 1894. White, Mr. G. H. D. Gossip; Black, Mr. Pollock.

Vienna Opening.

WHITE.	BLACK.	WHITE.	BLACK.
1 P-K4	1 P-K4	8 B-K3	8 PxP !
2 Kt-QB3	2 B-B4	9 BxB(D)	9 PxB
3 P-B4	3 P-Q3	10 Q-B2	10 Castles
4 Kt-B3	4 Kt-KB3	11 Kt-K2(E)	11 Q-K2(F)
5 B-B4(A)	5 Kt-B3	12 CastlesKR	12 BxKt
6 P-Q3	6 P-QR3(B)	13 PxB !	13 Kt-KR4 !
7 Q-K2(C)	7 B-KKt5	14 P-QR3 ?	14 QR-Qsq

Position after Black's 14th move.

BLACK.

WHITE.

WHITE.	BLACK.
15 Kt-B3	15 R-Q3
16 Kt-Q5	16 Q-Kt4ch
17 Q-Kt2(G)	17 Q-R5(H)
18 K-Rsq	18 R-Kt3(I)
19 QxR	19 RPxQ
20 K-Kt2	20 Kt-K4
21 B-Kt3	21 R-Qsq
22 QR-Ksq	22 P-QB3
23 Kt-B3	23 P-KKt4
24 Kt-K2	24 P-Kt5
25 PxP	25 KtxKtP
Resigns.	

NOTES.

(A) Black played the KKt first, because if QKt-B3, the B might pin. But here White might play 5 PxP PxP, 6 KtxP Castles (better for Black than Q-Q5), 7 Kt-Q3!

(B) Forstalling Kt-QR4.

(C) Kt-K2 is Steinitz's move.

(D) If 9 BxP Kt-Q5, 10 Q-Qsq Kt-R4, 11 B-KKt3 BxKt, 12 PxB Q-Kt4, with a strong attack.

(E) Castling seem advisable.

(F) Strong from every point of view. If KtxP now, Black rejoins KtxP.

(G) K-Rsq is no better.

(H) Q-R3 allows K-B2.

(I) Winning the Queen by force.

GAME 128.—Second of the match, played Tuesday, 18th December 1894. White, Mr. Pollock; Black, Mr. Gossip.

King's Bishop's Opening.

WHITE.	BLACK.	WHITE.	BLACK.
1 P-K4	1 P-K4	14 Kt-Q2	14 P-KR3
2 B-B4	2 Kt-QB3	15 B-K3	15 P-KKt4
3 Kt-K2	3 Kt-B3	16 K-R2	16 QR-Qsq
4 Castles	4 B-B4	17 P-Kt3	17 P-QR4
5 Kt-Kt3	5 P-Q3	18 P-B3	18 P-Kt4
6 P-QB3	6 Castles	19 Kt-B5	19 BxKt
7 P-Q3	7 Kt-KKt5	20 PxB	20 Kt-Q4
8 P-KR3	8 Kt-B3	21 Kt-Bsq	21 KtxP
9 B-Kt3	9 P-Q4	22 RxR	22 RxR
10 B-Kt5	10 PxP	23 Kt-Kt3	23 Kt-Kt5
11 PxP	11 QxQ	24 P-B6	24 B-Bsq
12 RxQ	12 B-K3	25 B-KB5	25 Kt(Kt5)-Q4
13 B-B2	13 B-K2	26 B-Q2	26 P-QKt5

S

138

WHITE.	BLACK.
27 P-R3	27 KtxP
28 PxP	28 PxP
29 B-Bsq	29 B-B4
30 B-B2	30 B-Q5
(See Diagram.)	
31 R-R6	31 P-K5
32 Kt-B5	32 B-K4ch
33 P-Kt3	33 Kt-K7
34 KtxPch	34 K-Kt2
35 Kt-B5ch	35 K-Bsq
36 QBxP	36 BxPch
37 KtxB	37 Kt-Q5
38 BxKt	38 KtxPch
39 K-Rsq	Resigns.

Position after Black's 30th move.

GAME 129.—Eighth of the match, played 29th December 1894-1st January 1895. White, Mr. Pollock; Black, Mr. Gossip.

King's Knight's Gambit.

WHITE.	BLACK.	WHITE.	BLACK.
1 P-K4	1 P-K4	24 P-QR4	24 K-Kt2
2 P-KB4	2 PxP	25 P-R5	25 R-Bsq
3 Kt-KB3	3 P-KKt4	26 K-Ktsq	26 R-B4
4 B-B4	4 B-Kt2	27 P-R6	27 Kt-B5
5 Castles	5 P-Q3	28 P-KKt3	28 KtxP
6 P-Q4	6 Kt-QB3		
7 KtxP(A)	7 BxPch		
8 K-Rsq	8 QxKt		
9 RxP	9 Q-Kt3(B)		
10 BxPch	10 QxB		
11 RxQ	11 KxR		
12 Q-R5ch	12 K-K2		
13 B-Kt5ch	13 B-B3?		
14 Kt-B3	14 B-K3		
15 R-KBsq	15 R-KBsq		

(See Diagram below.)

16 B-R4(c)	16 BxB
17 RxR	17 KxR
18 QxB	18 B-B2(D)
19 Kt-Q5(E)	19 BxKt
20 PxB	20 Kt(B3)-K2
21 Q-Q4	21 Kt-Kt3
22 QxP	22 Kt-B3
23 QxP	23 Kt-Ksq

Position after Black's 15th move.

WHITE.	BLACK.	WHITE.	BLACK.
29 P-R7	29 Kt-K6	32 K-R3	32 P-R4
30 P-R4	30 R-B8ch	33 P-R8(Q)(F)	Resigns.
31 K-R2	31 R-B7ch		

NOTES.

(A) This is quite premature. 7 P-B3 is necessary.

(B) An altogether unnecessary sacrifice, even though he remains with an equivalent for the Queen. A very good move here is P-B3, after which White's attack is utterly gone.

(C) Since his pecadillo on the seventh move White has certainly played irreproachably. The text move is not an obvious one.

(D) If KKt-K2, 19 Q-B6ch wins a piece.

(E) This move wins an important Pawn.

(F) In the nick of time, for if Kt-Kt5 White would reply Q-Kt2.

This match ended in a draw. Each scored six games, with five draws.

CONSULTATION GAMES.

GAME 130.—Fourth of a match, Mr. Pollock v. Messrs. Torsch and Schofield in consultation. White, Mr. Pollock; Black, The Allies.

Evans Gambit.

WHITE.	BLACK.	WHITE.	BLACK.
1 P-K4	1 P-K4	25 KR-Bsq	25 RxP
2 Kt-KB3	2 Kt-QB3	26 R-B3	26 R-K5
3 B-B4	3 B-B4	27 KtxR	27 PxKt
4 P-QKt4	4 BxKtP	28 B-R7ch	28 K-Bsq
5 P-B3	5 B-R4	29 B-K3	29 P-Kt6
6 P-Q4	6 PxP		
7 Castles	7 P-Q3		
8 PxP(A)	8 B-KKt5		
9 B-QKt5(B)	9 B-Q2		
10 P-K5	10 QKt-K2(C)		
11 BxBch	11 QxB		
12 Kt-Kt5	12 Kt-R3		
13 Kt-K4	13 Kt(R3)-B4		
14 P-Kt4	14 KtxP !(D)		
15 PxP	15 PxP		
16 B-Kt2	16 Kt(K2)-B3		
17 P-KR3	17 B-Kt3		
18 QKt-B3	18 P-KR4 ? ?(E)		
19 Kt-Q5	19 CastlesQR		
20 KtxB	20 PxKt		
21 BxKt	21 PxP		
22 BxQKtP	22 P-B4		
23 Q-B4	23 K-Ktsq(must)		
24 Kt-Kt3	24 QR-Ksq		

Position after Black's 29th move.

They are biting like a game and hardshell market crab. White now mates by force in eight moves, all checks. The mate is instructive and very pretty.

NOTES.

(A) White can get a strong attack by 8 Kt-Kt5, and if Kt-K4, 9 KtxBP KtxKt, 10 BxKtch KxB, 11 Q-R5ch, or 9 PxP KtxB, 10 Q-R4ch, &c.

(B) Or 9 Q-R4 B-Q2, 10 Q-Kt3, followed by Kt-B3, with a favourable position.

(C) 10 KtxKP would cost Black a piece in the following curious manner: 11 Q-K2 BxB, 12 QxBch Kt-B3, 13 P-Q5 P-QR3, 14 Q-R4 P-QKt4, 15 Q-R3 Kt-Kt5, 16 QxB Kt-B7, 17 Q-B3, &c.

(D) Highly ingenious, as if White takes Kt, the allies would draw by perpetual check, making their score 2½ to 1½, thus ½ a game nearer the goal of 5, with a P and move partie to follow.

(E) The allies are now two Pawns to the good, and here P-Q4 was not only essential, but left them with a distinct superiority every way.

(F) As a matter of course.

(G) After this solid defensive move (the Knight has an eye on the weak KRsq) White gets time to use his Rooks, and bring the contest to a rather pretty finale.

GAME 131.—One of six simultaneous (consultation) games played at Buffalo. White, Mr. Pollock; Black, Allies.

Two Knights' Defence.

Position after Black's 14th move.

WHITE.	BLACK.
1 P-K4	1 P-K4
2 Kt-KB3	2 Kt-QB3
3 B-B4	3 Kt-B3
4 P-Q4	4 PxP
5 Castles	5 KtxP
6 R-Ksq	6 P-Q4
7 BxP	7 QxB
8 Kt-B3	8 Q-KB4
9 KtxKt	9 B-K3
10 KtxP	10 KtxKt
11 QxKt	11 P-KR3
12 P-QKt3	12 P-R3
13 B-Kt2	13 P-QR4
14 QR-Qsq	14 P-KB3

(See Diagram.)

White mates in five moves.

CORRESPONDENCE GAMES.

GAME 132.—White, Mr. Pollock; Black, Mr. J. L. McCutcheon, Pittsburgh, Pa.

French Defence.

WHITE.	BLACK.	WHITE.	BLACK.
1 P-K4	1 P-K3	2 P-Q4	2 P-Q4

WHITE.	BLACK.	WHITE.	BLACK.
3 Kt-QB3	3 Kt-KB3	18 B-R5	18 BxP
4 B-KKt5	4 B-Kt5	19 BxPch	19 K-K2
5 P-K5	5 P-KR3	20 QR-Ksq	20 B-R3
6 B-R4	6 P-KKt4	21 P-B4	21 BxKt
7 B-Kt3	7 Kt-K5	22 PxB	22 Q-Q3
8 Kt-K2	8 P-QB4	23 RxB	23 KtxR
9 P-QR3	9 B-R4	24 Q-Q4	24 QxP
10 Q-Q3	10 PxP	25 BxKt	25 KR-KBsq
11 KtxP	11 KtxKt	26 Q-KB4	26 K-Q2
12 PxKt	12 Q-B2	27 QxP	27 Q-B4ch
13 Kt-Kt5	13 Q-B3	28 K-Rsq	28 Q-K2
14 B-K2	14 Kt-Q2	29 Q-Kt7	29 P-R3
15 CastlesKR	15 B-B2	30 BxPch	30 KxB
16 P-KB4	16 PxP	31 Q-Kt6ch	Resigns.
17 BxP	17 P-Kt3		

GAME 133.—A brilliant Muzio between the same players, Mr. Mc Cutcheon here playing White.

WHITE.	BLACK.	WHITE.	BLACK.
1 P-K4	1 P-K4	27 QxBch	27 Q-B2
2 Kt-QB3	2 Kt-QB3	28 Q-B8	28 P-R4
3 P-B4	3 PxP	29 R-K8	29 P-R5
4 Kt-B3	4 P-KKt4	30 R-Qsq	30 P-R6
5 B-B4	5 P-Kt5	31 RxBch	31 QxR
6 Castles	6 PxKt	32 R-Q8	32 PxPch
7 QxP(A)	7 Q-B3	33 KxP	33 QxR
8 Kt-Q5(B)	8 Q-Q5ch	34 QxQch	34 K-R2
9 K-Rsq	9 QxB	35 Q-R5ch	35 K-Ktsq
10 P-Q3	10 Q-Q5(c)	36 P-Kt6	Resigns.
11 KtxPch	11 K-Qsq		
12 BxP	12 P-Q3		
13 P-B3	13 Q-Kt2		
14 KtxR	14 B-Kt5		
15 Q-B2	15 K-Bsq		
16 P-Kt4	16 K-Ktsq(D)		
17 P-Kt5	17 Kt-Qsq(E)		
18 Kt-Kt6	18 PxKt		
19 QxP	19 Kt-K3(F)		
20 B-K3	20 Kt-B4		
21 P-Q4(G)			

(See Diagram below.)

	21 KtxP		
22 P-Q5	22 Kt-B4		
23 BxKt	23 PxB		
24 P-Q6	24 P-B3		
25 Q-Q8ch	25 B-Bsq		
26 QR-Ksq	26 BxP		

Position after White's 21st move.

BLACK.

WHITE.

Notes.

(A) The moves thus far, inclusive, were stipulated by White.

(B) Reckless of his minor pieces.

(C) If Kt-Q5, 11 PxQ KtxQ, 12 KtxPch K-Qsq, 13 KtxR Kt-K4, 14 BxP KtxP, and White will get the best of it.

(D) If QxP, 17 KR-Bsq QxKtP, 18 QxP, &c.

(E) If Kt-R4, White wins the Kt by the text continuation.

(F) Q-B3 is probably better, as the reply 20 B-K5 is not greatly to be feared.

(G) A very fine combination.

(H) Black has nothing better. Mr. McCutcheon finishes in great style.

GAME 134.—A Muzio Gambit. White, Mr. Pollock; Black, Mr. McCutcheon.

WHITE.	BLACK.	WHITE.	BLACK.
1 P-K4	1 P-K4	24 P-B3	24 P-KR4
2 P-KB4	2 PxP	25 P-KR3	25 P-R5
3 Kt-KB3	3 P-KKt4	26 K-B3	26 K-K3
4 B-B4	4 P-Kt5	27 K-K4	27 K-Q2
5 Castles	5 PxKt	28 R-KR8	28 B-Kt6
6 QxP	6 Q-B3	29 R-R7ch	29 Kt-K2
7 P-K5	7 QxP	30 P-B4	Resigns.
8 BxPch	8 KxB		
9 P-Q4	9 Q-KB4(A)		
10 BxP	10 Kt-KB3		
11 Kt-B3	11 P-Q3		
12 QR-Ksq	12 R-Ktsq		
13 Q-K2	13 Q-Kt3		
14 Kt-Q5(B)			

(See Diagram below.)

	14 QKt-Q2(c)
15 KtxP	15 R-Ktsq
16 Kt-K8	16 QxPch(D)
17 QxQ	17 RxQch
18 KxR	18 KtxKt
19 BxPch	19 Kt(K1)-B3(E)
20 BxR	20 KtxB
21 RxKtch	21 KxR
22 R-K8	22 B-Q3
23 RxB	23 Kt-B3

Position after White's 14th move.

Notes.

(A) Considered better than QxPch.

(B) See diagram of this remarkable position.

(C) If KtxKt, 17 B-R6ch Q-B4!, 18 RxQch BxR, 19 Q-R5ch, and must win.

(D) Again KtxKt loses through 17 B-R6ch.

(E) He cannot prevent the recovery of material whereby White remains with just enough superiority to win.

Result of Correspondence match (4 games): Pollock 3, McCutcheon 1.

GAMES PLAYED IN CANADA.

The following were played in a "simultaneous" at the Montreal Chess Club, March 1893.

GAME 135.—White, Mr. Pollock; Black, Mr. Robertson.

WHITE.	BLACK.	WHITE.	BLACK.
1 P-K4	1 P-K4	13 Kt-QB3	13 BxB
2 Kt-KB3	2 Kt-QB3	14 PxB	14 Q-R5
3 B-B4	3 Kt-B3	15 Q-Kt2	15 PxP
4 Q-K2	4 B-K2	16 PxP	16 P-R3
5 P-Q4	5 P-Q3	17 R-B3	17 Kt-B3
6 P-Q5	6 Kt-QR4	18 QR-KBsq(B)	18 Kt-R2
7 B-Q3	7 P-QKt3	19 R-R3	19 Q-K2
8 Castles	8 Castles	20 Kt-B3	20 Kt-Kt4
9 P-KR3	9 Kt-Kt2	21 R-R5	21 KtxKtch
10 B-K3	10 Kt-Ksq	22 RxKt	22 P-Kt3
11 P-KKt4	11 P-KR4(A)	23 R-Rsq	23 Q-Kt4
12 Kt-R2	12 B-Kt4	24 Q-R2	Resigns.

NOTES.

(A) A weak move and the beginning of Black's downfall.

(B) An excellent move. Black in reply cannot capture Pawn with Bishop on account of 19 KtxB KtxKt (if QxKt, 20 R-Kt3 Q-R5, 21 B-K2, and wins in a few moves), 20 R-R3 Q-Kt4, 21 R-B5 Q-Kt3, 22 R-Kt3.

GAME 136.—White, Mr. Babson; Black, Mr. Pollock.

Position after Black's 28th move.

The game continued:

WHITE.	BLACK.
29 RxR	29 KxR
30 K-Kt2	30 K-Q3
31 RxBch	31 RxR
32 BxR	32 KxB
33 K-R3	

and Mr. Pollock continued until the 49th move, when he resigned.

GAME 137.—White, Mr. Pollock; Black, Mr. Wheeldon.

WHITE.	BLACK.	WHITE.	BLACK.
1 P-KB4(A)	1 P-Q4	2 P-K3	2 B-B4

WHITE.	BLACK.	WHITE.	BLACK.
3 Kt-KB3	3 P-K3	18 QPxP	18 KtxKt
4 Kt-B3	4 Kt-KB3	19 PxKt	19 R-B4
5 P-QKt3	5 P-B3	20 QR-Ktsq	20 Q-K2
6 B-Kt2	6 B-Q3	21 PxP	21 R-B7ch
7 B-Q3	7 BxB	22 K-Q3	22 R-R7
8 PxB	8 Castles	23 R-Kt2	23 R-Qsq(B)
9 P-KKt4	9 KtxP	24 K-K2	24 B-Kt5
10 R-KKtsq	10 P-KB4	25 B-Q4	25 RxR
11 Kt-KKt5	11 P-KR3	26 QxR	26 P-K4
12 P-KR3	12 PxKt	27 P-Kt6	27 Q-K3
13 PxKt	13 Kt-Q2	28 R-KRsq	28 PxB
14 KtPxP	14 RxP	29 Q-Kt5	29 Q-B3
15 Q-Kt4	15 Kt-B4	30 Q-R5	30 P-Q6ch
16 K-K2	16 P-Q5	31 K-Qsq	31 Q-R8 mate.
17 Kt-K4	17 QPxP		

NOTES.

(A) This is the From Gambit, but it is often called Bird's Opening, probably because he adopted it as his favourite on many occasions. A defence much in favour is P-K4, 2 PxP P-Q3, offering a Pawn for a strong counter attack.

(B) All this part of the game up to the finish is played by Black in fine style.

GAME 138.—White, Mr. Pollock; Black, Mr. Beecher.

WHITE.	BLACK.	WHITE.	BLACK.
1 P-K4	1 P-K4	11 Kt-Kt5ch	11 K-Ktsq
2 Kt-QB3	2 Kt-KB3	12 Kt-K6 !	12 Q-Ksq
3 P-B4	3 B-Kt5(A)	13 KtxBP	13 Q-Qsq
4 PxP	4 BxKt	14 Kt-K6	14 Q-Ksq
5 QPxB	5 Kt-Ktsq	15 R-B8ch	15 QxR
6 Kt-B3	6 Kt-K2	16 KtxQ	16 KxKt
7 B-QB4	7 P-KR3	17 P-K6	17 K-Ksq
8 Castles	8 QKt-B3	18 Q-R5ch	18 P-Kt3
9 B-K3	9 Kt-R4	19 QxKt	
10 BxPch	10 KxB	and White won after a few moves.	

NOTES.

(A) Bad; P-Q4 is the best move.

GAME 139.—An interesting partie played at the Montreal Chess Club, 14th May 1895. The game is the more interesting inasmuch as Mr. Pollock, on being challenged to the conflict, observed that he and Mr. de Soyres had not enjoyed a game together for ten years. Mr. de Soyres, then in London, played two beautiful games with his present opponent in the first Congress of the British Chess Association, 1885. White, Rev. J. de Soyres; Black, Mr. Pollock.

Scotch Gambit.

WHITE.	BLACK.	WHITE.	BLACK.
1 P-K4	1 P-K4	20 B-Kt3(I)	20 Kt-K4
2 Kt-KB3	2 Kt-QB3	21 Kt-B4	21 K-Ktsq(k)
3 P-Q4	3 PxP	22 P-R4(L)	22 Kt-B3
4 B-QB4	4 B-B4	23 P-R5	23 Kt-Q5(M)
5 Castles	5 P-Q3	24 PxB(N)	24 KtxQ
6 Kt-Kt5(A)	6 Kt-R3	25 PxBPch(o)	25 KxP
7 P-KR3(B)	7 Q-K2	26 RxKt(P)	26 B-B3
8 P-QB3	8 B-Q2(c)	27 Kt-R5	27 R-QKtsq
9 B-B4	9 CastlesQR(D)	28 KtxB	28 PxKt
10 Kt-Q2	10 P-B3	29 RxPch	29 K-Q2
11 KKt-B3	11 P-KKt4	30 R-R3	30 R-Kt2
12 B-R2(E)			

Position after White's 12th move.

Position after Black's 30th move.

	12 PxP(F)	31 R-Bsq(Q)	31 KR-QKtsq
13 PxP	13 P-Kt5	32 B-B6ch(R)	32 K-Qsq
14 Kt-Q4(G)	14 KtxKt	33 R-Q3	33 R-Kt8
15 PxKt	15 BxP	34 RxR	34 RxRch
16 R-Ktsq	16 PxP	35 KxP	35 K-B2
17 Q-Kt3	17 B-Kt3	36 B-Q5	36 R-Kt5(s)
18 B-Q5	18 PxP(H)	37 R-B3ch	37 K-Ktsq
19 KR-Bsq	19 Kt-Kt5	38 R-B6	38 R-Kt3

and Black won after a few moves.

NOTES.

(A) White not having regained the Gambit Pawn, is almost "condemned" to a premature attack. If 6 P-B3 B-KKt5, 7 Q-Kt3 BxKt, with the advantage in every variation. However, 7 B-B4 has been tried without disadvantage for White, and perhaps it is a good move.

(B) In faint hopes that Black would Castle, when 8 Q-R5 would yield a formidable attack, the advance of the KBP following quickly.

(c) Black defends after the most approved fashion.

T

(D) If P-B3 at once, White might reply with Q-R5ch.

(E) White has the option of PxP, and, if Black recapture, of posting this B on K3 instead.

(F) Here P-Q6 has great merits, as it may give the second player later on more leisure for his K side attack.

(G) "Take all my Pawns, but let me have at your King!"

(H) Probably under-estimating the force of his opponent's designs.

(I) 20 Kt-B4 deserves consideration.

(K) KtxKt would give Black an easier defence.

(L) A very strong, if obvious, advance.

(M) Black's intention, if 24 Q-Kt2, was to play B-R6 (threatening mate on the move), and if 25 K-R2 Q-Q2, or if 25 Kt-Q2 Kt-K7ch, breaking the attack.

(N) This brilliant stroke almost deserved victory.

(O) If 25 PxRPch K-Rsq, 26 RxKt B-B3! and we cannot quite see a White win.

(P) If 26 KtxPch KtxR, 27 RxKtch B-B3, 28 Kt-B5ch Q-Q3, and Black wins.

(Q) White seems to miss his way to victory here; after 31 BxP! R-Kt8ch, 32 KxP QxB, 33 RxPch, Black is lost.

(R) BxR was surely better.

(S) Threatening to simplify matters by RxP.

GAME 140.—Played at the Cercle St. Denis, Montreal, 1895, at odds of Rook. White, Mr. Pollock; Black, Mr. B.

Remove White's Queen's Rook.

WHITE.	BLACK.	WHITE.	BLACK.
1 P-KB4	1 Kt-KB3	13 P-KKt4	13 KtPxP
2 P-K3	2 P-K3	14 KtxP	14 Kt-K4
3 Kt-KB3	3 P-Q4	15 PxP	15 KtxB
4 P-QKt3	4 Kt-B3	16 PxKt	16 PxP
5 B-Kt2	5 P-KKt3	17 K-Rsq	17 P-B3
6 Kt-B3	6 B-Kt2	18 R-Ktsq	18 R-KKtsq
7 B-R3	7 Kt-K5	19 Q-R5ch	19 Q-B2
8 KtxKt	8 PxKt	20 R-Kt6	20 B-Q2
9 Kt-Kt5	9 P-B4	21 Kt-K6	21 P-R3
10 B-B4	10 Q-B3	22 RxB	22 QxQ
11 Castles	11 P-KB3	23 R-K7 mate.	
12 Kt-R3	12 P-KKt4		

GAME 141.—Played in the Handicap Tournament, Montreal Chess Club, 1894-5. White, Mr. F. J. Marshall; Black, Mr. Pollock.

Odds of Pawn and two moves. Remove Black's KBP.

WHITE.	BLACK.	WHITE.	BLACK.
1 P-K4	2 P-Q3	6 P-B3	6 Kt-B4
2 P-Q4		7 P-KKt4	7 Kt-Kt2
3 B-Q3	3 Kt-QB3	8 P-B5	8 QPxP
4 P-K5	4 P-KKt3	9 PxP	
5 P-KB4	5 KtxQP(A)		

Position after White's 9th move.

WHITE.	BLACK.
20 Kt-Q4	20 B-Q4(G)
21 P-B4	21 BxB
22 KtxB	22 R-R4
23 B-B4ch	

Position after White's 23rd move.

	9 P-KR4(B)
10 Q-B3	10 Kt-B3
11 B-QB4(C)	11 Q-Q3
12 B-B7ch(D)	12 K-Qsq
13 Kt-Q2(E)	13 PxP
14 Q-Kt2	14 B-Q2
15 Kt-B4	

Position after White's 15th move.

	15 Q-B3(F)
16 QxQ	16 BxQ
17 B-Kt5	17 BxR
18 KtxP	18 P-B3
19 Kt-K2	19 K-B2

24 BxPch	24 RxB
25 KtxR	25 R-Ksq
26 K-Q2	26 RxKt
27 R-KBsq	27 B-K2
28 P-Kt4	28 BxPch
29 K-Q3	29 B-K2
30 P-QR4	30 P-R3
31 Kt-K2	31 K-Q3
32 Kt-B3	32 K-K3
33 R-QKtsq	33 P-Kt4
34 RPxP	34 RPxP
35 PxP	35 PxP
36 KtxP	36 K-B4
37 Kt-Q4ch	37 KxP
38 P-R4	38 PxP en pass.
39 Kt-B3	39 R-Q4ch
40 K-K2	40 B-B4
41 R-KRsq	41 Kt(Kt2)-R4
42 Kt-R2	42 Kt-Kt6ch
43 K-Ksq	

(See Diagram below.)

	43 Kt(B3)-K5(I)
44 Kt-B3	44 B-B7 mate.

Position after White's 43rd move.

BLACK.

WHITE.

NOTES.

(A) This capture is made for purposes of defence, to keep the Kt in play. If B-Kt2, 6 P-Q5 follows.

(B) At first sight the proper move seems to be P-R3. Obeying the principle formulated by Steinitz: "When you have found a good move, don't make it, look for a better one," Black changes the attack into a defence in a few moves.

(C) If 11 P-Kt5, Black replies P-K5. Truly a remarkable position.

(D) The attack now assists Black's defence.

(E) To obviate B-KKt5.

(F) This wins a clear piece.

(G) These few careful defensive moves were needed, and the rest, though slow, is pretty plain sailing.

(H) White overlooked this.

(I) The situations in this game are throughout remarkably curious and frequently beautiful.

GAME 142.—Played by Messrs. Palmer, de Bury, and Ring in consultation, against Mr. Pollock, during his visit to St. John, New Brunswick. White, The Allies; Black, Mr. Pollock.

Two Knights' Defence.

WHITE.	BLACK.	WHITE.	BLACK.
1 P-K4	1 P-K4	20 PxKt	20 QxPch
2 Kt-KB3	2 Kt-QB3	21 RxQ	21 BxRch
3 B-B4	3 Kt-B3		
4 Kt-Kt5	4 KtxP		
5 KtxKt	5 P-Q4		
6 BxP	6 QxB		
7 QKt-B3	7 Q-Qsq		
8 P-Q3	8 P-QKt3		
9 Castles	9 B-Kt2		
10 P-B4	10 P-B4		
11 Kt-KKt5	11 B-B4ch		
12 K-Rsq	12 Q-Q2		
13 PxP	13 CastlesKR		
14 B-B4	14 QR-Ksq		
(See Diagram.)			
15 Q-R5	15 P-Kt3		
16 Q-K2	16 Kt-Q5		
17 Q-Q2	17 Q-B3		
18 QR-Ksq	18 P-KR3		
19 Kt-B3	19 KtxKt		

Position after Black's 14th move.

BLACK.

WHITE.

WHITE.	BLACK.
22 Q-Kt2	22 BxQch
23 KxB	23 P-KKt4
24 B-Q2	24 P-B3
25 P-QR3	25 B-Q5
26 P-K6	26 R-B3
27 Kt-Qsq	27 RxP
28 RxR	28 RxR
29 K-Bsq	29 K-Kt2
30 P-B3	30 B-K4
31 K-Kt2	31 BxRP
32 Kt-K3	32 B-B5
(See Diagram.)	
33 KtxPch	33 K-B3
34 BxB	34 KxKt
35 B-Kt8	35 K-Kt5
and wins.	

Position after Black's 32nd move.

MISCELLANEOUS.

GAME 143.—A double blindfold game, played at the Baltimore Chess Club, 1892. The members of the Club were treated to a novelty by Lasker encountering Maryland's champion, Mr. Pollock, both playing without seeing board or men. A large crowd watched the progress of the game with interest, and when at the end of the partie a veritable race ensued between the opposite Pawns to be first at Queening, the crowd was wild with excitement. Lasker's final manœuvre, especially the intended sacrifice of his Queen, brought forth a volley of applause. White, Mr. E. Lasker; Black, Mr. Pollock.

Ruy Lopez.

WHITE.	BLACK.	WHITE.	BLACK.
1 P-K4	1 P-K4	17 RPxP	17 Kt-Q2
2 Kt-KB3	2 Kt-QB3	18 KtxKt	18 BxKt
3 B-Kt5	3 P-QR3	19 K-B2	19 QR-Bsq
4 BxKt	4 QPxB	20 K-Kt2	20 B-Q3
5 P-Q4	5 B-KKt5	21 Kt-Kt3	21 R-B2
6 PxP	6 QxQch	22 Kt-B5	22 BxKt
7 KxQ	7 B-QB4	23 KPxB	23 R-R7ch
8 K-K2	8 Castles	24 K-Ktsq	24 RxQBP
9 B-K3	9 B-K2	25 R-Q2	25 RxR
10 P-KR3	10 B-R4	26 BxR	26 R-Q2
11 QKt-Q2	11 P-B3	27 B-B3	27 B-B4ch
12 KR-Qsq	12 PxP	28 K-Kt2	28 B-Q5
13 P-KKt4	13 B-Ksq	29 BxB	29 RxB
14 KtxP	14 Kt-B3	30 R-Rsq	30 P-QKt4
15 P-KB3	15 P-KR4	31 R-R7	31 P-B4
16 Kt-Bsq	16 PxP	32 RxP	32 P-B5

WHITE.	BLACK.	WHITE.	BLACK.
33 K-Kt3	33 P-Kt5	38 RxRch	38 K-Kt2
34 P-B6	34 P-B6	39 P-B8(Q)	39 P-B8(Q)
35 PxP	35 PxP	40 Q-Kt4ch	40 K-B3
36 P-B7	36 R-Qsq	41 Q-Q6ch	41 K-Kt2
37 R-Kt8	37 P-B7	42 Q-Q5ch	Resigns.

GAME 144.—"Let us contrast the recipient and the attractive style—the heavy and the happy—and to do so I take a game played long ago between "Genius" and "Something Else," a game which is an example of the delightful style in vogue before the modern school had laid its withering hand on dash, on brilliancy, and on Chess. White, Genius; Black, Something Else.

Evans Gambit.

WHITE.	BLACK.	WHITE.	BLACK.
1 P-K4	1 P-K4	22 K-Rsq(M)	22 Q-R4(N)
2 Kt-KB3	2 Kt-QB3		
3 B-B4	3 B-B4		
4 P-QKt4	4 BxKtP		
5 P-B3	5 B-R4		
6 P-Q4	6 PxP		
7 Castles	7 B-Kt3		
8 PxP	8 P-Q3		
9 P-Q5	9 Kt-K4(A)		
10 KtxKt	10 PxKt		
11 B-R3(B)	11 B-Q5(C)		
12 Kt-Q2	12 BxR		
13 QxB	13 P-KB3		
14 P-B4(D)	14 PxP(E)		
15 P-K5	15 P-B3(F)		
16 Kt-K4	16 PxQP(G)		
17 Kt-Q6ch(H)	17 K-Q2(I)		
18 B-Kt5ch	18 K-K3(K)		
19 PxP	19 KtxP(L)		
20 R-Ksqch	20 Kt-K5		
21 QxP	21 Q-Kt3ch		

Position after Black's 22nd move.

White mates in six moves.

NOTES, by Professor Dryasdust.

(A) Kt-R4 is much superior. (B) An attacking move, but Kt-Q2 is safer. (C) We do not recommend this against such an opponent. (D) Best. (E) Black has no satisfactory line of play. (F) Weak. (G) ——. (H) ——. (I) ——. (K) ——. (L) The only move to prolong the game. (M) ——. (N) White here announced mate in six moves.

(The reader may imagine any amount of "dryasdust" analysis following each of the above notes.)

NOTES ALSO.

(A) The chivalrous Knight turns from his lowly foe and challenges one of his own size, is immediately slain, and as quickly avenged. He might have retired discreetly and with propriety to R4, and so have lived to fight another day.

(B) The White Commander now sends out skirmishers, and in doing so sacrifices a battalion. Had he been less of a strategist he would have advanced his remaining Knight to Q2.

(C) Black has yet to learn that a sprat is not a fair exchange for a mackerel, that "Give-um" is dead and "Lend-um" is very bad.

(D) He feels now particularly at ease, and proceeds to awaken the enemy from a deep dream of peace.

(E) "There's small choice in rotten apples," which, being interpreted, signifies that Black must lie down on the bed he has made for himself.

(F) This amiable and considerate procedure, yclept playing your opponent's game, is good when you have not one of your own to play.

(G) This appears to threaten a good deal, and White gives it his immediate attention, on the ground that it is as well to be civil, as the old woman said.

(H) He is evidently not much frightened, though he makes haste to get out of his way.

(I) And now the Commander-in-chief has to shut up his umbrella and take the field on his own account.

(K) He is not the first to find out that, though war is the sport of kings, only one of them laugh.

(L) He springs forth in time to avert a certain defeat in four, or the loss of his Royal Mistress.

(M) The King retires into his corner to laugh, offering thereby to his opponent the cup of Tantalus filled with the legacy of Philidor.

(N) The cup is smashed in sheer disgust and desperation, and White then proceeds to bring the encounter to a conclusion.

PHANTOM CHESS.

GAME 145.—The rule of this game is to commence with a clear or empty board, and place on pieces or Pawns as they are moved, &c. The following "Phantom" game was played at the Montreal Chess Club, 13th September 1894, between Messrs. G. H. D. Gossip and R. P. Fleming (White) consulting, versus Messrs. J. N. Babson and Pollock (Black). It is a splendid example of this kind of play.

	WHITE.		BLACK.		WHITE.		BLACK.
1	P-K4	1	P-K4	10	R-Ksqch	10	K-B2(D)
2	Kt-KB3	2	Kt-QB3	11	Q-Q5ch	11	K-Kt2
3	B-QKt5	3	Kt-B3	12	B-B4	12	Kt-B2
4	CastlesKR	4	KtxP	13	Kt-R4	13	Kt-K2(E)
5	P-Q4	5	Kt-Q3	14	Q-KR5	14	P-Q4
6	PxP	6	KtxB	15	R-R3	15	R-KKtsq(F)
7	P-QR4	7	Kt-Q3(A)	16	R-Kt3ch	16	K-Rsq
8	B-KKt5(B)	8	P-B3	17	QxKt	17	RxR
9	PxP(C)	9	PxP	18	RPxR, and wins.		

NOTES.

(A) KtxP is, maybe, a bit better.

(B) And yet White must commit him thus, or submit to a poor "Pawn minus" game.

(c) R-Ksq is unsound.
(d) Black's "sight" is quite poor.
(e) Very bad; he loses much time "preventing" R-QR3, a move made by White, nathless with winning. P-Q3 wins.
(f) Awfully weak, B-B4 is better.

QUEER MOVES IN CHESS.

IT is astonishing what bizarre and unexpected moves can be found right in the opening of a game—nay, as early as the first, second, or third moves. I refer to such as can be made without danger, and even with advantage. Anderssen made a great hit with 1 P-QR3 in his match with Morphy, and Boden took the great New Orleans player "out of the books" with good results by 1 P-KB3. Some moves that have occurred in my own experience will be less well known, and, therefore, amusing.

On entering Simpson's Divan one morning some years ago I gave out that I had discovered an entirely new move for White in giving the odds of a piece, viz., on the first move. Veteran Bird, who fears not to start a game with any move whatever, got up on his hind legs at this, but when I took off the QKt and moved the R to the vacant square he sat quite still. A gentleman shortly after came in, and a well-known professional player remarked "sotto voce" that he would like to tackle him for the customary shilling stake, but he always exacted the odds of a Knight, and was just strong enough to make it very poor market. "Go in and try my new move," said I, and he did so and won four games straight!

I once told Showalter that in the great New York Tournament of 1889 I played 1 P-Q4 against Weiss, who replied also P-Q4. "Now," said I (as soon as my old friend had acknowledged that he did not recollect the game), "I will give you 18 guesses as to what my second move was." He failed to guess it. The move was 2 Q-Q3. (A good game, too. See Tournament Book.) There must be some sort of mind reading in this kind of bluff, for I tried the same game on Arthur Peter, who won the "free-for-all" at Lexington, Kentucky, and his first guess was 2 Q-Q3.

Another time I allowed a young New York player (who was smart enough, anyway, to have gained one of Loyd's gold chess pins for solving), no fewer than 27 guesses as to what a certain new defence which I had discovered to the Ruy Lopez was. He did not find it, and finally besought me to tell him. It was 3 Kt-QR4! Quite a feasible move, too. I have played it against Lasker and Burn.

Now, Alapin, the Russian master, comes out with four or five pages of analysis in "La Strategie" to prove that the correct defence to the Ruy Lopez is 3 B-Kt5! It is even worse than my move, if only because less ridiculous.

Two or three years ago I showed Babson, the renowned problemist, a new opening which I had invented on the street. I called it the "King's Own Gambit." It was 1 P-K4 P-K4, 2 P-KB4 PxP, 3

K-B2! "I'll try it on Short" (a strong player with whom he had had little success), said he, and he won 11 games straight at the opening.

I have been reduced to such desperation when rendering the odds of Kt to a player who had "got on to" all my opening tricks that I have had to make double fianchettos with the Rooks instead of the Bishops, getting the latter on to the Rooks squares.

To get Staunton out of his grooves in the QP opening St. Amant repeatedly answered 1 P-Q4 with P-QB4. I played thus twice in the Hastings Congress and would do so again. I usually play the Kt to QR3, and subsequently to B2.

There is hardly any hopelessly bad move in answer to 1 P-K4, except it be 1 P-KB4. Delmar is fond of opening with 1 P-KKt4 in skittles, and 1 P-QKt4 has produced fine games.

Steinitz has been defending the Ruy Lopez with 3 B-B4 and 4 Q-B3 with excellent results in his matches.

I have seen the King moved—as Black's first move, i.e. 1 K-B2—as a defence in a Pawn and move game.

I have seen Bird win a dead-lost game in a handicap tournament by taking a Pawn "en passant" with a Rook; in other words, "jumping it." Neither player noticed it, and the bystanders thought they had no right to interfere.

And many other curious moves too numerous to be related here.

But I should like to see a position which Mr. Loyd told me he had constructed some years ago—or, at least, was constructing. It was a sort of problem in which both Kings were in perpetual check, and neither could escape, nor could either side either win or lose the game. He called it "The Whirlpool."

One of Alapin's leading variations is curious:—

WHITE.	BLACK.
1 P-K4	1 P-K4
2 Kt-KB3	2 Kt-QB3
3 B-Kt5	3 B-Kt5
4 Castles	4 KKt-K2
5 P-B3	5 B-R4
6 BxKt	6 KtxB
7 P-QKt4	7 B-Kt3
8 P-Kt5	8 Kt-R4
9 KtxP	9 Castles
10 P-Q4	10 Q-Ksq
11 Q-Q3	

Position after White's 11th move.

and White is made to get into trouble by P-KB4 and P-Q3. It is strange that so good a player should have failed to notice the great superiority of 11 R-Ksq. Many other of his variations are very ingenious, and more carefully worked out.—"Baltimore News."

END GAMES OF Mr. POLLOCK.

No. 1.
BLACK.

WHITE.

White mates in four moves.

No. 2.
BLACK.

WHITE.

White mates in seven moves.

No. 3.—B.C.A. Master Tournament, 1885.

Position after Black's 22 P(Q3)-Q4.

BLACK (Rabson).

WHITE (Pollock) to play.

Continued: 23 Kt-B5 PxP, 24 Kt-K5 B-Kt2, 25 KtxB QxPch, 26 K-Rsq KR-Ksq, 27 Q-Kt5 Q-R2, 28 R-B7 Q-R3, 29 Kt(K5)-B6 Kt-Q4, 30 QxQch BxQ, 31 R-R7 mate.

No. 4.—New York International Tournament, 1890.

Position after White's 19 R-Qsq.

BLACK (Pollock) to play.

WHITE (Mason).

The game now went on: 19 Kt-B5, 20 Kt-Q4 PxKt, 21 KBxKt(B4) PxP, 22 RxR QxR, 23 PxP P-Kt7, 24 B-R2 KtxKP, 25 B-KKt3 Q-K3!, 26 B-Ktsq KtxQBP, 27 QxQ R-Q8 mate. Steinitz terms this "a gem of a game on Mr. Pollock's part."

No. 5.

BLACK.

WHITE.

White mates in nine moves.

No. 6.

BLACK.

WHITE.

White to play and win.

No. 7.—Bradford International Master Tournament, 1888.

Position after White's 21 P-R5.

BLACK (Pollock) to play.

WHITE (Bardeleben).

Continued: 21 P-KKt4!, 22 B-K5 B-Kt4, 23 QxP B-R3, 24 B-B4 R-Bsq, 25 B-Kt3 Q-B3, 26 K-Qsq B-Q6!! (if PxB Black mates in three moves), 27 B-Q6 QxB, 28 Q-K5 QxQ, 29 PxQ RxP, 30 RxP RxP, 31 R-Kt8ch K-Q2, and **Bardeleben resigned.**

No. 8.—B.C.A. International Master Tournament, 1886.

Position after White's 45 K-Rsq.

BLACK (Blackburne) to play.

WHITE (Pollock).

Continued: 45 Kt-K5, 46 R-Kt6 (quite characteristic of Pollock's play. 46 Q-QR3 saves the exchange and leaves White with a good game) QxR, 47 PxQ KtxQ, 48 PxKt K-B2, 49 P-B5 K-Qsq, 50 P-B6 K-Ksq, 51 R-Rsq R-Q7, 52 P-B7ch K-K2, 53 R-Ksqch, and Blackburne resigned.

The following position occurred in a consultation game played at the Baltimore Club, 1890:

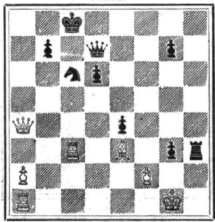

Mr. Pollock (White) here announced mate in nine moves.

The following fine ending arose in a game played in Pittsburg, between Mr. Pollock, of Albany, New York, and Mr. John L. McCutcheon.

Black drew elegantly, as follows: 1 Kt-Ktsq, 2 KxP Kt-Q2, 3 K-Kt5 Kt-B4, 4 P-R5 Kt-Kt6, 5 B-Q2 KtxB, 6 P-R6 K-K5, 7 P-R7 KxP, 8 P-R8(Q) K-K6, and the game is drawn.

The following interesting ending occurred between Messrs. R. Boyd and Pollock, when the latter was playing nineteen games at the Belfast Chess Club.

Continued: 16 Kt-B6, 17 Q-R6 R-Kt3, 18 Q-B4 K-Ktsq, 19 PxKt Kt-R4, 20 QxB RxQ, 21 PxR Kt-Kt2, 22 B-R6 Q-B3, 23 P-Kt5 Q-B6ch, 24 K-Ktsq Kt-B4, 25 Kt-Qsq Kt-Q5, 26 Kt-B3 Kt-K3, 27 P-Kt6 R-KBsq, 28 QR-Ksq R-B5, and Black mates in a few moves.

A highly amusing end-game at the Baltimore Chess Association.

Black played P-Q7 and drew, thus: 1. RxBch PxR, 2 R-Bsqch K-Q6, 3 R-B3ch

K-K5(A), 4 R-K3ch K-Q4(B), 5 R-K5ch K-B5, 6 RxPch K-Q6, 7 R-B3ch K-K5, 8 R-K3ch K-Q4(C), 9 R-K5ch K-Q3, 10 R-K6ch K-Q2, 11 R-K7ch K-Qsq, 12 R-K8ch K-B2, 13 R-B8ch K-Kt3, 14 R-B6ch and draws, for R checks all down B's file, drawing by perpetual check.

(A) If KxR White is stalemated.

(B) 4 K-B4 wins; for, after R-B3ch, Black can either move his King, or interpose; or, if R-K5ch K-B5, and there is no stalemate.

(C) Once more he has the same chance as pointed out in (A), and again fails to see it.

"In some positions the King should not always be 'checked to death,' or he may 'escape alive.'" The following is a very fine example, known in Dublin years ago as the "Monck Gambit":—1 P-K4 P-K4, 2 Kt-KB3 Kt-QB3, 3 B-B4 Kt-B3, 4 Kt-B3 KtxP, 5 BxPch KxB, 6 KtxKt P-Q4, 7 KKt-Kt5ch K-Kt3, 8 Q-B3 PxKt, 9 Q-B7ch KxKt:

BLACK (Amateur).

WHITE (Pollock).

White now mates in ten moves: 10 P-Q4ch K-R5 (if P-K6, the Q presently occupies KB3, instead of QKt3, a very pretty point), 11 P-KR3! B-Kt5ch, 12 K-Bsq! P-KKt3, 13 P-Kt3ch K-R4, 14 P-Kt4ch K-R5, 15 Q-Kt3 B-B6, 16 QxB P-K6, 17 QxP BxP, 18 PxBch KxP, 19 Q mates.

THE "HORRIBLE" FRENCH DEFENCE.

THE "Partie Francaise" or P-K3 defence has been persistently maligned, through the tameness of the early moves. It presents, however, from time to time, the most brilliant positions possible. The following one, though almost unknown, is quite a gem. Played at Simpson's Divan, London, January 1888. Messrs. Cook (author of Cook's Synopsis) and Pollock versus Lee and Muller, two well known and skilful "pros."

BLACK (Lee and Muller).

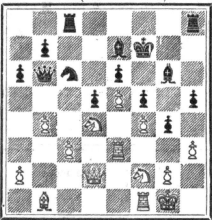

WHITE (Cook and Pollock).

White here played P-R3, saving a Pawn, but with a Machiavellian design beyond, whereat Black again attacked it by P-R4. Then came 2 KtxKP KxKt (innocent), and White gave mate in two moves.

A GOOD FINISH.

BLACK (J. D. Elwell).

WHITE (Pollock).

White mates in three moves.

PROBLEMS.

No. 1.
By W. H. K. Pollock.
BLACK.

WHITE.

White mates in two moves.

No. 2. *
By W. H. K. Pollock.
BLACK.

WHITE.

White mates in two moves.

No. 3.
By W. H. K. Pollock and Dr. S. Gold.
BLACK.

WHITE.

White mates in two moves.

No. 4.
By W. H. K. Pollock & T. B. Rowland.
BLACK.

WHITE.

White mates in three moves.

* This very peculiar and highly original problem was composed by Mr. Pollock on the occasion of giving a lesson on the art of composing at the Baltimore Chess Association.

SOLUTIONS.

END GAMES.

No. 1.—1 Q-R7ch KxQ, 2 PxPch K-Ktsq, 3 R-R8ch K-B2, 4 P-Kt8(Q) mate.

No. 2.—1 B-Kt8, 2 B-R7ch, 3 Kt-Kt6, 4 Kt-Q5 or B4ch, 5 Kt-K3, 6 Kt-B5 or Bsqch, 7 Kt-Kt3mate.

No. 5.—1 Kt-B4, 2 Kt-K6, 3 Kt-Kt3, 4 Kt(Kt3)-B5, 5 Kt-Q7, 6 Kt(K6)-B8, 7 K-B7, 8 Kt-B6, 9 Kt-Kt6mate. Moves 7 and 8 can be transposed.

No. 6.—1 P-Kt3ch PxPch, 2 K-Kt2 K-R4, 3 KxP K-Kt4, 4 P-B4ch PxPch, 5 K-B3 K-Kt3, 6 KxP K-B3, 7 P-K5ch PxPch, 8 K-K4 K-B2, 9 KxP K-K2, 10 P-Q6ch PxPch, 11 K-Q5 K-Ksq, 12 KxP K-Qsq, 13 P-B7ch K-Bsq, 14 K-K6 KxP, 15 K-K7 K-Bsq, 16 K-Q6 K-Kt2, 17 K-Q7 K-Ktsq, 18 K-B6 K-R2, 19 K-B7 K-Rsq, 20 KxP and easily wins.

PROBLEMS.

No. 1.—1 Kt-Kt5

No. 2.—1 Kt-Q6

No. 3.—1 K-Q3

No. 4.—1 Kt(R3)-B4 K-B3, 2 Q-Kt2ch, &c. If K-B5, 2 Q-Kt8ch, &c. If K-Q5 2 Q-Qsqch, &c. If any other, 2 Q-Kt5, &c.

INDEX.

PART I.

	Page.
Biographical Notes	2
In Memoriam	16

GAMES PLAYED IN ENGLAND.

Players.	Opening.	Played at.	Date.	
Bardeleben-Pollock	Irregular	Bradford	1888	64
Bird-Pollock	Giuoco Piano	London	1887	45
Bird-Pollock	Scotch	London	1886	34
Blackburne-Pollock	Ruy Lopez	Bradford	1888	66
Burn-Pollock	Ruy Lopez	London	1887	41
Burt-Pollock	Four Knights'	Bath	1884	21
Donisthorpe-Pollock	Irregular	London	1895	30
Erskine-Pollock	Muzio	London	1888	55
Gunsberg-Pollock	Four Knights'	London	1888	57
Gunsberg-Pollock	Vienna	Hastings	1895	73
Jacobs-Pollock	Vienna	Stamford	1887	50
Kvistendahl-Pollock	Evans	London	1885	31
Locock-Pollock	Ruy Lopez	Bath	1884	23
Loman-Pollock	Scotch	London	1887	42
MacDonnell-Pollock	Irregular	London	1885	29
MacDonnell-Pollock	Muzio	London	1887	43
MacDonnell-Pollock	Ruy Lopez	Stamford	1887	48
Mackenzie-Pollock	Irregular	Bradford	1888	66
Mason-Pollock	Greco Counter Gambit	London	1887	44
Mason-Pollock	Two Knights'	London	1888	56
Mortimer-Pollock	Two Knights'	Bradford	1888	71
Mortimer-Pollock	Two Knights'	London	1888	54
Muller-Pollock	Philidor	London	1888	63
Owen-Pollock	Irregular	Bradford	1888	65
Pearson-Pollock	Danish	London	1888	54
Pollock-Amateur	Irregular	London	1888	53
Pollock-Bird	Four Knights'	London	1888	59
Pollock-Bird	Sicilian	London	1885	26
Pollock-Bird	Sicilian	London	1886	38
Pollock-Bird	Sicilian	London	1888	59
Pollock-Blackburne	French	London	1886	35
Pollock-Blake	Four Knights'	Stamford	1887	49
Pollock-Blake	Two Knights'	Stamford	1887	51
Pollock-Burn	Four Knights'	London	1885	33
Pollock-Burn	Scotch	London		52
Pollock-Burt	Evans Gambit Declined	Bristol	1883	17
Pollock-Burt	Two Knights'	Bristol	1885	26
Pollock-Harsant	Four Knights'	Bath	1885	25
Pollock-Hirschfeld	Three Knights'	London	1887	47
Pollock-Lee	French	London	1887	40
Pollock-Lee	French	London	1888	62
Pollock-Lee	French	London	1889	72
Pollock-Locock	Vienna	Birmingham	1883	19

INDEX.

Players.	Opening.	Played at.	Date.	Page.
Ilock-Loman	Four Knights'	Bath	1884	24
Pollock-Loman	Sicilian	Bath	1884	21
Pollock-Mason	Evans Declined	Bradford	1888	70
Pollock-Mason	French	London	1886	37
Pollock-Mason	Irregular	Hereford	1885	32
Pollock-Mortimer	Three Knights'	London	1885	28
Pollock-Mortimer	Three Knights'	London	1887	43
Pollock-Schallop	Evans	Nottingham	1888	71
Pollock-Tarrasch	French	Hastings	1895	74
Pollock-Mr. W.	Muzio	London	1884	25
Pollock-Wildman	Four Knights'	Birmingham	1883	20
Pollock-Zukertort	Staunton	London	1887	46
Rynd-Pollock	Scotch	Nottingham	1886	39
Steinitz-Pollock	Giuoco Piano	Hastings	1895	77
Taubenhaus-Pollock	Four Knights'	Bradford	1888	69
Taubenhaus-Pollock	Thorold-Allgaier	Nottingham	1886	39
Thorold-Pollock	Irregular	Bradford	1888	67
Tinsley-Pollock	Queen's Fianchetto	Purssell's	1883	17
Zukertort-Pollock	Ruy Lopez	London	1886	34
Zukertort-Pollock	Two Knights'	London	1888	61

GAMES PLAYED AT ODDS.

Mr. —.-Pollock	Odds of KBP	London	1887	81
Mr. H.-Pollock	KBP	London	1887	82
Pollock-Mr. E.	QKt	London	1887	81
Pollock-Rumboll	QKt	Bath		79
Pollock-Rumboll	QKt	Bath		80

GAME PLAYED ON THE CONTINENT.

Pollock-Doppler	French	Hamburg	1885	83

GAMES PLAYED IN IRELAND.

Burn-Pollock	Irregular	Belfast	1886	86
Chambers-Pollock	English	Belfast	1886	85
Drury and Fitzpatrick-Pollock	Two Bishops	Dublin	1888	90
Harvey-Pollock	French	Dublin	1882	84
Morphy-Pollock	Two Knights'	Dublin	1887	88
Pollock-Blackburne	Evans Declined	Belfast	1886	87
Pollock-Stephens	Vienna	Clontarf	1888	89

PART II.

GAMES PLAYED IN AMERICA AND CANADA.

Blanchard-Pollock	Two Knights'	Chicago	1890	93
Delmar-Pollock	Dutch	Brooklyn	1892	98
Frere-Pollock	Ruy Lopez	Staten Island	1893	103
Gunsberg-Pollock	Ruy Lopez	New York	1889	92
Hanham-Pollock	Irregular	Staten Island	1893	102
Nedemann-Pollock	Staunton's Kt Game	Lexington	1891	95
Pollock-Anon	Giuoco Piano (sans voir)		1893	101
Pollock-Bonn	Allgaier	Brooklyn	1891	99
Pollock-Gossip	Evans Declined	New York	1893	104
Pollock-Gunsberg	Hamppe's Kt Game	Baltimore	1891	95
Pollock-Gwyer	KKt Gambit	Washington	1893	100
Pollock-Halpern	French	Staten Island	1893	102

INDEX.

Players.	Opening.	Played at.	Date.	Page.
Pollock-Hermann	Staunton's Kt Game	Chicago	1890	94
Pollock-Lissner	Two Knights'	New York	1893	106
Pollock-Pillsbury	Irregular	New York	1893	105
Pollock-Souweine	Evans	Brooklyn	1892	97
Pollock-Wilcox	Sicilian	Buffalo	1893	100
Showalter-Pollock	Two Knights'	Brooklyn	1892	99
Spencer-Pollock	Hamppe's Kt Game	Baltimore	1890	98
Weiss-Pollock	Ruy Lopez	New York	1889	91

GAMES PLAYED IN AMERICA AT ODDS.

Players.	Opening.	Played at.	Date.	Page.
Amateur-Pollock	Odds of R and P			107
Habershom-Pollock	KKt	Baltimore	1890	111
Loeb-Pollock	KBP	New York	1893	113
Maas-Pollock	QR	Baltimore	1891	110
Pollock-Dallam	QR	Baltimore	1890	107
Pollock-Henrichs	QKt			110
Pollock-Kemper	QR	Baltimore		108
Pollock-Torsch	QKt			112
Pollock-Uhtoff	QKt	Baltimore		108
Pollock-Uhtoff	KKt			109
Schofield-Pollock	KBP	Baltimore		112

MATCHES.

Players.		Played at.	Date.	Page.
Delmar-Pollock	(8 Games)	New York	1891	119-130
Gossip-Pollock	(3 Games)	Montreal	1894	136-138
Pollock-Moehle	(4 Selected Games)	Cincinnati	1890	114-118
Showalter-Pollock	(7 Games)	Georgetown	1891	131-135

CONSULTATION GAMES.

Players.	Opening.	Played at.	Date.	Page.
Pollock-Allies	Two Knights'	Buffalo		140
Pollock-Torsch and Schofield	Evans		1890	139

CORRESPONDENCE GAMES.

Players.				Page.
Pollock-McCutcheon	(3 Games)			140-142

GAMES PLAYED IN CANADA.

Players.	Opening.	Played at.	Date.	Page.
Babson-Pollock		Montreal	1893	143
De Soyres-Pollock	Scotch	Montreal	1895	144
Marshall-Pollock	Odds of P and 2	Montreal	1894	146
Palmer, de Bury, and Ring-Pollock	Two Knights'	St. John (N.B.)		148
Pollock-Mr. B.	Odds of QR	Montreal	1895	146
Pollock-Beecher		Montreal	1894	144
Pollock-Robertson		Montreal	1893	143
Pollock-Wheeldon		Montreal	1894	143

MISCELLANEOUS.

		Played at.	Date.	Page.
Double-Blindfold Game, Lasker v Pollock		Baltimore	1892	149
Game, Genius v Something Else	Evans			150
Phantom Chess, Gossip and Fleming v Babson and Pollock				151
Queer Moves in Chess				152
Game Endings ...	... ...			154
Problems ...	... ...			158
Solutions ...	... ...			159

Graphology.

Frideswide F. Rowland, the well known expert, sends full detail delineations of character from handwriting on receipt of stamped addressed envelope and 6d in stamps, or 1/- Postal Order by return post.

Address—

**6 RUS-IN-URBE,
KINGSTOWN.**

Card Tricks
AND
Puzzles,

By "BERKELEY" and T. B. ROWLAND.

One Shilling.

London:
G. Bell and Sons,
YORK STREET,
COVENT GARDEN.

Typewriting.

Authors' MSS., Circulars, &c., Typewritten at very moderate terms.

F. F. ROWLAND,
6 RUS-IN-URBE, KINGSTOWN, IRELAND.

KINGSTOWN SOCIETY.

A MONTHLY FAMILY JOURNAL.

Yatching, Boating, Cycling, Cricket, Chess, Shopping, and Society Notes.

YEARLY SUBSCRIPTION: 1s 6d POST FREE.

6 RUS-IN-URBE, KINGSTOWN, IRELAND.

Chess Problem tourneys, and solving competitions conducted by Mrs. Rowland.

A VALUABLE WORK FOR COMPOSERS AND SOLVERS.

NEW EDITION - - - 2s 6d.

The Problem Art,

A TREATISE ON HOW TO SOLVE AND HOW TO COMPOSE
CHESS PROBLEMS,

Comprising Direct-Mate, Self-Mate, Help-Mate, Retraction and Conditional Problems.

By T. B. ROWLAND and F. F. ROWLAND, Authors of "Chess Blossoms," "Chess Fruits," "The Chess Player's Annual," "Living Chess," &c.

SENT POST FREE, ON RECEIPT OF 2s 6d, by

F. F. ROWLAND, 6 Rus-in-Urbe, Kingstown.

Morgan's Shilling Chess Library.

Book I.—Games, Gossip and others. 1s.
Book II.—A selection of games from the Bradford International Tournament of 1888. 1s.
Book III.—A selection of games from the New York International Tournament of 1889. 1s.
Book IV.—A second selection of games from the New York Tournament. 1s.
Book V.—Globe Problem and Solution Tourney, No 2. Problems, Reviews, Solutions, &c. 1s.
Book VI.—A selection of games from the Breslau and Amsterdam Tournaments of 1889. 1s.
Book VII.—A selection of games from the Manchester International Tournament of 1890. 1s.
Book VIII.—The games of Gunsberg's matches with Tchigorin (1890) and Steinitz (1890-91). 1s.
Book IX.—How to solve a Chess Problem. By Bernard Reynolds. 1s. (In the press.)
Book X.—The games of Steinitz and Tchigorin. 1s.
Book XI.—In the Press.
Book XII.—A selection of Chess Problems of Philip H. Williams. 1s.
Book XIII.—A collection of fifty Blindfold Games, by the most famous exponents of the art. 1s.

Any of the above sent post free by the Publisher, W. W. MORGAN, Fleet Works, New Barnet.

W. W. MORGAN,

CHESS PRINTER, PUBLISHER, &c.,

CHESS PLAYER'S CHRONICLE WORKS, NEW BARNET.

Men, Boards, and every requisite for the game supplied. Chess printing a speciality.—Specimens, estimates, &c., on application. Authors assisted to publish works, on special terms.

CPSIA information can be obtained
at www.ICGtesting.com
Printed in the USA
LVHW020323250520
656513LV00009B/741